THE PRIMACY OF STRUCTURE

COMMENTARY

"Horner's perceptive observations on character and personality cover a wide range, including development, psychopathology, and treatment. The reader is provided with a lucid overview of object relations theory in health and illness. Horner elucidates the psychodynamics of commonly occurring syndromes, such as depression and bulimia, and such non-pathological states as creativity and passionate love. Her discussion of therapy provides much insight into the fundamental mental operations of patients with character disorders. *The Primacy of Structure* is full of material that all clinicians, from beginners to seasoned practitioners, will find thought-provoking and rewarding. It adds an important perspective to psychotherapy practice." **—Richard C. Friedman, M.D.**

"Immediately useful to the clinician, Dr. Horner's *The Primacy of Structure* boldly argues and elegantly demonstrates how object relations theory has practical applications to therapy. For me, for others who follow Dr. Horner's work, and for newcomers, this volume enriches our sense of the clinical enterprise and of that phenomenon that even the most experienced among us take too much for granted—a cohesive, object-related, reality-related self. How the vicissitudes of development lead to specific kinds of impairment and the kind of understanding necessary to provide good therapy is what this book is about." **—Douglas H. Ingram, M.D.**

"Dr. Horner has brought to her task of integrating object relations, self psychology, ego psychology, and drive theory in a structural–object relations approach, a wealth of scholarship, psychoanalytic sophistication, and much clinical experience. She shows how a patient's early experiences, interpersonal relationships, and defenses can be understood in structural terms. Throughout, she provides clinical examples from her practice to illuminate her perspective. She provides a thorough documentation of the clinical basis from which she draws her conclusions about patients' underlying character structure. Dr. Horner describes how the interpersonal and intrapsychic interact in ways that would be understandable to beginning as well as advanced clinicians. It was a pleasure reading this book and I recommend it to students, teachers, and all mental health professionals." **—Marion Solomon, Ph.D.**

THE PRIMACY OF STRUCTURE

Psychotherapy of Underlying Character Pathology

Althea J. Horner, Ph.D.

JASON ARONSON INC.
Northvale, New Jersey
London

The author gratefully acknowledges permission to reprint the following material:

Chap. 1. *International Review of Psycho-Analysis* 2:95–105. Copyright © 1975 Institute of Psycho-Analysis.

Chap. 2. *Issues in Ego Psychology* 3:27–35, 1980.

Chap. 3. *Journal of the American Academy of Psychoanalysis* 8:565–573. Copyright © 1980 John Wiley & Sons, Inc.

Chap. 4. *Dynamic Psychotherapy* 1(2):111–121. Copyright © 1983 by Brunner/Mazel, Inc.

Chap. 6. *Journal of the American Academy of Psychoanalysis* 18:223–232, 1990.

Chap. 7. *International Review of Psycho-Analysis* 1:337–340. Copyright © 1974 Institute of Psycho-Analysis.

Chap. 10. *Journal of the American Academy of Psychoanalysis* 17:491–493, 1989.

Chap. 13. The Lydia Rapoport Lectures Monograph Series, no. 10, Smith College School for Social Work, Northampton, MA, 1984.

Chap. 14. *Psychotherapy: Theory, Research and Practice* 10:83–86, 1973.

Chap. 15. *Journal of the American Academy of Psychoanalysis* 3:301–305. Copyright © 1975 John Wiley & Sons, Inc.

Chap. 16. *Contemporary Psychoanalysis* 16:186–203, 1980.

Chap. 18. *Contemporary Psychoanalysis* 19:471–482, 1983.

Chap. 19. *Journal of the American Academy of Psychoanalysis* 15:491–502. Copyright © 1987 John Wiley & Sons, Inc.

Library of Congress Cataloging-in-Publication Data

Horner, Althea J.
    The primacy of structure : psychotherapy of underlying character
    pathology / by Althea J. Horner.
        p. cm.
    Includes bibliographical references and index.
    ISBN 0-87668-748-6
    1. Object relations (Psychoanalysis). 2. Psychology, Pathology.
    3. Psychotherapy. I. Title.
    RC455.4.023H67   1990
    616.89'17—dc20   90-41165

Manufactured in the United States of America. Jason Aronson Inc. offers books and cassettes. For information and catalog write to Jason Aronson Inc., 230 Livingston Street, Northvale, New Jersey 07647.

This book is dedicated to the many patients and students from whom I have learned so much.

Contents

PART II: CHARACTER PATHOLOGY

PART III: TREATMENT OF CHARACTER PATHOLOGY

Preface

A Structural, Object Relational Approach to Clinical Theory and Practice

In my clinical work, teaching, and consultation, my emphasis is on understanding psychological behavior and clinical symptoms in terms of the patient's underlying character structure. The impact of the patient's early experiences, the meaning of behavior, particularly the nature of interpersonal relationships, and the function of the defenses can all be understood in structural terms. For example, we must distinguish between obsessive behavior that functions to hold together a fragile, inadequately integrated self, and obsessive behavior that defends against awareness of impulses that generate guilt or interpersonal anxiety. In discussing a patient's history and the particular trauma to which he was subjected, I will wonder: Who was the child to whom this trauma happened? Was this person a well-integrated and well-differentiated 7-year-old, or a borderline child already at risk because of failures of the primary caretaker in the first three years of life? And where was this individual along the developmental continuum at the time of this historical event? The implications of these facts are critical for the patient's treatment.

Psychic structure refers to an enduring organization of psychological elements, *enduring* being the salient word here. The structure we refer to as the self ideally encompasses all aspects of the psychophysiological self: somatic experience, affect, impulse, perception, and thought. The development of the mental structures we call the self and object representations takes place in the context of the primary caretaking relationship, as well as in the context of built-in schedules of maturation. What was first interpersonal becomes intrapsychic—that is, structured—and what is then intrapsychic is expressed interpersonally. The term *object relations* is a structural concept, referring to the inner mental structure of the self and object representations and their dynamic interplay, along with associated characteristic feelings, wishes, and fears. These mental representations develop in a manner outlined by Piaget in his description of the evolution of cognitive schemata (1934). The object relational situation, the inner psychological structure, becomes manifest in interpersonal relationships, the transference being one that is of particular interest to the therapist.

Sandler (1981) notes that every wish comes to include a representation of the person's own self and a representation of the object who has a role to play in the fulfillment of the wish. That is, the wish contains representations of both self and object in interaction. What is wished for is a specific interaction. By the same token, there may be a feared interaction that is warded off by a variety of defenses or strategies. The individual may attempt to make the wished-for interaction real either in fantasy or vis-à-vis the other, particularly the therapist. I have defined *transference resistance* as a way of managing the therapeutic relationship so as to bring about a wished-for interaction or to prevent a feared one.

My personal bent is an integrative one, which may be one reason I was drawn to object relations theory. The object relational perspective enables a theoretical integration of major principles of self psychology, drive theory, and ego psychology. It also clarifies the link between the family relational system and the intrapsychic makeup of the individual.

I see the view of those self psychologists who consider the object only in terms of its function as seriously limited. Stolorow and colleagues (1987) reject the notion that borderline personality disorder is a manifestation of pathological structure when they define "borderline" as an iatrogenic myth based on therapists' failures to function as an adequate selfobject with severely narcissistically vulnerable patients.

The importance of the object, or primary caretaker, goes far beyond the selfobject function as just described, although the holding, containing, affect-modulating, and mirroring functions certainly are an important aspect of the primary relationship. The primary caretaker is also a specific person with whom identifications will be made, who may be internalized as an unassimilated introject, or with respect to whom certain specific adaptations or modifications of the self will be made to secure the relationship. One of these adaptations is that of the false self, as first described by Winnicott (1965), which characteristically coexists with a split-off true self. All of these arrangements are set down in structure as central to the enduring organization of the mind, and they will be expressed in one way or another throughout life.

The primary caretaker is also the individual into whom the child will project its own impulses and feelings, as when a 5-year-old boy says to his mother, "You don't like me," when indeed, it is he who angrily denies his own love. The mother will also be confronted with the child's conflicted wishes, so evident in the 4-year-old boy who both yearns for and rejects his own passive-dependent attachment to her, who pushes away from her in the service of his individuation and sense of maleness. The view that development will go smoothly given a willing selfobject denies what I see as conflict that is intrinsic to the developmental process itself. It also denies how the child, with its cognitive limitations and primitive mental mechanisms, will participate in the creation of its own internal world, a world that is an amalgam of actual experience and perception. We need always remind ourselves of the distinction between narrative truth and historical truth.

The unique quality of the primary relationship will leave its mark on the individual's psyche. The shadow of this relationship will be manifest in all future significant interpersonal relationships.

What is at first interpersonal becomes structured as the enduring organization of the mind—that is, it becomes intrapsychic—and then what has become intrapsychic once again becomes expressed in the interpersonal situation. An object relations approach is inevitably an interpersonal approach, and in the clinical situation it will be expressed in the form of transference and countertransference. Attention to the interpersonal process is part of the object relations approach, in my view. Research findings indicate that patients benefit most from psychotherapy when the therapist correctly identifies their core relationship problem regardless of the presenting problem (Luborsky et al. 1988). This identification is enhanced by the therapist's understanding of the underlying structural situation in object relations terms. As such, interpretations formulated around wishes, fears, feelings, or impulses in the interpersonal context have a ring of truth for the patient inasmuch as he has experienced them even though he is unable to articulate them.

From this interpersonal, object relations perspective we can come to understand sometimes puzzling behaviors or symptoms. For example, a woman noted that when she was alone on weekends, she would become involved in a litany of self-criticism. One might be hard pressed to find the interpersonal wish in this report, yet exploration revealed that her mother's criticism of her was the most familiar and emotionally salient aspect of their relationship. By reenacting this interaction in her own mind, she in effect brought her mother to her and then felt less alone. This reminds us of Fairbairn's dictum that the child is object seeking rather than gratification seeking. In therapy, relinquishing the negative interaction, whether in fantasy or in fact, is likely to be accompanied by the experience of object loss. The apparent resistance to change may be a defense against that loss and an underlying depression; as one woman put it, "There would only be blackness and emptiness." The pathological attachment cannot be relinquished until a healthy one has been established. This, of course, is often the most critical aspect of the therapeutic relationship. Healthy, depression-free individuation requires a structured good object, a loving internal presence.

Looking for the embedded interpersonal metaphor frees us from unproductively joining the patient in obsessional thinking or behavior. I see bulimia as essentially a manifestation of a failed schizoid defense, a situation in which the pull of the exciting objects—the intensely needed but disappointing preoedipal mother and the overly sexual oedipal father of many female patients—is countered by the coexisting danger of moving in either direction. The obsession with food and weight, like any other obsession, serves to divert and bind the anxiety that belongs elsewhere—in this case, in a highly conflicted and intensely ambivalent interpersonal situation. One such patient noted at the outset of treatment that she didn't want me to matter too much because she was sure I would disappoint her, and then she would be so angry that she might tear my office apart. We observe the object hunger and the attempted schizoid defense against its dangers not only of intrusion, but also of abandonment rage and incestuous sexuality. The symptoms can be understood in terms of the underlying character structure and the double approach–avoidance conflict and its dynamics.

Other examples of the structural, object relations approach to understanding symptoms would be instances in which patients believe that they have been poisoned or that they are possessed, where this belief is a manifestation of the patients' experiences of having been made the container of maternal projections, of one or more of the mother's disavowed self or hated object representations. It is difficult for the child to establish boundaries between the self and those projections and identifications with what was projected. One woman described herself as the "family garbage pail," into which both parents projected hated aspects of self; they then attempted to eradicate these projections in the patient. Dreams of overflowing toilets may also represent the individual's sense of holding what parents have projected of their own internal world.

Projective identification is an object relations concept. It entails projecting one part of a split representational world—one or more self representations or one or more object representations—into the other and then relating to that person as though she were, in fact, the projected self or the projected object. My patient's father projected into her his own hated and shamed fearful self, sadistically placing her in dangerous or frightening situations, demanding that she be brave, and then ridiculing her for her fear.

Another parent with a problem of low self-esteem may simultaneously project into a child both the hated helpless self and a grandiose self, with ensuing double-bind communications to the child.
Children who have become the containers and personifications of
these parental projections have difficulty developing their own
identity and feel frightened and mystified as to what is real about
them and what is not. They increasingly turn to others to define
reality for them, making themselves susceptible to becoming the
container for projections in later relationships. One has to be
careful about making interpretations that then become for patients
yet another external definition of who they are. The self psychology
concept of failures of parental empathy, although valid, is of little
help in understanding and working with the specific and idiosyncratic nature of the patient's internalizations and identifications.

Although I do not believe that we can ignore the drives, I do
not view them as prime movers unless there has been a failure to
structure them within a cohesive self in early development. Instinctual drive is one aspect of experience that must be integrated within
the self along with other aspects of experience, both internal and
external. The capacity for control of the drives—one of the functions of the ego from an ego psychology perspective—is an outcome of this integration. Failure to achieve control of instinctual
drive suggests a failure of the organizing processes that lead to the
structuring of the self. The structuring of drive, or the structuring
of affect, relates to their integration within a cohesive, object-
related self representation. It marks the difference between the
individual who indiscriminately shoots down everyone in sight and
the person who can say, for example, "I hate my father because he
hurt my feelings."

It is useful to map, so to speak, the specific set-up of the self
and object relational world in order to understand shifting ego
states within the treatment hour. For each state there is a self
representation/predominant affect/and object representation gestalt. The evoking of any aspect of the gestalt is likely to evoke its
counterparts. An example of one patient's complex intrapsychic
arrangement is as follows, in the order of downward, regressive
movement:

1. inadequate false self/insecure, dependent/superadequate object
2. unhappy self/missing, yearning and angry/unattainable object
3. the true self/overwhelming sadness/amorphous object
4. paranoid, undifferentiated bad self/hate, fear/bad object
5. autistic self/anaclitic depression/no object

The major defensive structure was that of a split-off schizoid self, a state which this patient found intolerable. The patient's closest relationship with his actual mother is as the container of her inadequacy as well as of her grandiosity—that is, through a false self. When she becomes unavailable, he cannot sustain the connection apart from their interaction. First he yearns for her, and then he denies that he wants her as a defense against the intolerable pain and to ward off anger. The denial leads to the experience of object loss and the overwhelming sadness, a state he reports as feeling most real. If reparation is not made by the other at this point, there is a split between the good and bad object, and the patient is left with his rage at the bad, abandoning object. His rage annihilates the object altogether, and he sinks into an anaclitic, vegetative depression, with no sense of an object of any kind. The malignant regression would occur as a result of the therapist's failure to discern the emergence of the sad, true self and to connect empathically.

The major therapeutic task is to establish a positive attachment with the true self—to join the patient in his sadness—and to interpret when the observing ego is available. This patient is, in effect, a well-functioning individual in the outer world.

If we view the self as developing within the context of the mother–child matrix—and this includes all facets of that self, including the way it controls its impulses, uses its potential intellect, or structures reality—then we can expect to find a correspondence between disturbances of that psychological self and the nature of the relationship with the primary mothering person or persons. This will be manifest in the patient's developmental history, in the nature of his inner representational world, in the quality of present-day relationships and functioning, and in the quality of his relationship with the therapist.

In the treatment of character disorders, the therapeutic matrix can be viewed as analogous to that provided by the good-enough mother of the early years. It is a relationship within which repair of an impaired structure may take place. Within the therapeutic interpersonal matrix, various split-off aspects of self can be experienced, expressed, and integrated. The treatment relationship facilitates the attachment process, which will eventually provide the basis for the internalization of maternal–therapist functions and interactions and for the further integration of the self within a context of human relatedness. The therapeutic matrix facilitates differentiation, the structuring of the boundaries of the self, the achievement of identity coupled with the achievement of object constancy, and the structuring of a guiding and loving superego. With structural repair and growth, the archaic images of self and object, which were theretofore played out in interpersonal relationships in the here and now, will loosen their grip on the patient's life and fade into the realm of the archaic unconscious, perhaps to reappear in dreams or artistic creation.

The chapters in this volume were selected from a larger group of papers that were written over the past twenty years. They were selected for this book because the issue of structure was clearly relevant in each. Inevitably, there will be some repetition of ideas as they are reworked and expanded over time, sometimes with changes that evolve by virtue of clinical experience. Long-term treatments afford us the opportunity to observe the process of structural change and the concomitant changes in the patient's way of being in the world. Psychoanalytic theory is an ever-evolving system of concepts that becomes richer as new insights are integrated and old ones modified.

In Part I, "Development of Character," I have included the following material:

Chapter 1, "Stages and Processes in the Development of Early Object Relations and Their Associated Pathologies," became the nucleus for my book *Object Relations and the Developing Ego in Therapy* (1979). It marks my continuing attempt to understand psychopathology in structural, object relational terms. There were some modifications in my thinking by the time I wrote that book, and the original diagram has been replaced here by a later one from the book.

In Chapter 2, "Object Relations Theory and the Primacy of Structure," I explore patients' awareness of structural aspects of the self and its deficiencies.

Chapter 3, "The Roots of Anxiety, Character Structure, and Psychoanalytic Treatment," approaches the question of anxiety from a structural point of view.

Chapter 4, "Refusal to Identify: Developmental Impasse," examines the structural and characterological implications of a defense against identification with the mother.

In Chapter 5, "The Idealization and Sexualization of the Power Attributed to the Male Figure," I note that love, as a combination of intense positive affect and emotional attachment, is experienced at every level of development. Its quality in the transference will depend on the patient's level of development in structural terms.

Chapter 6, "From Attachment to Identification: The Female Analyst and the Female Patient," discusses problems associated with the conflicted identifications of some female patients vis-à-vis the oedipal and postoedipal mother as well as the father. In these instances we see how conflict interferes with structure, with the ultimate consolidation of ego and superego identifications.

In Part II, "Character Pathology," I have included the following:

Chapter 7, "Early Object Relations and the Concept of Depression," is an attempt to understand the symptom of depression from an object relations point of view. In the current climate of biological emphasis and pharmaceutical treatment, it is important that we not forget about the earliest developmental situation that sets into motion the depressive process and the characterological aspects of depression. We know that just as the physical state can affect the mind, so can one's mental state exert a profound effect on one's physiology. When the only way a child can connect with its depressed mother is to join with the mother in her predominant mood, we will miss the structural implications if we treat the mood alone without understanding and psychological treatment of the characterological pathology.

Chapter 8, "Bulimia: A Complex Compromise Formation," addresses the subject of bulimia as a failed schizoid defense. The presence of a grandiose self is also considered.

In "Pathology of Gender Identity Development," Chapter 9, I discuss gender identity development as an aspect of the early structuring of the self representation.

In Chapter 10, "Pseudoschizoid Development: The Little Boy's Dilemma," I make the distinction between the schizoid personality and schizoid-like defenses of the healthier male patient.

Chapter 11, "The Double Approach–Avoidance Conflict and Obsessive Disorders," notes that obsessive disorders may manifest a double approach–avoidance conflict at various structural levels. Stage-appropriate interpretations of the underlying developmental dilemma lead to a resolution of the developmental impasse and an abatement of the obsessive symptoms.

Chapter 12, "Creativity and Pathological Solutions," explores a number of variations of pathology of the structure of the self: the false self (Winnicott), the as-if personality (Deutsch), the constructed self (Horner), the self-effacing personality (Horney), and the factitious disorders (DSM-III).

In Part III, "Treatment of Character Pathology," the following material is covered:

Chapter 13, "The Creative Alliance," speaks to the importance of the integration of the various psychoanalytic theories for the full understanding of the individual and his character structure, and for doing the work of psychoanalytic treatment.

Chapter 14, "Ego Boundaries and Resistance," notes how structural pathology and the need to defend against its associated vulnerabilities stand as a source of resistance in the treatment situation.

"A Characterological Contraindication for Group Psychotherapy," Chapter 15, was written at a time (1975) when many group psychotherapists were failing to address the growing body of theory concerning character disorders. Many patients with narcissistic personality disorders were referred to group treatment on the basis of a need for confrontation—a situation that often proved to be nonproductive for the patient at best, and destructive for both the patient and the group at worst.

In Chapter 16, "Object Relations, the Self, and the Therapeutic Matrix," I specify the need to relate the treatment to the underlying character structure. That is, an accurate assessment of character strengths and vulnerabilities must inform the treatment.

Chapter 17, "Innovative Techniques in Work with Character Disorders," encourages the therapist to be creative in the treatment situation but notes the importance of that creativity's being informed by and appropriate to the patient's specific needs.

"Will, Transcendence, and Change," Chapter 18, discusses the concept of will and its relation to structural pathology.

Chapter 19, "The 'Real' Relationship and Analytic Neutrality," discusses the importance of the patient's relationship with the therapist insofar as it serves as an alternative to the childhood relationships that were structured in early development. This alternative then becomes the basis for new identifications and structural change.

In Chapter 20, "Object Relations and Transference Resistance," I directly address the effect of structural pathology on the therapeutic process. "Resistance" may function to preserve the self.

Chapter 21, "The Oedipus Complex," is included here in the interest of following the early developmental process along with its structural implications through this critical phase, which overlaps with the rapprochement phase of the separation–individuation process.

Finally, Chapter 22, "Preoedipal Factors in Selection for Brief Psychotherapy," considers the use of brief-psychotherapy techniques in patients with structural deficit.

PART ONE

Development of Character

1

Stages and Processes in the Development of Early Object Relations and Their Associated Pathologies

In its attempt to understand and classify the psychological disorders of childhood, taking into account the many psychosomatic, developmental, and psychosocial factors that may be operative, the Group for the Advancement of Psychiatry (1966) observes that "no classification can as yet be made of childhood psychological disorders in relation to specific pathogenic characteristics of the parent–child relationship" (p. 200).

Although this may be true with respect to certain child-rearing behaviors, we can say that we most certainly can make such a classification if we have as our focus the development of object relations along the continuum from the normal autism at birth, through the process of attachment to the mothering object, and

3

from this point through the process of psychological individuation from the object and establishment of the self as a separate, yet related, individual. It is my contention that specific kinds of disturbances will be associated with either maternal failure and/or inability of the child to respond to normal mothering at any of these developmental stages or during the transitional processes that lead from one stage to the next.

The ego psychologists, as represented by Hartmann, define the ego in terms of its functions. These are as follows: (1) relation to reality, (2) regulation and control of instinctual drives, (3) object relations, (4) thought processes, (5) defense functions, (6) autonomous functions, and (7) synthetic function (Beres 1956).

What is not taken into consideration here is the essentially hierarchical aspect of these functions. The synthetic function seems most clearly related to the innate competency of the organism itself, its ability to assimilate, organize, and integrate its experiences from the very start. Differences in the extent of this innate competency may well explain why one child can master, at least relatively successfully, unfavorable environmental factors, while another child cannot. When the ability to process experience in this way is impaired at the very outset because of innate limitations of the organism, we will expect to find grossly disturbed behavior and functioning at all levels of development.

So far as the remaining functions are concerned, it seems equally clear that *object relations development is primary*, providing the matrix within which the other functions develop.

In a study of language and communication disorders in children, Wyatt (1969) concludes that the

> optimum condition for successful language learning in early childhood is a continuous, undisrupted, and affectionate relationship between the mother and child, manifested in frequent and appropriate communication, both nonverbal and verbal. Such communication is appropriate for the child if the mother takes her cues from the child's behavior and verbalizations and provides the child with corrective feedback. [p. 19]

And further,

> We assume . . . that for a young child languages are not abstract
> symbolic systems which can be interchanged at will; the mean-
> ing of language for the child . . . and the learning of language is
> embedded in a concrete total relationship. [p. 39]

By the same token, the development of the sense of reality takes
place within and through the relationship with the mother; ". . .
the most important transitory step in the adaptation to reality . . ."
is that step "in which the mother is gradually left outside the
omnipotent orbit of the self." Here Mahler (1952) is referring to
individuation and separation out of the symbiotic merger with the
mother.

If we view the ego as a self that develops within the context of
the mother–child matrix—and this includes any facet of that self
(such as how it controls its impulses or uses its potential intellect,
or structures reality, all defined by ego psychologists as functions
of the ego)—then we can expect to find a correlation between
disturbances of that psychological self or ego and the nature of the
relationship with the mother. The problem has been to adequately
conceptualize that relationship within a developmental framework
to allow for the drawing of such connections.

Guntrip (1971) traces the evolution of object relational thinking from early psychoanalytic theory and presents a view of what he
calls the person-ego (which he characterizes as a psychodynamic
view), as opposed to what he calls the system-ego (and characterizes
as a structural approach). The latter is exemplified by Hartmann.
Although he eschews the structural approach as essentially nonpersonal, he presents us with what is, in fact, another structural view,
only this time it is the structure of the ego rather than of a
departmental psyche. He expands Fairbairn's differentiation of the
libidinal ego, the antilibidinal ego, and the central ego to include
what he describes as the regressed schizoid ego. These aspects of
self bear a striking resemblance to Freud's id, superego, and ego
along with the concept of what Winnicott (1965) calls the "true
self." The only true departure from the essentially early analytic

view is his discussion of how the structure is evolved. He sums this up, saying, "A human infant can only grow to be a person-ego, a self, out of his original state of total mergence in and identification with his mother . . . [and] through the period of his separating out from her mentally" (Guntrip 1971, p. 124). But, in effect, he skims briefly over the vicissitudes of this critical process, focusing more on the outcome of that process. He then views pathology as a split (and conflict) between the separate aspects of self as reflected in external and internal object relations.

Mahler has, perhaps more than anyone else, recognized that it is the vicissitudes of this developmental process that constitute the critical factor in the understanding of certain kinds of disturbances (1952, 1971). A comprehensive theory of object relations must integrate both the developmental process and the resulting ego structure.

In an earlier work (Horner 1974), I addressed the limitations of the disease entity model for the understanding of that which is labeled "depression." I explained it from the vantage point of object relations theory *in its developmental aspects* and examined its relevance to the concept of libidinal object constancy. It is this developmental process itself which is too quickly dismissed by earlier object relational thinkers, despite Klein's and Guntrip's delineation of "positions."

Freud's concept of fixation is still valuable when seen as a developmental impasse to be resolved in treatment. Even with individuals who appear to be well beyond the early attachment–individuation struggle, its derivatives are frequently still evident.

A distinction must be made between what is essentially a description of process and its deviations, and statements about etiology. Whether we are talking about a failure to develop attachment to the object, an inability to differentiate self from object, or a failure to separate and individuate from the object with the concomitant development of object constancy, causative contributions can be made by either the infant or the mother or both.

There may be a biological incompetency on the part of the child, such as an organically based inability to process and integrate incoming perceptual data, or a failure of the mother to provide what Winnicott calls "good-enough mothering." Whatever the etiology, a clear understanding of what has gone wrong in the developmental process is basic to an understanding of the individual, how he functions, how he relates, what goes on in therapy, and in some general way, how therapy should be conducted.

Where the nature of the etiology is most significant, perhaps, is in the formulation of a prognosis. It would make sense to expect that the greater the contribution of organismic incompetency, the poorer the prognosis and the more limited the treatment goals. An exception to this would be environmental failures at certain early critical stages that, at this point of knowledge, produce irreversible personality damage. This would pertain, for instance, to children raised in institutional settings where the opportunity to attach to a single mothering figure was absent and the ability to attach at all was irrevocably lost. Mahler (1952) states:

> In cases of symbiotic infantile psychosis the development of individuation has been missed at a time when essential basic faculties of the ego are usually acquired within the somatopsychic matrix of the primal mother–infant unit. In our experience, if and when differentiation in this matrix, highly specific for promoting sound individuation, is missed, the ego remains irreparably warped, narcissistically vulnerable, unstructured, or fragmented. [p. 303]

With respect to etiology, it is also important to consider that what was *at one time* a causative factor may no longer be operative— much as the polio virus which caused paralysis is no longer active. Where an early lag in neurological maturation interfered with optimal personality integration at the very outset, it does not make sense to direct therapy toward an organic factor that has ceased to be operative; its developmental residua need, instead, to be the focus of intervention.

A criticism of the object relations school is its failure to take into account the contribution of the child (except for Melanie Klein, who makes the reverse error). But there is nothing inconsistent with a recognition of the child's own givens and their contribution to the developmental process, and an object relational approach to the understanding of both normal and pathological development, for the potential of the autonomous functions requires, as stated earlier, the matrix of the object relationship in which to unfold and develop.

I will touch upon a number of pathological developments as they relate to the developmental stages of the relationship of the self to the object in the progression from the normal autism at birth (referred to by Kohut as the stage of the fragmented self and by Freud as the stage of autoerotism), through the process of attachment to the stage of symbiosis; and from the stage of symbiosis through the process of separation and individuation to the stage of being a separate individual who has a firm sense of self and other, who is able to relate to others as whole persons rather than just as need-satisfiers, who can tolerate ambivalence without having to maintain a split into good and bad objects, and who has the ability to sustain his own narcissistic equilibrium, or good self-feeling, from resources within the self, which are the outcome of the achievement of libidinal object constancy.

Again, in brief, these stages and their intervening processes are as follows:

Stage I   *Normal autism*

    Process A   Attachment

Stage II   *Symbiosis*

    Process B   Separation and individuation

Stage III   *Separate individual with firm sense of self and other, etc.*

It is hoped that this presentation will provide a paradigmatic framework for further conceptualization and for the understanding of psychopathology.

AUTISM AND THE FAILURE TO ATTACH

The most clearly stage-related pathology is that of infantile autism, in which the child remains fixed at this earliest stage of development and makes no move toward attachment. Infant observation studies (Szurek 1973) show that attachment-seeking behavior is innate.

> The neonate has as its behavioral equipment, its early responses to people, such as its tendency to orient toward them, the head-turning and sucking (rooting), grasping, clinging and reaching (the Moro response of embracing), and especially the development of smiling. [p. 205]

When such attachment-seeking behavior is innately lacking, whatever is available as response or stimulation from the environment remains unassimilated.

Rimland (1964) presents a convincing argument for understanding infantile autism as the result of a biologically based inability to think conceptually and thus to integrate experience into a comprehensible whole. The child cannot organize his pleasure experiences or his mother experiences into a meaningful gestalt, and, as Rimland concludes, is unable to build an organized and unitary "ego." He points out, moreover, that autistic children are behaviorally unusual from the moment of birth, citing the absence of one particular form of attachment-seeking behavior—the adaptation of the body to that of the adult when being carried or held. Mahler (1952) too sees constitutional factors as operating in childhood autism and comments on the fact that there is no anticipatory posture at nursing, no reaching-out gestures, and no specific smiling response. What is lacking is attachment-seeking behavior, and thus the mother–child matrix, which fosters ego development, is nonexistent.

When the response of the *mother* is inadequate or unpredictable, the child may retreat into secondary autism (Mahler 1952, p. 259). This kind of regression is also seen in older patients who have been unable to form a stable attachment because of the emotional unavailability of the mother. Later on they continue to behave in an attachment-seeking way, but since the environment cannot possibly respond in a way that is commensurate with their needs, they react to environmental failure with regression into an autistic shell.

> Sixteen-year-old Mary, a member of a girls' therapy group, was described by the therapist as being "depressed" and apparently unable to become attached to the group or anyone in it, although she continued to come to the sessions. She would respond eagerly when her therapist reached out to her with an offer of an individual session. Mary ate poorly and was significantly malnourished. It was suggested that the group setting was inappropriate, since the facilitation of attachment had to be the immediate therapeutic goal, and her contact with the therapist was too dilute in the group setting.

Later I will differentiate between symbiotic merger at the somatic level and at the psychic level. They are often combined as "somatopsychic" merger, but by differentiating the two aspects of attachment, we can understand why some patients can experience a cohesive body-self and thus not be prone to fragmentation under conditions of autistic regression.

Yarrow (cited by Szurek [1973]) provides us with an operational definition of what Winnicott calls good-enough mothering, which is essential to the normal attachment process. On the basis of his research into infant development, he noted that:

> Significantly high correlations were found between the child's ability to cope with frustration and stress and such characteristics of maternal behavior as: the amount of physical contact mother gave the infant; the degree of her holding the child [which] was adapted to his characteristic rhythms; the extent of the effectiveness of her soothing techniques, and [her] stimulating and encouraging him to respond socially to express his needs or to make developmental progress; . . . by the provision of materials and experiences provided that were suitable to his individual potentialities; and finally the intensity and frequency of positive expressions of feelings toward him by mother, fa-

ther, and others. . . . The highest coefficients of correlation, however, were found to be between the infant's capacity to cope with stress and the degree of the mother's adapting herself effectively to the infant's rhythms and development. [p. 258]

Bowlby (1969) emphasizes the degree to which an infant himself plays a part in determining his own environment. Certain kinds of babies who tend to be overreactive or unpredictable make it difficult for the mother to provide that good-enough mothering. But Bowlby concludes that the mother has a much larger role than the infant by the end of the first year in the determination of the quantity as well as the quality of the transactions that occur between them. When mothering is inadequate or unpredictable, the child may persist in his efforts to engage the mother, with alternating reaching out, angry disappointment, and defensive detachment.

Bowlby (1969) describes separation distress which . . . is characterized first by protest, then despair, and finally detachment. Although his conclusions were based on the observation of infants who had suffered a single traumatic separation from the mothering person, we can apply these conclusions in the context of what Khan (1963) refers to as "cumulative trauma." This concept is relevant to the formation of characterological defences against the repeated experiences of separation distress by the infant. . . . The repeated nonresponsiveness of the mother is experienced as repeated abandonment. [Horner 1974, p. 337]

Masterson (1972) sees the psychopathology of the sociopath as a manifestation of the use of detachment to deal with repeated separations from the mother. The inability of the sociopath to form attachments is well known, and it is striking to observe the intensity of the underlying despair in such an individual when it momentarily breaks through.

If maternal failure during the process of attachment can be hypothesized as the significant factor in the formation of the sociopathic character, we might wonder why such a child is not instead plunged back into a reactive autism with fragmentation of the self. Perhaps this can be understood if we differentiate two separate aspects of symbiotic merger. Mahler (1952) refers to the demarcation of the body ego from the nonself as taking place within the stage of somatopsychic symbiosis. If we suppose that somatic symbiosis and psychic symbiosis are not necessarily tied to each other, although they ordinarily occur contemporaneously, then we can see how the infant can possibly assimilate and integrate body-self experiences and come to differentiate them from non-body-self without necessarily ever achieving affective attachment and, thus, psychic symbiosis. The greater the failure of the mother to provide those good-enough experiences in which she attunes herself to and responds to the child's state of being, the less likely it is that affective attachment will develop. Again we must refer to the competency of the organism itself and the synthetic function of the ego as being the significant factor in deciding the outcome of a failure of the environment during the attachment process. When the innate givens are optimal, we can expect to find the establishment of a reality-delimited sense of self and nonself, albeit without libidinal attachment.

SYMBIOSIS AND THE FAILURE TO INDIVIDUATE

A disturbance or failure of the stage of symbiosis represents either failure at the inception of the stage with disturbances of attachment, or a disturbance toward the end of the stage in the form of an inability to move toward or complete the process of separation and individuation. Mahler's work (1968) on the symbiotic infantile psychosis addresses itself to the latter. She describes children in whom constitutional factors seem preeminent, as well as those in which the extrinsic factor, parental psychopathology, is prominent. "In these . . . symbiotic cases the adult partner very often seems to be able to accept the child only as long as it belongs as a quasi-vegetative being, an appendage, to her or his body" (1952, p. 293). This type of severe disturbance

> becomes apparent either gradually or fulminantly at such cross-roads of personality development at which maturational function of the ego would usually effect separation from the

mother. . . . As soon as ego differentiation and psychosexual development confront the child and thus challenge him with a measure of separation from and independence of the mother, the illusion of the symbiotic omnipotence is threatened and severe panic reactions occur. [Mahler 1952, p. 292]

Any pressure in the direction of sudden separate functioning must be cautiously avoided in the symbiotic child. If the ego of the symbiotic type is overrated and expected to be able to cope with reality without continuous ego infusions from the therapist who substitutes for the mother, the panic reactions and acute hallucinations may cause regressions and withdrawal into stuporously autistic states or hebephrenic deterioration. [Mahler 1952, p. 303]

These observations not only apply to children but are also seen to occur in adult patients who have managed a precarious adjustment for many years until life changes precipitate just the kind of break Mahler describes.

A 35-year-old woman patient, a brilliant graduate student, had managed a marginal social adjustment by means of a circumscribed delusional system which contained the nucleus of the symbiotic merger with her schizophrenic mother, a mother who was able to accept her only as long as she continued to function as a quasi-vegetative being, an appendage "to her . . . body." For this reason, the delusional material itself was not dealt with directly or confronted in treatment. Rather, work focused on the issue of separation and loss with respect to the mother, with an attempt to establish a substitute relationship in the transference. At the beginning of summer, the patient was confronted with the termination of her studies, the termination of her period of training, and the vacation of this therapist all at the same time. Realizing the panic that this was sure to produce, I made it possible for her to both see and call me during the four weeks I would be away from my office. However, she experienced this offer as an "insult," a blow to her precarious self-esteem, and as a threat to her determination to become independent. The latter push toward growth also constituted the main source of resistance to establishing the therapeutically necessary attachment to me. Within two weeks she was hospitalized with a fulminant psychosis. Her release was obtained by a relative, who brought her to see me. By this time there was no observing ego, and I had become incorporated within the delusional system. Despite the intensity of her struggle to individuate, the severity of the separation panic precipitated a regressive merger with the mother and a reentry into the mother's delusional world.

In the symbiotic stage, the mother is experienced as part of the self. Since experience of both self and other must emerge from this stage through the process of separation and individuation, it is logical to assume that a disturbance of the symbiotic relationship will lay the groundwork for difficulties in the process of separation–individuation.

According to the theory of unconscious object relations, as developed by Klein and Fairbairn:

> Object relations exist within the personality as well as between the personality and the external world, [and] the inner world of object relations determines in a fundamental way the individual's relations with people in the external world. This inner world of objects—more strictly object relations—is basically the residue of the individual's relations with people upon whom he was dependent for the satisfactions of primitive needs in infancy and during early stages of maturation. . . . The first simple technique of maintaining a good relationship with the object by incorporating the "good' and rejecting the "bad" according to whether it is a satisfying or a frustrating object are differentiated *pari passu* with the development of the ego capacities of the individual. [Phillipson 1955, p. 7]

I will offer here an alternative explanation for what is called the introjection of the good or bad object, and splitting of the object as a defensive maneuver to protect the good object from the anger toward the bad.

The development of object relations depends upon the ability of the infant to process stimuli coming from both the internal and the external environments. This process will involve the ability to receive stimuli, to differentiate one stimulus from another, to recognize patterns and relationships of these stimuli, and to form meaningful associations between these patterns—in short, to achieve some kind of meaningful gestalt from a body of discrete experiences. A deficiency of the organism in any of these abilities will necessarily interfere with the most rudimentary steps in the development of a cohesive sense of self and of normal object relations. It is not surprising that we frequently find evidence of organic factors in psychotic children. Mark, a 12-year-old psychotic boy, showed both positive findings upon neurological examination and severe deficiencies on the Illinois Test of Psycholinguistic Abilities in those sensory and associational processes that involve meaning. His unusually good memory and imitativeness enabled him to develop a social facade and an apparent brightness that, for a time, obscured the diagnostic picture.

The environment may also contribute to a disturbance of this early process, and we can see how what eventuates in what is seen as object splitting has its origins here.

Piaget (Phillips 1969) refers to the development toward the end of the first year of life of symbolic meaning and causality, and describes how "more and more stimulus patterns are assimilated, with coordination of various schemata as functional relationships are developed among them" (p. 19).

Pleasurable experiences become organized into one gestalt; displeasure experiences into another. What comes to be the good object is part of the first gestalt; what comes to be the bad object is part of the second. Where mothering is, for the most part, good enough, and where displeasure experiences do not attain significant salience, they will not be organized out as a significant constellation of experience (or vice versa—i.e., pleasure experiences). An attitude of basic trust (or distrust) will also emerge from these early constellations. Where self and object merger experiences are significantly discrepant, usually reflecting maternal ambivalence, synthesizing them is a task too monumental for the infantile ego, and both kinds of experience will acquire a compelling salience. The infant will then organize all aspects of experience, including the perceptual, kinesthetic, and physiological, into two discrete categories, good and bad. Thus there will be, during the symbiotic stage, a self–good object merger based on good mothering experiences, and a self–bad object merger based on unsatisfactory mothering experiences. The origins of the split in the relationship with the object, and thus in the self, arise from the disparity of experience, which is too extensive for the child to form into an integrated, single, self–other experience. To separate out of the dual symbiosis would require two parallel processes, since integration at this stage of perceptual-cognitive development is impossible.

Should the differentiation of self from nonself be from the bad object only, the merger with the good object remains and will be the basis for later attempts to establish symbiotic relationships with idealized others, alongside a paranoid view of the now separated-out bad mother–world.

Should the differentiation of the self be from the good object only, we might be likely to find an idealized view of the external world alongside a tendency to seek out a symbiotic relationship with a bad or hurtful other, a possible etiological factor in masochism. Here we see developmentally the origins of what Fairbairn observed structurally. Mahler (1971) sees as characteristic of borderline transference (1) coercive behavior designed to force the mother to function as the child's omnipotent extension, and (2) splitting of the object world permanently into good and bad. She describes one patient's longing for the symbiotic other half of self side-by-side with the rage and hatred felt toward the bad mother of separation. My patient, Carol, a woman in her thirties, has since childhood sought out and found warm and sympathetic women to function as her idealized good mother. At the same time, she is drawn into exciting and intense sadomasochistic relationships with cold and rejecting men, turning to them instead of the available good mothers at the times of her greatest need and yearning to be loved by and reunited with her rejecting actual mother.

It seems more parsimonious to understand the splitting of the object, and thus of the self counterpart, in terms of these relatively simple aspects of early cognitive organization of experience into meaningful patterns rather than in terms of later introjections and defensive splittings, although later derivatives may appear to be theoretically consistent with such hypotheses.

Although the separation–individuation phase is the point at which the split becomes apparent, its genesis is earlier: during the time of symbiotic merger with the ambivalent object.

The narcissistic personality, as described by Kohut (1971), represents a fixation at the latter phase of symbiotic attachment. Mahler (1971) discriminates between individuation, which is the evolution of intrapsychic autonomy, and separation, which involves differentiation, distancing, boundary-structuring and disengagement from the mother, and she points out that the two processes run on two intertwined but not always synchronized developmental tracks (p. 407). Although the narcissistic personality has achieved secure body-boundary structuring with differentiation of self from nonself, he has not yet achieved intrapsychic autonomy. Kohut (1971) says:

> It is important to realize that these patients have specific assets which differentiate them from the psychoses and borderline states. Unlike the patients who suffer from these latter disorders, patients with narcissistic personality disturbances have in essence attained a cohesive self, and have constructed idealized archaic objects. And, unlike the conditions which prevail in the psychoses and borderline states, these patients are not seriously threatened by the possibility of an irreversible disintegration of the archaic self or of the narcissistically cathected archaic objects. [p. 4]

Kohut (1971) describes the progressive components of the narcissistic segment, which marks the end of the symbiotic stage, as it is evidenced in the transference.

> In its most archaic form, the cognitive elaboration of the narcissistically cathected object is least in evidence: the analyst is experienced as an extension of the grandiose self. . . . The patient expects unquestioned domination of the therapist.

[In the next, less archaic form] the narcissistically cathected
object is experienced as being like the grandiose self or as being
very similar to it. . . . The patient assumes that the analyst is
either like him or similar to him, or that the analyst's psychological makeup is like, or similar to, that of the patient.

[And then in] the most mature form . . . the analyst is experienced as a separate person. He is, however, important to the
patient only, and accepted by him only . . . as was the mother
during that stage of development, so is now the analyst an
object which is important only insofar as it is invited to participate in the child's narcissistic pleasure and thus to confirm it.
[pp. 114–116]

Moving out of this realm of narcissism involves going with the
process of defining self and object as fully separate. Ideally this
occurs gradually enough and with sufficient maternal support to
allow for the internalization of maternal functions (i.e., the development of object constancy) and a transformation of narcissistic
grandiosity into healthy self-esteem. The object is then loved not
only for its need-satisfying function, but because of its own unique
attributes.

The kind of rage and claims of entitlement expressed by the
narcissistically fixated patient suggests a highly dysphoric rupture
of the symbiotic bond, possibly by circumstances and/or maternal
psychopathology. Thirteen-year-old Carlos, who expressed his rage
by fecal soiling and messing, as a baby was kept inappropriately
close (sleeping next to his mother), and for too long. His mother
cathected him narcissistically and gratified herself through him. He
was abruptly displaced, at the age of 2, by the next baby, who
served mother's symbiotic needs better, and then further by several
subsequent children. He continues to rage at inequality and unfair-
ness and demands continuous compensation for his bill of grievan-
ces. He is able to extort unreasonable indulgences by inducing guilt
in the mother, and she is further motivated to reward his demands
because of her still existing narcissistic cathexis of him.

Manic-depressive psychosis, the thorn in the side of theorists
and frequently explained in terms of hereditary tendencies, can be
understood instead as representing the pivotal position between the

self object merger and omnipotence of symbiosis (manic phase), and the sudden experience of object loss that accompanies recognition of separateness in the earliest phase of the separation–individuation process (depressive phase).

Maternal failure at this junction, whether because of rigid child-rearing practices or because of the mother's own depression and consequent emotional unavailability, will predispose the individual to the latter reactivation of this sequence when inner or outer stressors exert a regressive impact on a reasonably stabilized borderline character structure.

The appearance of this syndrome for the first time in later years in persons apparently normal up to that time has contributed to its puzzlement. Hypothesizing a stabilized borderline character makes the "breakdown" theoretically comprehensible.

Masterson and Mahler both pinpoint failure of the separation–individuation phase as the crux of the pathology of the borderline patient. He is caught on the horns of a dilemma, the engulfment of symbiosis if he moves toward the object, the experience of loss and abandonment if he moves away. In such instances, we often find a mother who withdraws love at the child's first move to define himself as separate from her. Her emotional unavailability if he attempts to individuate prevents the achievement of object constancy, which would allow him to sustain for himself his narcissistic equilibrium. Instead, as he moves away, he experiences object loss and depression (Horner 1974). Masterson defines as the hallmarks of the borderline syndrome abandonment depression and a narcissistic oral fixation. To defend against the terror of abandonment, the borderline patient "clings to the maternal figure, [and] thus fails to progress through the normal developmental stages of separation–individuation to autonomy" (p. 19).

Tolpin (1971) equates the achievement of object constancy with the achievement of a cohesive self, an equation certainly not upheld by Kohut's work. The achievement of object constancy is a task of the process of separation and individuation, which follows the point at which a cohesive sense of self has been established. However, the issue of object constancy is as critical in development as is that of the cohesive self, and it deserves the attention Tolpin gives it.

She describes the kind of "developmental leap" that occurs during the separation–individuation phase, the successful outcome of which depends upon the gradual internalization of equilibrium maintaining maternal functions that lead to a separate, self-regulating self. This is the essence of what is meant by object constancy.

Burgner and Edgcumbe (1972, p. 328) refer to "the capacity for constant relationships" and see this as "a crucial switch point in the development of object relationships." They describe this capacity functionally as "the capacity to recognize and tolerate loving and hostile feelings toward the same object; the capacity to keep feelings centered on a specific object; and the capacity to value an object for attributes other than its function of satisfying needs." Anna Freud (1968) wrote, "Object constancy means . . . to retain attachment even when the person is unsatisfying."

Tolpin (1971) describes how the transitional object eases the stress of transition to object constancy.

> [It] promotes internalization of the mental structure on which object constancy depends—the inner structure now performs for the self some of the equilibrium-maintaining regulations which depended at first on the need-satisfying object. [p. 328]

The transitional object itself is eventually put aside as its functions become internalized. Tolpin (1971) comments:

> When a structural deficit is incurred during [this] period of infancy . . . a fixation on the need for the functions of the idealized parent imago occurs, and the personality is "addicted" to the function of the external regulator. The clarification of the function of the transitional object may assist in understanding disorders like addiction and fetishism in which this is the case. [p. 331 fn]

The transitional object can be used in therapy with the patient who has not achieved full libidinal object constancy. I will, at times of separation such as vacations, give such a patient something of mine to keep as a transitional object, or suggest that he or she sit down and write to me when the sense of loss of connection with me starts to develop.

And in working through the separation–individuation process with a patient, I will suggest an attempt to regain and consider as many early nurturant memories as possible, these memories themselves functioning as very effective transitional objects. With all the focus in therapy on anger, anxiety, and defense, the importance of positive memories in the maintenance of object constancy is often overlooked.

PSEUDOINDIVIDUATION: THE SCHIZOID SOLUTION

Guntrip speaks of the need–fear dilemma of the separation–individuation phase, a dilemma which the borderline patient seems unable to resolve. Some individuals escape from it by means of schizoid withdrawal. Although he characterizes this as a regression, I have described it (Horner 1974) as a

> flight forward, a premature severing of the symbiotic bond, in a kind of pseudoindividuation. Since the separation process is, in this instance, so precipitous, it does not allow for the gradual internalization of the libidinal object which culminates in what is referred to as object constancy. [Although] attachment has been achieved with the schizoid individual . . . it is later denied in the effort to escape the engulfment of symbiosis. [p. 338]

Shirley, the 28-year-old mother of two boys, who maintained her schizoid detachment through a series of sexual encounters, attributes her fear of letting herself become attached to anyone, including me, as a fear that, were she to do so, she could no longer be Shirley, but would then have to exist to meet the needs of the other. Now, as she is becoming more and more aware of her longing for attachment and sharing, her anxiety is becoming intense. The nonattachment of this kind of patient is qualitatively different from the *inability* of the sociopathic individual to experience attachment.

Also, the level of functioning in other areas of the ego is significantly different from the patient who *regresses* from the danger of engulfment into autistic withdrawal. Because a cohesive sense of self and other (although there is no object constancy) has been achieved, there is no danger of psychotic fragmentation. The main complaint of the schizoid patient is his loneliness and his feelings of emptiness, all of which are manifestations of the absence of object constancy and the denial of the wish to reach out affectively toward others. Treatment is difficult because this patient

> will have to undergo a painful regression in order to reconnect with the libidinal object, thence to individuate once again, only this time gradually enough to allow for the development of object constancy. This view makes understandable the schizoid patient's massive resistance to change, since such a move must surely be experienced as a regressive loss of autonomy which threatens other areas of ego functioning. Without his schizoid defenses, such an individual will more closely resemble the borderline patient, and he will have to experience, once again, the severe anxiety of this position. [Horner 1974, p. 339]

A successful negotiation of the process of attachment, and then of separation and individuation, with the achievement of the psychological status of a separate individual who has a firm sense of self and other, who is able to relate to others as whole persons rather than solely as need-gratifiers, who can tolerate ambivalence rather than maintaining a split into good and bad objects, and who can sustain his narcissistic equilibrium from resources within the self that are the outcome of the achievement of object constancy, brings a child to the stage of a reasonably healthy ego formation, where further developmental tasks do not lead to serious depression, paranoia, or fragmentation.

It is more and more my belief that an incomplete working through of these early challenges underlies all later neurotic disturbances, and that psychoanalysis and psychotherapy must address themselves to a resolution of these tasks. Perhaps it is a naive belief that persons who, in certain aspects of their life—their work life in particular—function at high levels of achievement and effectiveness cannot have residual pockets of such early pathology that keeps the therapist from entertaining and exploring such hypotheses. If such exploration is not undertaken and early developmental impasses are not resolved, treatment may go on and on, with certain isolated derivatives of these impasses continuing to interfere in interpersonal relationships. A theoretical orientation that takes into account both the developmental and structural aspects of object relations will allow for a richness of understanding and interpretation that will enhance the effectiveness of therapy and the possibility of change on the part of the patient.

In summary, Figure 1–1 presents the stages and processes of early object relations and their related pathologies:

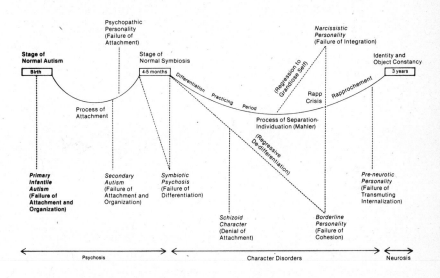

Figure 1-1. Stages and Processes in the Development of Early Object Relations and Their Associated Pathologies (Revised).
From Horner, A. (1979), *Object Relations and the Developing Ego in Therapy.* New York: Jason Aronson.

2

Object Relations Theory and the Primacy of Structure

Guntrip (1971) notes that Freud takes the whole self for granted and that he does not discuss it specifically "as the one psychic phenomenon that matters most of all" (p. 74). He adds that "the problem of having an unquestioned possession or else a lack of a sense of personal reality and selfhood, the identity problem, is the biggest single issue that can be raised about human existence" (p. 119).

Guntrip (1971) rejects Freud's concept of an "Id-plus-Ego-control apparatus" and calls for what he terms a personal theory, by which he means one that focuses on "the object relational life of meaningful and motivated relations between persons, beginning with parents and child" (p. 30). He sees a dichotomy between a structural theory and a personal theory. I do not believe that we can have one without the other. The very term *object relations* implies structure—the structure of the self and object representations as well as their dynamic interplay. The origin, development, and the pathology of these structures come out of the interpersonal and the developmental, and our concept of structure must be in harmony with both factors. The concept of a self structure with its own developmental vicissitudes allows for a clinically fruitful integration of both lines of thought.

Although Guntrip takes issue with what he sees as a mind–body dualism in Freud's work, he does find acceptable a concept of structure as defined by Fairbairn (1954)—that is an "arrangement of mental phenomena into functioning structure groups" (p. 128). In other words, a mental structure is an enduring organization of psychological elements, *enduring organization* being the key phrase. Guntrip writes further of Fairbairn's work:

> To emphasize the ego and its search for security, which it can find only by dealing satisfactorily with its bad objects and maintaining reliable relations with its good objects, is to bring the whole problem of object relationships into the very center of psychoanalytic inquiry. It also lifts psychoanalysis above psychobiology to the level of a true psychodynamic theory, that is, a theory of the person, not simply of the organism. [Guntrip 1971, p. 230]

Psychoanalytic object relations theory has taken two separate paths, each deriving, of course, from Freud. One follows his early psychology of the id, with its focus on the instincts. Melanie Klein is an example of this group of theorists. The second path follows Freud's later concern with the ego. Its advocates, like Fairbairn, view the individual as primarily object seeking and not gratification seeking. Fairbairn regards aggression as primarily a reaction to the frustration of object seeking on the part of the ego.

In Klein's view (Segal 1964), the ego deflects the death instinct which has been transformed into aggression, and the anxiety it evokes, by projecting it outward toward the external object, the breast. The breast is bad and threatening to the ego. At the same time, libido is also projected onto the breast, creating the good breast. The subsequent introjection of the ideal and persecutory breasts lays the groundwork for the inner world of good and bad object. Thus, Klein begins with an orthodox instinct theory but eventually comes to an object relational view of the psyche. Although external objects are not valued as objects in themselves, but as receptacles for projection, what ultimately develops is an inner world of fantasy that is object relational.

The Fairbairn–Klein disagreement with respect to the role of aggression is echoed today in that between Kohut and Kernberg. Kernberg (1974), like Klein, stresses the importance of the aggressive drive per se, and its own vicissitudes in the genesis of pathological narcissism. He views self and object splitting as a defense that protects the positive images from the destructive forces of the negative images. Kohut (1971), on the other hand, views aggression as reactive to failure of the environment during the stage of normal developmental narcissism.

I also see the gratification-seeking versus object-seeking dichotomy as theoretically nonproductive. If the infant's needs are not tended to by the object it seeks, there will be rage, which will attach to the object that comes to be perceived as frustrating.

OBJECT RELATIONS AND EGO PSYCHOLOGY

In an object relations or self theory—that is, an ego psychology and not an id psychology—instinctual drive is regarded as only one aspect of experience. That aspect must be integrated within the self representation along with other aspects of experience, whether they be of internal or environmental origin. This is consistent with Fairbairn's (1952) view that instinct is a function of the ego. That is, instinct is not a stimulus to psychic activity; it *is* the activity. It is the integration of this experience that originates with the organism or person that is the basis for the structuring of drive, as well as of affect. Once structured as an integral part of the self representation, drive and affect can be understood in psychodynamic terms. Unstructured drive and unstructured affect are subject to neither ego nor superego controls. They lead, instead, to an overwhelming of the ego, and disorganization, or to a distortion of the ego in an attempt to counteract their disruptive impact. This often takes the form of schizoid detachment.

The function of the ego, according to Freud, is to be aware of realistic environmental circumstances so that it may plan behavior aimed at gratifying somatic needs. Although Freud's ego is concerned with the achievement and maintenance of object relationships, it seeks these objects for the sake of the id. The id is governed by the needs of the biological organism. For Fairbairn, on the other hand, the ego is not dependent upon the id, and its primary concern is to serve itself (Sullivan 1963). He sees the internalized object as a structural aspect of the psyche. This is in contrast with Freud, who notes that libidinal attachments are *between* the ego and its objects.

According to Fairbairn, there is a structure, a unitary ego, or ego potential, present from the beginning of life. We can assume that from the beginning, if not in utero, there is an experiencing organism, and that this experiencer is the primordial ego, or self. The infant demonstrates two kinds of behavior from the start: attachment-seeking behavior, manifest in intense eye contact and interest in the human face (Fantz 1966), and what Mahler (1968) calls normal autism, when the perception of the newborn is inwardly focused. Nonetheless, these two alternating states must be viewed as experiences of that primordial self, and in that respect, unified.

Fairbairn notes that split ego development arises out of bad object relations in real life. The bad object mother is internalized in an effort to control her. The now internalized bad object is further split into an exciting and a rejecting object. At the same time there is an emotionally neutral idealized mother with whom the child conforms to gain approval. With this object splitting there is a parallel ego splitting into an infantile libidinal ego, which dependently craves the object; an infantile antilibidinal ego, which is identified with the rejecting object and which is the basis for an immature, severe conscience; and a central ego, which conforms to the idealized parents. The central ego assumes the ascendency while the emotionally disturbing aspects of both object and ego have been split off and repressed.

In my own work (1979) I have attempted an approach to object relations theory that is a more fully articulated ego psychology—one that takes into account more specifically what earlier ego psychologists spoke of as the various functions of the ego, by which it was defined (Beres 1956, Hartmann 1954), and one that brings them under the aegis of a structured self with its cognitive, affective, impulse-related, and perceptual correlates. This self-representation develops within an object relational matrix, although ideally it emerges from that matrix as an autonomous psychic structure. With a focus on the developmental vicissitudes of the self both as a structure and as a person, we move closer to what might be termed *self theory.*

According to Beres (1956), the functions of the ego are (1) relation to reality, (2) regulation and control of instinctual drives, (3) object relations, (4) thought processes, (5) defense functions, (6) autonomous functions, and (7) the synthetic function. A shift from the ego psychology of Hartmann and others to an object relations theory comes with the emphasis on the central role of object relations development in the overall structuring of the ego.

The synthetic function is the link between the biological organism and the psychological person. It is manifest in the innate tendency and capability of the infant to assimilate, organize, and integrate its experiences from the very beginning. Although this tendency is innate, even in an organically competent infant these capabilities can be overwhelmed by excessively chaotic or disruptive environmental conditions.

As far as the remaining functions are concerned, the emerging organization and patterning of the self and object representations provide the matrix within which they unfold. All aspects of ego functioning become organized *within* the self representation in healthy development and cannot be separated from it. They are all experienced and understood as aspects of an integrated self. The failure of such organization is viewed as a manifestation of pathology of the self.

Thus we have an organizer, and experiences of both inner and environmental origins to be organized, a process that will lead to that enduring mental structure we call the self. The combination experiencer and organizer is Fairbairn's primordial unitary ego.

Only by examining this process with microscopic care can we detect certain defects in the organization and integration of the self in the earliest stages of its evolution, defects that will be revealed later on when the thrust of development will be impeded by their existence.

REQUIREMENTS FOR HEALTHY ORGANIZATION

As I see it, the three desiderata of the organization of the self are cohesion, reality-relatedness, and object-relatedness. The cohesive self is characterized by an adequate integration of affect, impulse, perception, and cognition, and it is not subject to fragmentation or disorganization.

Deficits of cohesion, in my view, characterize the borderline personality. In a more evolved character structure, under the impact of intrapsychic conflict, integrated feelings, wishes, or thoughts may become subject to repression. Their reemergence into consciousness will result in guilt or anxiety and not in disorganization. The borderline's deficits in cohesion are the basis for the excessive dependency upon the object. The sense of connection with the object has an integrating effect; the object serves as an intrapsychic prosthesis for a structurally vulnerable self. It is because of this excessive dependency that differentiation and object loss are traumatizing for the borderline patient. They result in the dissolution of the self.

A reality-related self not only has adequate reality testing; there is also a firm sense of a real self in contact with the external world, and particularly with the interpersonal environment. In the false-self organization described by Winnicott (1965), there is a deficit in the reality-relatedness of the true self. The false-self identity is consolidated around the infant's *reactions to* the object, who may be either abandoning or impinging. The true-self identity is consolidated around that which originates from within and to which the object responds empathically. Thus, the responding object is a bridge between the inner world of experience and the outer world of reality. A self-representation that is cut off from reality-relatedness and is in autistic isolation is potentially a delusional self.

The object-related self is characterized by internalizations and identifications that, in optimum development, lead to libidinal object constancy, to a well-secured identity with the capacity to regulate one's narcissistic equilibrium from resources within the self, to the capacity for signal anxiety, and, finally, to the structuring of the superego.

Failure of object-relatedness characterizes autism in the extreme, as well as schizoid detachment in which a pathological self and its corresponding pathological object are split off and repressed early in development. With pathological detachment there can be no achievement of object constancy and its desired correlates. Since the individual who uses these character defenses is thrown back into a state of excessive emotional reliance upon an essentially impoverished self, the pathological grandiose self takes on important defensive and compensatory functions.

THE ORGANIZING MATRIX

The self develops within the context of the maternal matrix, and the primary mothering person is viewed as the mediator of organization. The consistent and predictable presence of the good-enough mother throughout the early months of life serves to tie the infant's universe of experience together in a particular way. First of all, she prevents the traumatic emotional states that overwhelm the ego and impede organization. Then, it is through her that the body, impulse, feeling, action, and eventually thought become organized as part of the self and integrated not only with one another, but also with external reality of which she is representative. The mothering person not only mediates this process of organization and reality relatedness, but her image as manifest in the nature of characteristic interactions is also part of what is organized and is the basis for the development of object relatedness as well. When early development within the maternal matrix goes well, the outcome is the achievement of a cohesive, reality-related, object-related self. Under these same optimal conditions, the stages and processes of object relations development that are part of the separation–individuation process (Mahler et al. 1975) will entail ever greater differentiation of self from object, integration of disparate self and object representations under the aegis of the concepts "baby" and "mama," and the gradual internalization of maternal functions into a now differentiated and psychically autonomous self representation.

Failure of cohesion, failure of reality relatedness, or failure of object relatedness each has its specific consequences in terms of character pathology, symptoms, and implications for treatment. We do not find a one-to-one correlation between them, and there may be an unevenness in any of the three domains. It is essential that we be able to construct, as accurately as possible, a structural diagnosis in terms of these three factors for any given patient. If we determine, for example, that a patient's obsessive–compulsive behavior provides an external structure that holds together a potentially fragmented self, we will not make the interpretation that this behavior serves as an ego defense against unacceptable id impulses. Rather, we will understand this behavior as a defense against the dissolution of the self, and we may therefore choose not to interfere with it at the moment. Many such patients, wrongly diagnosed as neurotic, have done poorly with analytic treatment aimed at uncovering repressed feelings, thoughts, or impulses, as well as with some of the newer therapies, which tend to override the defenses.

The character structure of our adult patient, as it is manifest in symptoms, in disturbances of interpersonal relationships, or in the transference, will be directly related to the relative successes or failures of early development. The earlier the interference with the organization processes and with the steps in object relations development, the more serious the psychopathology.

Developmental failure at any given stage will affect the structure, and deficits of structure will be a deterrent to subsequent development. In the face of structural deficit, even normal maturation can act as a stressor. For instance, if there is an inadequately organized selfobject representation at the undifferentiated stage of symbiosis, cognitive development, which is the outcome of neurological maturation, will confront the child with an awareness of separateness that actually traumatizes him, necessitating pathological defenses against that awareness. This may be a major issue of the crisis in some instances. The developmental tasks of adolescence notoriously stress a fragile structure. The changes in body image and the upsurge of sexual and aggressive impulses may disrupt a tenuously organized self.

Our treatment plan should always be consistent with our structural diagnosis. When we have determined that a failure or defect has occurred in the organization of the self, we can view the most important function of the therapist as analogous to that of the primary mothering person of infancy—that is, as the mediator of organization.

DEFENSIVE AND COMPENSATORY STRUCTURES

Kohut (1977) points out the difference between the primary structures of the self, which develop out of the early processes of organization within the symbiotic orbit of the maternal matrix, and later compensatory structures, which make up for defects in the primary ones. These are based upon later identifications, often with the father, and on the development of the so-called autonomous functions as well as that of ambitions and ideals. He notes the necessity of determining whether the pathology of the primary structures should be addressed, or whether the therapeutic task should be the firming up of the compensatory structures. An unwise pursuit of primary pathology with an inappropriate focus on the transference may lead to a psychotic transference. It says to the patient, "You must be aware of me and my impact on you." On the other hand, if we do not correctly assess the strengths as well as the deficits of the primary structures, we may well do the patient a disservice by avoiding such pursuit.

The grandiose self often stands as a significant defensive structure in character disorders. A major difference between the borderline patient and the narcissistic personality is the relative cohesion of this structure and its ability to withstand the impact of reality without further deterioration. With the borderline patient, underlying deficits of cohesion contribute to a fragility of the defensive structure as well. Confrontation of the grandiosity may lead to a paranoid reaction with both patients, but the narcissistic personality does not disorganize. The paranoid reaction of the borderline is part of the reactivation of the undifferentiated bad selfobject representation, which also evokes a disorganizing fear or rage in addition to the loss of differentiation.

For Klein, Fairbairn, and others, structure is explained on the basis of psychodynamic formulations. The internal bad object of Klein is said to be the outcome of projection of innate aggression in order to deflect it and the anxiety it evokes, and the subsequent internalization of what was projected. For Fairbairn, internalization of the bad mother is *motivated by* the wish to control her. According to Kernberg, splitting is a defensive maneuver *aimed at* the protection of the good object. This approach to understanding structure is a teleological one in which the ego is *motivated* to act upon its own structure for a psychological gain.

DEVELOPMENTAL OUTCOME
OR DEFENSE MECHANISM

With a more developmental view of the process of structuralization, I see structure as the outcome of basic processes of organization under the aegis of the synthesizing capabilities of the organism. These processes involve assimilation, accommodation, generalization, differentiation, and integration, as described by Piaget (1936) in his conceptualization of cognitive development and the formation of the cognitive structures he called *schemas*. The cognitive structures we refer to as the self and object representations have their affective, cognitive, and perceptual concomitants as well.

I see the internal bad object as the outcome of the organization of experience around unsatisfactory object-relating reality. I see splitting as originating in the separate organizational schemas that consolidate around contrasting positive and negative experiences. In optimal development, the positive far outweigh the negative, and with their integration, with further maturation and conceptual development, the hate associated with the negative experiences is mitigated by the love associated with the positive ones. The failure of such integration and the use of splitting as a defense, in my view, comes after the fact of the early structuralization.

This is in accord with Atkin (1974), who views splitting as a manifestation of developmental arrest. He says, "Where no knitting into a whole has taken place there can be no 'split' in Kernberg's sense" (p. 13). He adds that only after some maturity of the ego is achieved as the result of analysis does anxiety occur when the discrepancies are analyzed. "Only then was the disjunction used as a defense, with resistance to giving it up."

Structure is the anatomy of the personality. Psychodynamics constitute the physiology. Just as we can only understand the physiology of the body in terms of its anatomical underpinnings, so the psychodynamic situation must always be examined and understood in the context of psychic structure. Technical decisions in the treatment situation will be determined primarily by the diagnosis of structure. The focus of our interpretations will depend upon whether or not structural deficits are in evidence and, if they are, what they may be. Is the immediate danger for the patient the eruption of anxiety along with the memories or associations of repressed oedipal fantasies? Or is the immediate danger the terrifying experience of the dissolution of the self? Do we support a decision to cut down on the number of sessions of a borderline patient who cannot tolerate the intensity of frequent contact, or do we interpret this decision as resistance? When can we count on the integrity of the ego to carry the patient through a difficult moment and when do we step in to function as an auxiliary ego?

STRUCTURAL ISSUES IN TREATMENT

Patients sometimes reveal an awareness of structural aspects of the self and its deficiencies. The following dream illustrates one woman's awareness of the internalized powerful object of symbiosis, the traumatic states associated with maternal failure, and the defensive grandiose self structure. The threat to that defense she felt therapy posed is also evident in the dream.

In my dream, Bob was convinced that the ruins of a Minoan temple were under the foundation of the house. He wanted to dig it up and find it. I accepted it as inevitable and was only annoyed when he told someone it was a temple of Pergamam.

That was a real Asian city that was the most powerful city before the Hellenistic period. I insisted it was Minoan. A few years ago I read about an ancient society with mother-goddess cults. It was also a civilization that was destroyed by a mysterious event, a tidal wave or earthquake.

When asked what she thought the dream meant she replied, "I feel shaken—my foundation and the superstructure—the impermanence of them. Order is necessary to my sense of knowing what is going on. When that's threatened, I am too."

In a later session, exploring her terror of death, she reveals a sense of fragility in the structure of her self.

Sometimes I worry a lot about death—not dying, but being dead. (What is your fantasy of what it is like?) The ultimate loss. I have a sense of what it is not to be; a complete disintegration of your self. It's the not-being. The vision of cremation is devastating. Scattering ashes is the ultimate disintegration. For me there are degrees of death. If you are scattered how do you find yourself again? Being reincarnated would be OK— me, being a whole cow. Things wouldn't end. Sometimes I get the feeling just from hearing someone tell about a place or event that I have actually been there. (Do you feel as though you have already seen death?) The experience is as valid. I know the distinction. What I heard and experienced is close enough to it. I haven't died but I've been dead.

Winnicott (1974) writes of the fear of breakdown in which the ego organization is threatened. He includes in his list of "primitive agonies" the fear of a return to an unintegrated state and says, "I contend that clinical fear of breakdown is *the fear of a breakdown that has already been experienced*. It is a fear of the original agony which causes the defense organization which the patient displays as an illness syndrome" (p. 104).

Winnicott says that at such moments the patient needs to be told that he has indeed already experienced that which he now fears; that this is a fact that was buried in his unconscious when the ego was immature. Too immature to gather all the phenomena into the area of personal omnipotence—that is, into a cohesive self-object representation characteristic of a healthy symbiosis.

In the treatment situation, the patient must reexperience that which is dreaded, with the therapist assuming the auxiliary ego-supporting function of the mother.

Noting the difference between the traumatic state and signal anxiety, Krystal (1978) describes psychic trauma as the outcome of being confronted with *overwhelming* affect. He points out that in this situation the "affective responses produce an unbearable psychic state which threatens to disorganize, perhaps even destroy all psychic functions" (p. 82). The ego is overwhelmed. In the case of signal anxiety there is a sense that something bad is *about* to happen, and if adequate defenses can be mobilized, the something bad can be averted. With the failure of defense, anxiety can escalate to panic and become a traumatic state.

Repeated traumatic states in the first year or so of life have developmental implications with respect to the organization of a cohesive self structure (Horner 1980). Khan (1963) attributes what he calls cumulative trauma to the failure of the mother to function adequately as a protective shield for the child. This may be due to her failures of empathy, or it may be due to illness and pain in the child which she is unable to alleviate. Whatever the reason, the child is subjected to repeated traumatic states, which interrupt and interfere with the building organization of the ego and the synthesizing of a cohesive self representation. Krystal notes that in adult life, the fear of affect may represent a dread of the return of the infantile type of trauma. I have found this with some patients in whom repression of the bad self and object representations and the associated traumatic, disorganizing rage, served not so much to protect the positive object relation, as Fairbairn would say, as to protect the cohesion of the self. What was feared was not the loss of the good object but the dissolution of the self.

The defenses erected against the traumatic state in early life lead to pathology of structure even as they protect it. This is unlike the defenses put into operation by an already structured and differentiated ego, as is the case with anxiety, which is the outcome of the achievement of object constancy at the end of the separation-individuation process. The primitive defense against the traumatic state in infancy is not derived from the object relationship. In fact, it may be manifest in a schizoid development which emotionally excludes the object. As Tolpin (1971) remarks, "The infantile psyche begins early to resort to pathogenic mechanisms" (p. 336). One patient complained of a poor memory, of having no thoughts of his own, of a lack of creativity, and of an inability to start a session on his own. These felt defects were all the outcome of a fear of looking inward lest he also become aware of potentially disorganizing affect.

There is a specific danger to the integrity of the self with each stage in object relations development. Freud (1926) describes a sequence of danger situations that can be conceptualized from the perspective of the structure and integrity of the self.

The first he viewed as overwhelming excitation. This relates to the infantile traumatic state which overwhelms the young ego. Next is the loss of the object. The undifferentiated object of symbiosis and of the earlier stages of the separation–individuation process holds the budding organization of the self together. Object loss at this stage is a threat to the cohesion of the self (Sandler 1977).

Next Freud notes that there is the danger of the loss of the object's love. With this danger there is a threat of emotional abandonment at a point when the object is still needed to alleviate distress and to prevent the emergence of the traumatic state.

Castration anxiety of the oedipal period signifies a threat to the integrity of the bodily self and to the body ego. Finally, the danger of loss of the superego's love carries the threat of the loss of internal harmony within the self structure—a loss of integrity that does not carry the danger of the dissolution of the self, but a loss of integrity nonetheless.

There are other dangers to the integrity of the self. For example, the anxiety of humiliation may be a manifestation of threat to the grandiose self structure, which itself may stand as an important defense against the dissolution of the self that goes with object loss. We see this with the borderline patient. Splitting of self and object representations creates an intolerable sense of intrapsychic nonintegration and conflict, which is alleviated by projective identification. Externalization and acting out promote the illusion of intrapsychic unity and harmony. The anxiety of shame comes with the

awareness of the discrepancy between the ego ideal and the immediate perception of the self. Schecter (1979) comments that "Resistance often functions in the service of maintaining a sense of self-
constancy and continuity, warding off a sense of discontinuity in
one's identity."

*Defenses can be viewed in general as those available behaviors that
will restore the sense of integrity of the self,* be it schizoid withdrawal,
which shuts out the object and its distressing and traumatizing
impact, all the way up to repression, which prevents awareness of
intrapsychic conflict between structured aspects of the self.

Psychoanalytic teaching has always emphasized the importance
of the analyst as the guardian of autonomy. I would add that it is
critical that the therapist also bear the responsibility of being the
guardian of the self in the treatment of the character disorder.

I believe that the single most critical and powerful message that
one can communicate to the borderline patient—or to any patient
with a character disorder—is one's concern for, and dedication to,
the survival of the self. The therapeutic alliance depends ultimately
upon this fundamental trust. Khan (1974) cautions us that we must
not be omnipotently curative at the cost of the person of the
patient (p. 128). I will often comment of the character defenses
that they were adaptive at one time and are an indication of the
person's determination to survive. This recognition enhances the
self-esteem, which is bruised by the awareness of the pathology of
the self.

Patients with characterological problems are acutely sensitive
to what goes on in their interpersonal relationships. When the
observing ego is primarily a defensive ego, it is not available for
analytic work. Such patients have a stance of vigilance (Giovacchini
1979, p. 439). If, in treatment, it becomes clear that here the self
will not be impinged upon or humiliated, nor will autonomy be
abrogated, the observing ego will be released from its defensive
vigilance and will become available to the working alliance.

The analytic setting is an instrument par excellence for the
mediation of organization. The consistent, reliable empathic, and
nonintrusive presence of the therapist mediates organization and
integration, and contributes to the structuralization of an autonomous self.

3

The Roots of Anxiety, Character Structure, and Psychoanalytic Treatment

In delineating the kinds of anxiety characteristic of the stages of attachment and of the separation–individuation process, David E. Schecter (1980) pinpointed missing someone who is loved as the key to the understanding of anxiety. Love, for the infant, he notes, "means the security of empathic responsiveness to his needs by the mothering one." Both the mothering one and the analyst are characterized as providing the steady holding environment that enhances the integration of the self.

Whereas Dr. Schecter emphasizes the importance of the relationship per se, I want to consider the relationship in terms of its developmental function—that is, the promotion of structuralization—and to reconceptualize the key to the understanding of anxiety as any danger to the integration of the self.

Schecter alludes to this view when he differentiates traumatic anxiety from signal anxiety: with traumatic anxiety, "the ego is overwhelmed or disorganized." He later notes that "resistance often functions in the service of maintaining a sense of self-constancy and continuity, warding off a sense of discontinuity in one's identity."

Following this line of thinking, I will approach the question of anxiety from a structural point of view. That is, I will consider the developmental roots of anxiety from the perspective of the implications for adult character structure and for the psychoanalytic treatment of character disorder. I am concerned with the structuring of affect (as well as the structuring of drive and thought) within a cohesive, reality-related, object-related self (Horner 1979).

I find it useful to consider anxiety from the broad general perspective as a concomitant of any threat to the integrity of the self. The specifics of this threat will depend upon the character structure of the individual. In the more primitive character in which there is a deficit in the cohesion and differentiation of the self structure, the threat may be to the structure itself. That is, the threat may be one of disorganization, or of what Kohut (1977) refers to as the dissolution of the self. In a more evolved character in which ego and superego structuralization has taken place, the threat may be to the sense of consonance and internal harmony of the structure—the structural and dynamic underpinning of neurotic conflict. Basch (1976) comments: "Emotions are subjectively experienced states and always related to a concept of self vis-à-vis some particular situation" (p. 768).

Perhaps the most important distinction that needs to be made here is that between the traumatic state and signal anxiety. Krystal (1978) describes psychic trauma as the outcome of being confronted with *overwhelming* affect. He notes that in this situation the "affective responses produce an unbearable psychic state which threatens to disorganize, perhaps even destroy all psychic functions" (p. 82). That is, the ego is overwhelmed. In the case of signal anxiety there is a sense that something bad is *about* to happen, and if adequate defenses can be mobilized, the something bad can be averted. With the failure of defense, anxiety can escalate to panic and become a traumatic state.

DEVELOPMENTAL IMPLICATIONS
OF INFANTILE TRAUMA

Let us consider the developmental implications of repeated traumatic states in the first year or so of life. Khan (1963) attributes what he calls cumulative trauma to the failure of the mother to function adequately as a protective shield for the child. This may be due to her failures of empathy, or it may be due to illness and pain in the child that she is powerless to alleviate. Whatever the reason, the child is subjected to repeated traumatic states that interrupt and interfere with the budding organization of the ego and the synthesizing of a cohesive self representation. Krystal notes that in adult life, the fear of affect may represent a dread of the return to the infantile type of trauma. There is not only a dread of the return of the traumatic state; there is an *expectation* that it will occur (p. 98). Winnicott (1974, p. 103) views the fear of breakdown in a similar way. He says, "The ego organizes defenses against breakdown of the ego organization and it is the ego organization that is threatened."

The defenses erected against the traumatic state in early life lead to pathology of structure even as they protect it. This is unlike the defenses put into operation by an already structured and differentiated ego, as in the case of signal anxiety. The primitive defense against the traumatic state in infancy is not derived from the object relationship. In fact, it may be manifest in a schizoid development that emotionally excludes the object. As Tolpin says (1971, p. 336), "the infantile psyche begins early to resort to pathogenic mechanisms . . . that are expedient substitutes for maternal buffering."

ORIGINS OF SIGNAL ANXIETY

Anxiety as a signal is derived from the gradual internalization of the comforting functions of the primary mothering person. This comes about when the good-enough mother characteristically intervenes so that the experience of distress or unpleasure is consistently followed by the experience of being comforted *before* a traumatic state can develop. In this manner, affect becomes structured within the emerging selfobject representation and does not remain unstructured or lead to disorganization. Tolpin describes the role of the transitional object (Winnicott 1951) in the developmental shift from dependence upon the mothering person for the alleviation of distress to the achievement of signal anxiety. The child "usually creates this object"—that is, the transitional object— "when he has emerged enough from the symbiotic state to begin to perceive his mother as the chief instrument of his sense of well-being and relief from distress" (p. 321). He has endowed the blanket with her functions. She notes that "although the infant begins to perceive the mother as a not-me . . . by the time the transitional object is formed, her soothing functions are perceived as part of the self" (p. 326). That is, experiences vis-à-vis the object of the stage of symbiosis are self experiences as well, and they are retained as part of the self representation even as differentiation from the object proceeds.

The blanket, or teddy bear, is decathected little by little as its soothing functions are further internalized. With fixation at the transitional object level of dealing with anxiety, the individual still needs something from outside. This dependency may be on food, which functions as the transitional object, or upon an idealized other. The degree to which the child is able to successfully soothe himself with the blanket, or to which he clings anxiously to it with little comfort, will affect the outcome of the internalization process. The quality of the comforting interaction with the mother affects the quality of the interaction with the transitional object. Tolpin notes that the "demanding and possessive behavior of the child during the separation–individuation phase is thus seen as the expression of the phase-appropriate psychic organization that treats the mother's activities and functions as the child's own until they can be acquired from her to form the emerging self" (p. 341). The mother is narcissistically viewed as an extension of the self at this time. The mother's capacity to tolerate this phase with equanimity and empathy enables the child to move beyond it.

Part of this process of the assimilation of maternal comforting functions into the self is the achievement of a sense of mastery. When the mother is responsive to the child's cry, the child can connect its own activity to relief from distress. When the mother is not responsive, the child must passively endure. Since this situation can lead to the traumatic state, passivity, which is enforced at this stage of development, comes to be associated with anxiety and panic. I have noted that several patients who do not have that sense of mastery and potential effectiveness with activity, and who do passively endure with anxiety, report severe anxiety upon awakening in the morning as long as they remain in bed. They feel better as soon as they get up and begin to get themselves organized for the day.

The process beginning with distress, followed by maternal comforting, lays the groundwork for the gradual internalization of comforting functions, for the achievement of ego defenses against anxiety, which functions as a signal, and for the development of basic trust. It is also critical for an image of an effective self that has the capacity for active mastery. Tolpin notes that with the emergence of the transitional object, the child now actively does for himself that which previously had to be done for him. The very issue of taking active charge of the comforting situation, I believe, relates to the sense of mastery that comes with being able to have an effect upon the mother in a positive way. The child who knows he has an effect upon her in a negative way may become frightened of his power to destroy.

The development of signal anxiety is a concomitant of the achievement of object constancy. The end of the separation–individuation process is marked by the further assimilation of maternal (or parental) functions into the self even as the object is separated out as fully differentiated from the self. This involves the assimilation of nurturant and executive modalities (Giovacchini 1979), as well as the assimilation of the imperatives that leads to the structuring of the superego. Schecter (1979) speaks of the formation of the superego as "the organization of experience in the imperative mode."

With the structuring of the superego, a new danger to the self emerges. Indeed, for each of the stages in object relations development, there is a specific danger to the integrity of the self. Freud (1926) describes a sequence of danger situations that can be conceptualized from the perspective of the structure and integrity of the self.

SOURCES OF DANGER TO THE SELF

The first he viewed as overwhelming excitation. This we can relate to the infantile traumatic state, which overwhelms the budding ego. Next is the loss of the object. The undifferentiated object of symbiosis and of the earlier substages of the separation–individuation process is essentially a prosthesis that holds the budding organization of the self together. Object loss at this stage is a threat to the cohesion of the self. Schecter (1980) spoke of the infant's fear of the strange. I see this as related to the developmental and structural immaturity of the child for whom the external structure, including the interpersonal environment, still functions as an organizer. When there are internal structural defects, this dependence upon external structure may become manifest in what is referred to as culture shock. The autistic child's pathological need for sameness is probably in this same category.

Next Freud notes that there is the danger of the loss of the object's love. With this danger there is a threat of emotional abandonment at a point when the object is still needed to alleviate distress and to prevent the emergence of the traumatic state.

Castration anxiety of the oedipal period signifies a threat to the integrity of the bodily self and to the body ego. Finally, the danger of loss of the superego's love carries the threat of the loss of internal harmony within the self structure—a loss of integrity that does not carry the danger of the dissolution of the self, but a loss of integrity nonetheless.

Departing from Freud's formulation and thinking in terms of present-day object relations theory, we can make note of other kinds of dangers to the integrity of the self. For example, the anxiety of humiliation is a manifestation of threat to the grandiose self structure, which itself may serve as an important defense against the dissolution of the self that goes with object loss. We see this with the borderline patient. Splitting of self and object representations creates an intolerable intrapsychic disharmony that is alleviated by projective identification. Externalization and acting out promote the illusion of intrapsychic unity and harmony. The anxiety of shame comes with the awareness of the discrepancy between the ego ideal and the immediate experience of the self.

Schecter (1980) commented that "resistance often functions in the service of maintaining a sense of self-constancy and continuity, warding off a sense of discontinuity in one's identity."

Defenses can be viewed in general as those available behaviors that will restore the sense of integrity of the self, be it schizoid withdrawal, which shuts out the object and its distressing and traumatizing impact, or repression, which prevents awareness of intrapsychic conflict between structured aspects of the self.

TREATMENT IMPLICATIONS OF THE STRUCTURAL VIEW OF THE SELF AND ANXIETY

The consistent and predictable presence of the primary mothering person throughout the early months of life serves to tie the infant's experiences together in a particular way. It is through her that the body, impulse, feeling, action, and eventually thought become organized as parts of the self and integrated, not only with one another, but also with external reality, of which she is a representative. The mothering person is a bridge between the child's inner world of experience and the outer world of reality. She not only mediates this process of organization and reality relatedness, but her image is part of what is organized and is the basis for the development of object relatedness as well. When early development within the maternal matrix goes well, the outcome is the achievement of a cohesive, reality-related object-related self.

Within this context, early primitive distress does not result in traumatic states that overwhelm the budding ego organization but are gradually transformed into signal anxiety. With this structuralization, anxiety is no longer associated with a threat to the very structure of the self. It will instead be associated with a threat to the sense of harmony and consonance within the structure, and the ego will have developed a repertoire of defenses against it.

What the therapist does, or should do, in any given treatment situation must bear directly upon the developmental, structural diagnosis. This diagnosis will take into consideration the qualities of cohesion and integration, of reality relatedness and object relatedness. When it has been determined that there has been a failure or deficit in the organization of the self, we can view the major function of the analyst as analogous to that of the primary mothering person or persons of infancy—that is, as the mediator of organization within the therapeutic matrix.

This therapeutic matrix sets the stage for the repair of the deficits in the character structure. It facilitates organization and integration of the various aspects of the self, some of which may have been cut off, denied, or repressed and which may have a disorganizing impact when experienced. With such disorganization we will observe, not anxiety, which can be interpreted, but panic, the traumatic state that goes with the experience of the dissolution of the self.

To the extent that we are unable to alleviate the traumatic state readily and effectively within the context of continuing structuralization, the experience of anxiety as a signal will gradually come to replace the experience of panic. The therapeutic matrix facilitates the attachment process, which eventually provides the basis for the internalization of maternal–therapist functions.

The single most critical and powerful message that we can communicate to the borderline patient—or indeed to any patient with a character disorder—is our concern for and dedication to the survival of the self. The therapeutic alliance depends ultimately upon this fundamental trust. As we monitor the patient's level of anxiety, we can also assess our relative success or failure in this regard.

THERAPEUTIC MANAGEMENT OF ANXIETY

If our goal is to further ego development and the structuralization of the self, then the way in which we manage the patient's anxiety level will be a central concern. Do we, like the nonempathic mother, allow it to escalate into a traumatic, ego-overwhelming state, or do we step in so as to begin the process of pairing distress with our alleviation of distress, a process that we hope will eventually become internalized? Alleviation of distress refers to whatever technique is indicated. It may take the form of an empathic statement or of an interpretation that promotes structuralization.

Clearly we must have an accurate picture of the patient's character structure and of the deficits in the self structure so that we will be able to distinguish that which produces tolerable anxiety from that which produces traumatizing anxiety.

It is my guess that many so-called negative therapeutic reactions are reactions to something the therapist does or says that is a threat to the integrity of the self. Thus the term *negative therapeutic reaction* is a misnomer. The reaction may instead be due to a therapeutic error. There is a class of therapeutic errors in which something we say or don't say, something we do or don't do, traumatizes the patient. By "traumatizing the patient," I mean we endanger the structure of the self. Panic reactions, with flight from treatment or acting out, may ensue. If we do make such an error, it is critical that it be verbalized to the patient in such a way that we restore the patient's sense of safety and thereby also restore the therapeutic alliance. Properly managed, such errors and their sequellae can be put to therapeutic use. The empathic recognition of the traumatic experience will alleviate the traumatic state, while subsequent interpretation of the event will promote structuralization. This is not to say that we should deliberately induce trauma. Basic trust is always at stake in this situation, and cumulative trauma in the treatment situation will eventually necessitate flight from it.

4

Refusal to Identify: Developmental Impasse

Identification is the process common to the completion of separation–individuation and to the resolution of the Oedipus complex. The end of the separation–individuation process (Mahler et al. 1975) is marked by a relatively secure sense of a separate self and identity, and object constancy. These are the outcome of a series of identificatory internalizations in which aspects of the relationship with the primary attachment object are made part of a fully differentiated self. That which the other provided vis-à-vis the self now resides within the self. This would include comforting functions and executive modalities (Giovacchini 1979, Tolpin 1971). Identification with the anxiety-reducing object leads to the development of signal anxiety (Horner 1980).

Freud (1923) wrote that with the dissolution of the Oedipus complex there is a father identification as well as a mother identification. The father identification preserves the object relation to the mother that belonged to the positive complex (in males) and, at the same time, it replaces the object relation to the father that belonged to the inverted complex. "The same will be true, *mutatis mutandis*, of the mother identification" (p. 34).

Freud saw the broad general outcome of this phase as the formation of a precipitate in the ego that consists of these two identifications in some way united with each other. This modification of the ego then "confronts the other contents of the ego as an ego-ideal or superego."

Developmental identifications thus play a major role, first, in the achievement of identity and object constancy with the completion of the separation–individuation process, leading to the emergence of intrapsychic autonomy; and second, in the resolution of the Oedipus complex in a manner that allows the individual to give up the parent as the object of libidinal strivings and yet to retain the relationship intrapsychically in the form of the mature superego. Thus, identification is a process that leads to the structuralization of both the ego and the superego.

We need to clarify the term *identification* and to distinguish the primary identifications of early object relations development from later identifications. We also must distinguish identification as a process leading to a change in the structure of the ego from the kind of gross identification that serves as an ego defense against object loss or other dangers to the ego. The internalizations that allow one to *give up* the object—as with the completion of the separation-individuation process and with the resolution of the Oedipus complex—are not the same as the identifications that *defend against* the anxiety and depression of loss. One woman, with the death of her mother when she was a young adolescent, essentially *became* her mother, a defense that propelled her into an incestuous relationship with her father. Identification with the aggressor defends against the anxieties inherent in the role of passive victim. One patient, attempting to resurrect his relationship with his beloved grandfather, developed Parkinsonlike tremors. These identifications, like any other ego defense, need to be analyzed.

Defensive identification does not lead to a structural change in the self representation; developmental identifications do. In his discussion of the relationship between identification and individuation, Schecter (1968) defines the process of identification as "the means by which part of the psychic structure of one person tends to become like that of another to whom he is emotionally related in a significant way" (p. 50).

Schecter also distinguishes the conscious wish to become like another person, as happens in the formation of one's ideals, from the actual tendency to become like another—that is, from the basic developmental processes leading to structural likeness. He also distinguishes both of these from pseudoidentification, which involves an attempt to reconstruct an internalized object with which the self may then fuse. "The severely disturbed, often psychotic patient attempts to cling to the internal object, to fuse with it, to 'become' it, or to destroy it" (p. 74).

Schecter concludes that identification grows out of primarily active and relatively conflict-free individuating processes, that it contributes to the ego structure or strength that is necessary for the gradual relinquishing of the more primitive object ties. "Identification and the partial loosening of primitive object attachments may be simultaneous and part and parcel of the same individuation process" (p. 64). When Freud (1923) wrote that the ego is a precipitate of abandoned object cathexes, he noted that it may be that "identification is the sole condition under which the id can give up its object" (p. 29). When this process of identification loses its conflict-free status, when identification stands in conflict with gender identity or the ego ideal or both, there is a developmental impasse.

CLINICAL IMPLICATIONS

Of the stages of the separation–individuation process, the end point, the achievement of object constancy and of an autonomous identity, has perhaps been given the least attention in the literature. I have become increasingly aware of a group of patients who fall just short of the completion of this developmental task, a developmental failure that prevents the achievement of dependable intrapsychic autonomy. Although they are not borderline or narcissistic personalities, they have not yet achieved the degree of intrapsychic structuralization and individuation that is assumed in the neurotic character as contrasted with the character disorder.

From an object relational viewpoint, failures of identification result in an ego insufficiency that constitutes the port of entry to pre-oedipal symptoms in a regressive fashion under the impact of oedipal anxieties. The insufficiency—the incomplete securing of object constancy and emotional autonomy—is the basis for an ongoing dependency vis-à-vis the object, for the lack of intrapsychic autonomy that generates fears of abandonment, separation anxiety, and depression (Horner 1979). Inevitably, the competitive strivings of the Oedipus complex will stand in conflict with the dependency strivings.

Anything that interferes with the identification process will prevent the completion of the separation–individuation process and the resolution of the Oedipus complex. In the clinical setting, we see such an interference in the form of a steadfast "refusal" to identify, a refusal which operates in the service of protecting gender identity or the ego ideal or both.

These patients present with a picture of exaggerated dependency and depression in the context of a relatively well-differentiated and structured ego. These dependencies are played out in current adult interpersonal relationships in which oedipal issues are also prominent. These same dependency strivings will be manifest in the transference and often constitute a major source of transference resistance.

Because of the regressive potential, these patients are frequently misdiagnosed as more primitive than they are, partially as a consequence of current focus on the character disorder. Parameters more appropriate for the borderline or narcissistic personality disorder are contraindicated, but are frequently inappropriately applied. Although these patients may use the language and vocabulary of the more serious disorders, the cohesiveness or differentiation of the self is rarely, if ever, in actual jeopardy.

IDENTIFICATION AND OBJECT CONSTANCY

The early self and object representations develop hand in hand out of the undifferentiated image of the normal stage of symbiosis. *Primary* identifications are those that are the outcome of the separation–individuation process, at the end of which identifications with the *primary attachment object* lead to the intrapsychic autonomy of a fully differentiated self. Through this process, through "transmuting internalizations" (Kohut 1971), part of the earlier undifferentiated object representation becomes part of the self representation, even as the self is being differentiated from the object. We see this shift in the making in the toddler's relationship with a transitional object (Winnicott 1951). Unlike the condensation of object attributes into the self, as is the case of the pathological grandiose self, in which the object is then *excluded* emotionally and cognitively, with the identificatory processes that mark the end of the separation–individuation process in which object attributes become part of the self representation, the object is both differentiated from the self and *preserved* emotionally and cognitively.

The issue of the identification with the *primary* attachment object, who is usually the mother, is especially relevant to the issue of gender identity for the male and, as I will discuss later, becomes one source of conflict that leads to a defensive refusal to identity.

Mahler and colleagues (1975) describe object constancy in terms of the internal good object, the maternal image that is psychically available to the child just as the actual mother was previously available for sustenance, comfort, and love. They comment that object constancy seems to come about to a significant degree during the third year, and that, with this achievement, the mother can now be substituted for in part by the now reliable internal image. The security that comes with this step toward intrapsychic autonomy makes it possible for the child to sustain the anxieties of the oedipal conflict and thus to maintain the forward thrust of development. Fears of abandonment or fear of the loss of the object's love heighten the anxieties of the competitive situation.

The further delineation and enrichment of the self goes on at this time, and the establishment of individuality is the developmental task that is paired with the achievement of object constancy. The self representation is enriched with the assimilation of maternal functions into the self. Giovacchini (1979) focuses on the connection between the self representation and the nurturing modality of the maternal introject. "The evaluation of the ego's functional capacity becomes incorporated into the identity system and contributes to the self's feelings of confidence, security, and esteem" (p. 276). This assimilation of caretaking activities into the self representation is an important factor in the structuring and equilibrium of the self representation.

And so the end of the separation–individuation process is marked by this assimilation of maternal functions into the self even as the object is separated out as fully differentiated from the self. The assimilation of the "imperatives" that leads to the structuring of the superego (Schecter 1979) is an integral aspect of the resolution of the Oedipus complex as well.

The assimilation of the functions and qualities of the object into the self representation—that is, *the process of identification*—is thus a sine qua non for the achievement of intrapsychic autonomy and for increasing autonomy vis-à-vis the object relationships of the oedipal period.

During this same period, identifications with other important attachment objects, particularly the father, can be noted. Beyond separation and individuation, later identifications continue to modify the self representation throughout life. The identifications with father and with the later mother of reality (as contrasted with the personifications of the object constructed by the infant and toddler in the earliest months), with a loved grandparent, with heroes or heroines, or with other important models continue throughout the life cycle. Identification is an important aspect of analytic treatment, in which the functions of the analyst that develop within the working alliance are taken into the self and eventually enable the individual to become his own therapist, as it were.

THE REFUSAL TO IDENTIFY: GUARDIAN OF GENDER IDENTITY

I have observed in the male patient that the need to protect the sense of masculinity is a deterrent to the assimilation of identifications with mother, with the primary attachment object. This active refusal to identify must, at some point in treatment, become the focus of interpretive interventions.

Greenson (1968) writes of the importance for the little boy of disidentifying from mother in the service of securing his male gender identity. Greenson uses the term *disidentify* in his discussion of the little boy's struggle to free himself from the early symbiotic fusion with mother. "The male child's ability to disidentify will determine the success or failure of his later identification with father. These two phenomena, disidentifying with mother and counteridentifying with father, are interdependent and form a complementary series" (p. 306). The outcome of this process is determined by the mother's willingness to let the boy identify with the father figure, the father's availability, and the motives the father offers the child for identifying with him. Part of the motivation to identify with father also arises out of mother's love and respect for the father. This process is often made nearly impossible when the real qualities of the father—for example, alcoholism—make him unacceptable as a model for the boy. In instances of loss of the father through death or separation before the resolution of the Oedipus complex, the question of maleness is bound to be an issue when there are no other available male figures to take his place.

Greenson poses the question, What happens to the original identification with the mother? He wonders if it disappears or becomes latent. And, he asks, "How much of the boy's identification with father is a counteridentification, actually a 'contra'-identification, a means of counteracting the earlier identification?" (p. 312). Greenson postulates that it is in this area that we may find an answer as to why so many men are uncertain about their maleness.

I believe that it is this very need to disidentify with the mother to protect the sense of maleness that precludes the achievement of object constancy and intrapsychic autonomy in many males. The process of differentiation from mother is precipitate, and with the denial of the inevitable identifications with the former object of symbiosis, the achievement of object constancy is aborted. In adult life there will be islands of emotional dependency that may seem inconsistent with the rest of the character. This vulnerability may not be exposed until there is an experience of actual loss of an emotional partner.

Case Example

A 35-year-old unmarried man complained of not being able to establish a lasting relationship with a woman. On the basis of his identifications with his loved and admired father, he was able to achieve a high level of business success. However, he still maintained a posture of inadequacy with respect to certain executive functions and strengths attributed to the mother, a posture he played out in his relationships with women, inviting their domination and contempt. The issue of his fear of both identifying with mother and the dangers associated with his oedipal fantasies had been under exploration for some time. He also had been describing his pseudoidentifications, his attempts to gain the power of the other by becoming like the other. These attempts would lead to a felt confusion of identity. This was operative in the transference.

> **Patient:** I need to identify the elements of my dependency and work on them. In enough of my relationship with you I feel inadequate. I wish your strength to be mine; I rely on your judgment.
>
> **Therapist:** The trick will be to learn from my strength and make it part of you and still be able to maintain your sense of separateness from me.
>
> **Patient:** I still need to identify what you got that I ain't got, and why I feel I don't have it. If I can come to terms with it I will have the ability to relinquish my need to acquire your strength, yielding the separateness.
>
> **Therapist:** Because you had to hold on to your sense of maleness as a boy, you couldn't let yourself acquire your mother's strength.
>
> **Patient:** The achievement of maleness is also the problem of losing the strength she represents to me in terms of self-sufficiency. Like my apartment—if I wasn't fearful of identifying with her I would have been able to acquire her strength in this area. I saw *not* taking care of my apartment as a rebellion and as positive. I was determined to be male and to be independent.

Oedipal issues were predominant for this man. Fantasies of intercourse with mother led to fantasies not only of castration *by mother*, but also of annihilation of a separate self. This is an example of the appearance of the terminology of the border-line experience in a nonborderline patient. Fantasies of killing father so he could have mother evoked anxiety because he perceived his father and his identification with him as rescuing him from the engulfing preoedipal mother. This is a good example of how the developmental dilemma persists, even in the presence of an available, loved, and admired father. The patient remained dependent because he could not allow the identifications with mother that would lead to autonomy. With the dependency, he perceived her (women) as strong, and he wanted her (their) strength. He could only imagine his gaining it through an identificatory merger (pseudoidentification) with a felt annihilation of the self as a result, which led to anxiety, or by destroying the woman and stealing her power from her, which led to feelings of guilt.

Loewald (1979) pays attention to the interaction of oedipal and preoedipal issues, and notes that the incest barrier is a barrier between identification and object cathexis. Particularly in the boy, "the preoedipal stage of primary lack of subject/object differentiation is evolving into the object stage. . . . The incestuous object, thus, is an intermediate, ambiguous entity, neither a full-fledged libidinal *objectum* nor an unequivocal identification" (pp. 766–767). In the treatment of the patient just described, the fears of annihilation beyond castration that went with the fantasies of intercourse with mother illustrate the more terrifying oedipal dangers for the boy. Only with the interpretation of the developmental dilemma and the conflicts associated with it was he able to assimilate what he had perceived as mother's strength into his self representation and to move into more mature relationships.

IDENTIFICATION AND THE STRUCTURING OF THE SUPEREGO AND THE EGO IDEAL

According to Freud (1923), as the object cathexes of parental objects are relinquished, they are replaced with identifications that form the nucleus of the superego. The superego takes over the father's severity and his prohibitions against incest, securing the ego from the return of the libidinal object cathexis. "The libidinal trends belonging to the Oedipus complex are in part desexualized and sublimated . . . and in part inhibited in their aim and changed into impulses of affection" (p. 176).

Here we see how identification in the resolution of the Oedipus complex leads to the structuralization of the superego and a concomitant more realistic and appropriate relationship with parents. At the same time, identifications originating out of the primary object attachment lead to a further structuralization of the self representation and to the capacity for mature relationships. They are parallel processes that facilitate each other in a reciprocal fashion. On the less favorable side, an impediment in one will constitute an impediment for the other.

Loewald (1979) notes that the essence of the superego as an internal agency involves owning up to one's needs and impulses as one's own. This is a necessary step in the uncovering phase of treatment. He comments that this involves facing and bearing guilt for acts we consider criminal, even if these acts exist only in fantasy. The criminal acts he refers to are the incestuous fantasies of the Oedipus complex, and what he characterizes as a form of parricide: the murder of parental authority and the assumption of responsibility for one's own life that takes place with the severing of the emotional ties with parents. That is, incest is the "crime" associated with oedipal wishes, and parricide is the "crime" associated with the resolution of the Oedipus complex. "Not only parental authority is destroyed by wresting authority from the parents and taking it over, but the parents, if the process were thoroughly carried out, are being destroyed as libidinal objects as well" (p. 757).

Loewald sees the repression of the Oedipus complex as avoiding the emancipatory "murder" of the parents and as a way to preserve infantile, libidinal-dependent ties with them. When there has been a failure to achieve the intrapsychic autonomy of a fully differentiated self, this "murder" has terrifying consequences. Loewald notes that when parricide is carried out, "aspects of oedipal relations are transformed into superego relations [internalization], and other aspects are, qua relations with external objects, restructured in such a way that the incestuous character of object relations gives way to novel forms of object choice" (p. 758). Even so, he tells us, these novel choices will still be under the influence of those internalizations.

Freud's concept of the ego ideal changed over time. In his "Introductory Lectures" of 1917, he wrote that the ego ideal is created "for the purpose of recovering thereby the self-satisfaction bound up with the primary infantile narcissism, which since those days has suffered so many shocks and mortification" (1917b, p. 429). In object relational terms, this view of the ego ideal is related to the grandiose self, the defensive and compensatory structure that may be activated by those very "shocks and mortification." A defensive and compensatory ego ideal must be distinguished from that of the mature superego, which is the outcome of the transmuting internalizations of parental imperatives (Schecter 1979) at the end of the separation–individuation process, and of the parental identifications that are part of the resolution of the Oedipus complex.

Freud made that shift in 1933, in the "New Introductory Lectures," when the superego was referred to as the "vehicle of the ego-ideal, by which the ego measures itself, towards which it strives and whose demands for ever increasing affection it is always striving to fulfill." He viewed this ego ideal as a "precipitation of the old idea of the parents, an expression of the admiration which the child felt for the perfection which it at that time ascribed to them."

Sandler and colleagues (1963) relate the ego ideal to the ideal self, which they view, in object relational terms, as one of the shapes that the self representation can assume. They trace the development of a mature, reality-oriented ideal self as it takes place in the healthy individual. The ideal self contains a solid core of identifications with the admired parents of the earliest years. However, "in the well-adapted individual the content of the ideal self will undergo continuous modification in the light of the person's experiences in reality" (p. 154). Parental ideals are modified and displaced over time and integrated wtih ideals taken over from other figures throughout life. The authors note that in states of regression, the ideal self will approximate more closely to aspects of the idealized pregenital objects.

THE REFUSAL TO IDENTIFY:
GUARDIAN OF THE EGO IDEAL

The disparagement of the mother as a model worthy of identification has several determinants for the little girl. First of all, the inevitable maternal failures in the earliest years yield a reservoir of resentment. Maternal power is viewed as bad insofar as it was experienced as in opposition to the wishes of the self. Second, just as the boy must move away from mother in the service of differentiation and individuation, so must the girl. The deidealization of her mother and the concomitant disparagement enable this process. Freud (1931) says that the view of mother as castrated contributes to the deidealization of the mother. In addition, mother is also disparaged as a rival for father, and there are typical fantasies of a nicer, more attractive self who will be preferred. The oedipally fixated female patient characteristically describes her mother as unattractive and sexless. The refusal to identify with the disparaged mother protects the developing ego ideal. At the same time, this refusal interferes with the achievement of object constancy. Interpretation of these dynamics is essential for the full resolution of both the separation–individuation process and the Oedipus complex with the female patient.

Case Example

It became clear in the course of psychoanalytic psychotherapy with a middle-aged homosexual woman that her relationships with women were based upon a felt dependency on and fear of them, and upon her attempts to placate them. Her associations, memories, and dreams strongly suggested a heterosexual character.

The departure of the father from the home when she was 5 years old threw her back upon her dependent tie with a narcissistic and exploitative mother. Her relationships with women were predominantly masochistic, with a hope that by pleasing and placating, she would be loved and not abandoned. As Freud (1931) notes, when the father is disappointing, the little girl will return to the attachment to the mother and to the sexuality of the "negative Oedipus complex."

In treatment, this patient experienced severe anxiety whenever she reported a pleasant or gratifying experience of any kind. Transferentially, the therapist was experienced as the envious mother who would not tolerate her having anything good. She tended to offer gifts in a seductive manner when her own anger threatened to emerge from repression. Inevitably she blamed the maternal figure for the deprivations that were the outcome of her own placating renunciations.

As termination began to be discussed, she reported two dreams:

One dream was violent. Someone had been killed and I needed a note to say that I wasn't present. In the second dream I was in a therapy session. The therapist didn't look like you, but it was you. There were a lot of people around. I got angry. I said I wouldn't pay when I had to share and be interrupted.

Her anger at her mother, who failed to meet her needs, who went out with male friends and left her with the responsibility of younger siblings, is evident in these dreams. She experienced the idea of termination as an abandonment, even though she had initiated the topic. The patients who would be staying in treatment with the therapist were the envied siblings. The guilt and the need to deny the anger were expressed in the first dream.

Toward the end of her treatment she became romantically involved with a man. He responded to her in a manner that allowed her to reexperience the lost bond of tender affection and sexuality she once had with her father. At this time she began to experience the coming termination of her treatment as punishment for her relationship with a man. She reported being strongly drawn to a woman and offered dreams that said, in effect, "I still only want women—that is, I still only want you, Mother." Interpretation mitigated the anxiety and the flight from her emerging heterosexual interests.

It also became clear that her renunciation of strength, with all its feared ramifications, left her dependent upon the powerful maternal figure. The renunciation was partly due to her fear of her own aggression as well as her view of her mother's aggression as bad. In all events, she would be "nicer" than her mother was. Her need to hold on to an image of herself that she came to characterize as "goody two-shoes" prevented the identification with and internalization of mother's strength in its positive and effective significance. The need to protect this image of an unrealistic "sanctified" self was addressed throughout the course of her treatment.

That the inhibition of aggression was also tied to oedipal issues is clear from the following dream:

There was a woman, my mother. She was pregnant and married to her second husband. In the scene I seduced him. I kissed him and held his body close to mine. I enjoyed it. I didn't care that my mother was there.

After relating the dream she asserted rather fiercely that she had no intention of letting her mother keep her from what she wanted in life any more. It should be noted that her mother was no longer living at this time, testimony to the fact that she had internalized the prohibition. Her aggression had been tied not only to her anger at the maternal failures, but also to carrying out the forbidden oedipal wishes. We shouldn't forget the principle of overdetermination. With the acceptance of the real mother and a more realistic view of her own nature, the patient was able to accept the identifications with mother's strengths, strengths that had been allowed only to mother and that had also been viewed as bad. With this shift she began to think in terms of ending treatment with far less ambivalence and with a sense of accomplishment.

I find in many instances that the woman's continued stance of dependency is a direct consequence of her rejection of maternal *power*, which is experienced as bad since it has been experienced as in opposition to the wishes of the self. The good nonpowerful self, in addition, will be preferred by Daddy and is more consistent with her developing ego ideal. At the same time, with the rejection of the identifications with the now disparaged mother, the little girl may identify with a now idealized father. She strives not only to be specially loved by him, but also to be like him. The identifications with mother and father are now experienced intrapsychically as conflicting in a manner that reflects the conflict of the original interpersonal situation. To be intellectual and professionally successful, or to stay home and be a mother—currently psychosocial issues and role conflicts—may be further derivatives of the internalized oedipal conflict.

Loewald (1979) concludes that oedipal issues are new versions of the basic union–individuation drama. I do not think that they can be that neatly equated. Their complex interrelationships must be understood. The failure to achieve object constancy and emotional autonomy will interfere with the resolution of the Oedipus complex, and wishes and anxieties relevant to oedipal strivings will interfere with the achievement of object constancy and emotional autonomy. And the converse also obtains: achievement of either developmental goal, in whole or in part, facilitates the achievement of the other. They go hand in hand and affect each other reciprocally. The accuracy of our interpretations, and thus their effectiveness, will depend upon the precision of our understanding.

5

The Idealization and Sexualization of the Power Attributed to the Male Figure

As clinicians, we see the many pathological forms that can be taken by what people call "love." The experience of falling in love has frequently been interpreted as a manifestation of pathology in the analytic literature. However, it can also be an accompaniment of a structural shift leading to a higher level of organization.

CLASSICAL VIEWS: ELATION AND FINDING THE LOST OBJECT

In his consideration of the affect of elation, which he also refers to as *joy, bliss,* or *euphoria,* Lewin (1951) notes that it is a task of psychoanalysis to determine the antecedent *anlagen* of the defenses. He says that elation is a narcissistic neurosis, as is depression, and that both have their roots in oral eroticism; he adds that in elation we find the denial of the emotional impact of reality. Lewin notes that a state of elation is a manifestation of what Freud (1915) called the "purified pleasure-ego"—that is, the fusion of the self with the good object that feeds it and brings it pleasure. The ecstatic mood repeats or relives the nonverbal or never-verbalized experiences of union at the breast. Lewin cites a patient's description of the experience of coitus, in which she says that she "melts into" the other person. "There is a oneness," she tells him, "a loss of my body in the other person, as if I were part of him without my individual identity, yet in him part of a larger whole. At other times," she adds, "I am the dominant individual and he the lost one, so that I become a perfect whole." Lewin quotes an ancient charm that invokes an intimate union with the deity: "I in thee and thou in me." His patient observed that when her partner entered her, she gained his attributes.

In "Being in Love and Object Loss" (1973), Bak likens being in love to mourning and melancholia, noting that in all three there is a narrowing of the field of consciousness through an all-exclusive concentration of interest on the object. And, he adds, in all three conditions, forms of identification with the object take place. Whereas in melancholia the lost object is regained through identification, the person who suffers from being in love finds a substitute object. In this way the loss is undone and the object is replaced or resurrected. Bak concludes that being in love is a uniquely human, exceptional emotional state that is based on undoing the separation of mother and child. He adds that this feeling state is also directed at undoing later separations and losses of important objects. From this standpoint, the passionately loved oedipal father represents a refinding of the passionately loved good mother of symbiosis, while being in love represents a refinding of the passionately loved oedipal father. Thus Bak implies that being in love is an indication of a state of deficit.

I want to suggest the possibility of a more positive view of passionate love. When we see evidence of early structural and dynamic issues, need we assume that there is a defensive regression? This may be an accurate interpretation in some cases, but we can also see the possibility of higher-level phenomena as derivatives of the early self and object set-up, but derivatives that are character-ized by significant developmental transformations over time. We need to maintain a clear distinction between "same as" and "analo-gous to," lest we fall into the trap of inaccurately pathologizing certain aspects of human behavior or inappropriately reducing them to their developmental origins.

Just as falling in love need not represent a reunion with the lost good mother of symbiosis, it also need not simply be the narcissis-tic delight of being perfectly mirrored by a selfobject (in self psychology terms). When is there a transcendence of the primitive or the pathological, with a new synthesis that is the outcome of the reworking of the developmental *anlagen* referred to by Lewin? When is passionate love a manifestation of a new synthesis that creates a heightened potential for a mature and intimate relation-ship between a man and a woman? Do we have to remain a little neurotic in order to experience passion or ecstasy? The fear that resolution of conflict may lead to a diminution of the intensity of the love experience has validity insofar as a reawakened primitive idealization is the major fuel for the passionate attachment. Freud (1914a) postulated that when one falls in love, one essentially loves a sexualized version of one's own ego ideal. Others also emphasize the role of idealization in falling in love. In individuals with devel-opmental arrest, passionate attachments are more clearly narcissis-tically determined. Bergmann (1980) makes the distinction be-tween needing, which is based on inadequacy in any one of the subphases described by Mahler (1968), and loving, which is the emotional experience of the more evolved individual. Arlow (1980), in exploring the many complex patterns of loving, con-cludes that "It would be impossible to reduce the complexities of object-finding and gratification to any of the simple basic formulas proposed by several of the proponents of object relations theory" (p. 125).

AN ALTERNATIVE VIEW

Perhaps we can view passionate love in a more open-ended manner that allows for a nonpathological and nonreductionistic interpretation. Such love is, indeed, a state of disequilibrium, but one in which there is potential for reorganization—reorganization that allows either for repair of felt deficit or for a new synthesis in which a widened and enriched sense of self may emerge. In *The Sandcastle*, Iris Murdoch (1957) writes:

> He wondered for the hundredth time what it was that he wanted from her. . . . He wanted to be the new person she made of him, the free and creative and joyful and loving person that she had conjured up, striking this miraculous thing out of his dullness. [p. 238]

Murdoch describes the reintegration of repressed aspects of the self of her character, whose name was Mor, within an interpersonal context.

Rather than being defensive, the state of passionate love is more likely to be accompanied by a massive lowering of defenses, with an inordinate degree of trust—sometimes poorly placed, to be sure—in a context of heightened vulnerability to loss or humiliation. It is in the temporary letting down of the defenses that a reorganization becomes possible, a state in which libidinal and object-seeking strivings are in ascendence. The excitement of falling in love accompanies the thrust toward a sometimes only dimly perceived wholeness and integrity of the self within a context of human relatedness. A more successful integration may remain as a permanent aspect of character, even after there is a diminution of the early passion. When passionate attachments are more narcissistically determined, although there may be opportunity for reorganization, this potential may be aborted because of depression or rage at the failure of the idealization of the partner.

In *Mourning and Melancholia*, Freud (1917) made note of the "normal" model for mania, saying that all states such as joy, exultation, or triumph depend upon the fulfillment of a particular economic condition in the subject's mind (p. 254), and that with this fulfillment the person is in high spirits on one hand, and uninhibited in action on the other. Must we limit this "economic condition" to loss and the wish to re-find? Indeed, Freud gives us a more generic organizing principle. Should we not wonder about the possibility that there are growth and creative and integrative economic conditions that, when satisfied, will also be accompanied by high spirits and uninhibited action? Waelder (1930) viewed love as an act of integration of a very high order. Whatever the regressive, restitutive, or defensive aspects of passionate love, there may also be progressive, creative, and structure-building aspects as well. The affective component, the joy or elation, may just as well signify progression as regression. The creative writer or artist will frequently describe the creative process in terms of passion, likening it to the experience of being in love. One is reminded of Karl Buhler's (1927) concept of *Funktionlust*, or function pleasure. In our clinical work, we have to be cognizant of and acknowledge the thrust toward health, whatever form it takes. When we pathologize or negate it by reducing it to its genetic roots, do we not risk becoming a destructive force in the individual's struggle to evolve?

Viewed from this perspective, passionate love, with its accompanying feelings of joy or elation, marks the temporary triumph of trust over mistrust, of love over hate, and of hope over despair. The loosening of defenses allows for an integration of new or previously split-off and repressed aspects of self within a context of interpersonal relatedness. The reorganization of attachment, affectional-affiliative, and sexual strivings under the auspices of a new organizing principle is manifest at successive developmental stages and at ever higher levels of organization.

A DEVELOPMENTAL VIEW

If we think about the developmental milestones that are accompanied by feelings of elation, we can see that each of them is a time of organization and of reorganization. The first is the bliss of the perfect oneness with the symbiotic partner, the developmental basis for the capacity to love. The first passionate love is that for the mother of symbiosis. The infant's delight at her appearance is manifest throughout its entire being, emotional and physical.

During the practicing period (Mahler et al. 1975), the child seems intoxicated with her own expanding ego and the unfolding of the autonomous functions. Narcissism is at its peak. Joy and elation mark the reorganization of the practicing period as the power of the symbiotic partner is now experienced as belonging to the self.

In the rapprochement phase, the mother is idealized when the loss of infantile omnipotence is accompanied by conscious recognition of the relative helplessness and powerlessness of the self vis-à-vis the powerful maternal object. The mother's smile and words of encouragement add to the child's joyful self-expansion, bringing the developing sense of self once again within the sphere of human relatedness. The father becomes increasingly important in this respect as well, as an emerging other of importance in his own right.

With the full flowering of the Oedipus complex, the little girl's state of elation at her father's love for her and his appreciation of her marks the linking of pride in her femininity to his reciprocation of her passionate love for him. Here the capacity for heterosexual love is established. Subsequent reorganizations occur with the crushes of the so-called latency period, and the never-to-be-forgotten first love of adolescence. Just as the small girl must disengage from mother and, in so doing, turn to father and a new synthesis of love and eroticism, so the adolescent must disengage from his or her parents to find a nonincestuous object who provides the interpersonal context within which love and adult sexuality may become integrated. Whatever the extent to which there may be a refinding of a lost object, there is also a new level of integration and the creative synthesis of a new structure, or at least the potential for it. Later passionate attachments may serve to bring ego achievements of later stages of life into the realm of love and relatedness, mitigating against the possibility of a later-developing split between feelings and intellect. Falling in love in the later years of life is likely to be accompanied by a reawakened sexuality and femininity in the woman, and renewed masculine potency in the man, as well as by a sense of future which counteracts the awareness of the limits of time remaining. That is, it reorganizes time itself so that the skew to the past and what has been lost is counteracted by a forward vision.

I want to consider one particular way-station in the transformation of the "purified pleasure-ego," the ecstasy of union at the breast. At this way-station in the development of the little girl, there is a further elaboration of this affect state under the aegis of the Oedipus complex.

Freud (1931) wrote that while a woman's husband is meant to be the inheritor of her relationship to her father, in reality he becomes the inheritor of her relationship to her mother (p. 231). We might amend this by saying that there is an intermediate phase in which her father stands as the inheritor of her relationship to her mother. The relationship with father, already carrying the earlier idealization of mother, now also becomes infused with a new sexuality. It is at this point that eroticism and the power now attributed to father become wedded. This imago then becomes the template for later passionate attachments, although it contains embedded in it the earlier relationship with mother.

In non-neurotic development, subsequent experiences of falling in love will offer the opportunity for the reorganization of libidinal and object-seeking strivings within the nonincestuous context, although there will inevitably be derivatives from both infantile love relationships. I suggest that the degree of passion and elation in the little girl's adoration of her father and the degree of passion and elation associated with one's first love of adolescence reflect the excitement of a new experience of self as much as it does a restitution of the lost object of symbiosis.

Freud (1931) cited the range of motives for the young girl's turning away from her mother: the mother's failure to provide a penis, her failure to feed sufficiently, her failure to fulfill the little girl's expectations of exclusive love, and her contradictory arousal and forbidding of sexual activity. Elsewhere (Horner 1984) I have noted that other motives for devaluing the mother include the facilitation of individuation by denial of loving (also a dynamic for the little boy) and the fantasy elimination of the mother as a rival in the service of the illusion of oedipal triumph. The oedipally fixated woman characteristically describes her mother as unattractive, as sexless, and as cold and unloving. The impact of her daughter's rejection may actually bring about maternal hurt, anger, and withdrawal, which is experienced by the child as punishment. Positive feelings toward the earlier good-enough preoedipal mother are generally recovered with the resolution of the Oedipus complex. The father inherits the earlier idealization of the powerful rapprochement mother, which then becomes condensed with sexuality, leading to a new structure in which there is an eroticizing of the power that is now attributed to him and associated with his maleness. Gorkin (1985) notes that while female hysterics may have masochistic fantasies, such fantasies "are accompanied more by the wish to experience the man's power and strength than a wish to be injured and humiliated. In the masochist, punishment and woundedness are far more entwined as part of the sexual experience" (p. 432).

Case Examples

The following dream was reported by a 35-year-old woman as the hold of her jealous, abusive alcoholic mother was loosening and as she was extricating herself from a sadomasochistic love relationship. She was realizing that her mother was who she was, that she herself was who she was, and that they were separate; she was in the process of sadly acknowledging that there was no way she could reach either her mother or the man with whom she had been involved for many years. The daughter's need to placate her mother, who showed her anger by acting as though the daughter literally did not exist, driving her to desperation, had led to the renunciation of her gentle and loving father, who had recently died. The powerful, sadistic mother continually demeaned the father, spoiling his image for the little girl. Here is the dream:

> There was a house surrounded by acres of land. There were black panthers, and I was trying to get away from them. A man rode up on a powerful horse that ran at great speed. He was a powerful man. Both the man and the horse were wild-looking. The man said, "I'll save you." I said, "I'm afraid of the horse and the speed." He said he would help me get away. I wanted to go with him, but I was scared by the speed. It was the wildest, most exciting man and horse, the essence of power.

Then she reported another scene in the dream, to which she associated the memory of being injured in an accident as a child, and her father's calm strength in the face of her mother's hysteria. We see that, at this point in her therapy—with the giving up of the need to placate the dangerous mother and the fantasy of becoming perfect enough to finally win her approval and be safe from annihilation—the powerful, idealized oedipal father was regained. This then enabled her to make his love part of her own loving superego and to mourn his loss.

Another young woman, in brief psychotherapy that focused on her oedipal conflicts, recalled the sudden loss of her sexual feelings toward her father when she realized that he was powerless to protect her in a dangerous situation at her high school. Unlike the perversion in which sexuality becomes condensed with the power of the sadistic mother, with accompanying feelings of hatred and shame (as was true of the woman in the previous example), in normal oedipal development the eroticizing of the father's power is imbued with love and a sense of pride. When the Oedipus complex remains unresolved, self-esteem may continue to be dependent upon having a special relationship with an idealized male, such as a teacher, mentor, or lover.

To the extent that there is an unresolved and virulent envy of the power of the preoedipal mother, as is the case when the mother fails to use that power benevolently as a source of security and self-esteem for the child, the father will also be the inheritor of that envy. The envied power is likely to become associated with his very maleness and may be expressed concretely as penis envy; or, less specifically, this power may be explained and rationalized in sociological terms—a defense that, whatever its validity, avoids the developmental and interpersonal issues.

One woman recalled how she had wanted to show that her father had done something bad, "maybe to break away from the feeling that he was wonderful," she said. "I didn't want to think it. It was babyish, or I was ashamed of how I felt about him. It was a weapon he had. If I cared about his feeling for me, he could control me. I looked for a reason not to care." When I suggested, based on this disclosure and on previous material as well, that she envied what she admired and thus needed to bring it down, she said, "I could see that in relation to his being male—the envy. I tried to show him as less." Later she commented, "I don't want to be a man, but I want to have—the aggressiveness. I think I'm developing it more. But the conflict is deep and severe and mysterious" (Horner 1985).

She believed that I had a secret power I would not share with her, and it became evident transferentially that I was a condensation of the father with the magical penis and the mother who possessed it; that I was both the denier and the denied.

The more normally developing oedipal girl, although not structurally split in the primitive sense, will still be using the more primitive defenses against what is becoming an intolerable ambivalence toward her mother and a conflict of object choice. The father, who is now the predominantly more exciting and gratifying object, becomes the repository for idealized love. At the same time, the more ambivalently experienced mother, who—from weaning onward—has been the source of as much frustration as gratification, becomes the repository for hostility and resentment. When the splitting is defensive and not characterological, the focusing of the child's libidinal charge on her father permits the welding of sexuality and love within the context of a significant attachment. Of course, this creates a subsequent developmental task—namely, the undoing of the defensive rejection of the mother to allow the necessary identifications and internalizations essential to the firming up of object constancy and an unconflicted feminine identity. Without object constancy there will be a continued predisposition to depression; and without the freeing from conflict and firming up of the inevitable identifications with the defensively devalued mother, there will be a continuing predisposition to shame.

With the dissolution of the Oedipus complex, father and his power are no longer idealized, and the wish to be his preferred other is also relinquished. Mother's real power, which was eschewed in the service of maintaining the ego ideal—a self who is nicer and thus preferable in father's eyes as well—must also be internalized if the woman is to achieve any degree of psychic autonomy (Horner 1984). She will no longer have to attach herself to a man who is perceived as powerful in order to maintain her security and self-esteem. Elsewhere (Horner 1989) I have referred to this healthy, or "intrinsic," power in terms of identity (I Am), competence (I Can), and intentionality (I Will). A female patient of mine rejected the idea of trying to be "one of the guys" as a way to get ahead in her field. She decided she would have to find her "own path"—one that did not require what she saw as masculine behavior, yet one that also did not require that she be an adjunct to a powerful man. She reported a dream in which she was explaining that "the battery pack consisted of being and will." This insight in her dream was a reflection, not of something I had said, but of her own discovery.

THE UNRESOLVED OEDIPUS COMPLEX

The unresolved Oedipus complex leads to the reestablishment of similar passionate attachments when the woman falls in love. It is the oedipal idealization, the inheritor of the idealization of the preoedipal mother, that renders the failure of the relationship a painful narcissistic wound.

Women fixated at this phase of development tend to devalue all women and thus will rarely choose a female therapist. However, the eroticized attachment to a male therapist's power often constitutes a formidable transference resistance. On one hand, this stance may be relatively invisible. It is simply how she feels in the presence of the powerful male. It is old and familiar and may not be explicit in the content. Because of unconscious or preconscious countertransference gratification, the therapist may not perceive the resistance. If he does and it is analyzed, its analysis may be experienced as a narcissistic wound, the oedipal defeat she refuses to contemplate.

Anger toward the disillusioning father is frequently more intense than that toward the rejecting father. The element of betrayal is present when the idealization is not supported by the father's behavior or character. Notable in the analyses of such women is the father who submitted to the mother's disapproval of his closeness with his small daughter. Although the father continues to be yearned for, his love is now a source of shame, as the idealized power has been returned to the resented mother. In later love relationships, there is an ongoing conflict between the wish for love with a man and the need for self-esteem. Mother continues to be hated, while her power evokes envy and anxiety. Father is loved, but also looked upon with low regard or with contempt, as are future male partners. Intense ambivalent friendships with women

take precedence over the relationship with the devalued male sexual partner. Developmentally, the narcissistic, dyadic relationship
with mother exists side by side with oedipal strivings that are
rejected in the service of security and self-esteem. A higher level of
psychological organization is aborted by a combination of the
father's failure as an oedipal object and the mother's sabotage of
the father–daughter relationship.

The pessimistic view of elation as necessarily a manic-like
defense against the depression associated with object loss neglects
the experience of this affect as an accompaniment of the achievement of something new, be it the developing ego functions, a more
complex object relationship, or the integration of the sexuality that
is one aspect of passionate love. In all of these situations, self-
esteem is greatly enhanced. It is just because self-esteem is tied to
these times of reorganization and enhanced functioning that their
failure will predispose to the loss of that esteem, to feelings of
shame and depression, and to the erection of a variety of defenses
against the anxiety associated with these feelings.

Love, as a combination of intense positive affect and emotional attachment, is experienced at every level of development. Its
quality in the transference will depend on the patient's level of
development in structural terms. Considering the positive transference as an integral aspect of the therapeutic alliance, we do not
interpret it until and unless it creates a resistance, as when it must
be protected by screening out whatever may endanger the emotionally positive connection with the therapist. The unspoken fantasies
of specialness that may lurk within the positive transference have to
be interpreted at some point in treatment, although the timing will
depend upon the patient's capacity to work with transference issues
without being traumatized by that work.

Love for the therapist may also be a concomitant of the
patient's enhanced experience of herself as a result of therapeutic
gains within the interpersonal matrix of the therapeutic relationship, an enhancement that is leading toward a greater degree of
structural integrity as well. The capacity for gratitude comes with
the transformation of primitive narcissism to healthy self-esteem
and positive regard for the therapist as a fully differentiated other.
This gratitude may be experienced by the patient as love. Once

again, the joyful affect will accompany a new synthesis of the self at a higher level of organization. From this point of view, the work of analysis calls for interpretation and resolution of transference and resistance. This should lead to a deidealization and desexualization of the patient's love for the therapist. However, this love may also be a concomitant of a successful analysis, not to be pathologized or reduced to its developmental origins, and not to be analyzed away in the pursuit of some mythical "complete analysis."

6

From Attachment to Identification: The Female Analyst and the Female Patient

Can a male therapist enable the female patient's integration of aggression, or power, and femininity? Possibly, as long as the apparent dilemma is attended to analytically. But I think it is more likely that the task will be complicated by the very fact of his maleness. Even if his power is experienced as benevolent and is internalized, can it be integrated with her femininity, or will it be associated with maleness? Will she maintain her femininity with an unresolved idealization of her father's power, which she shares through her relationship with her therapist? Are there some provisions that only a mother can supply for her daughter, and are there some provisions that only a father can supply for his son? As analysts, we need to give full attention to the impact of the therapist's gender on the outcome of treatment.

In my early days as a therapist, I found I was being referred patients on the basis of their supposed "need for nurturance." Because I was a woman, it was assumed that this would be the major thrust of my work. The hard analytic stuff was sent to my male counterparts. And inasmuch as psychological development— both in the earliest years and through psychotherapy—comes about within an interpersonal context and is profoundly affected by that milieu, the gender of the therapist cannot be without some significance, not only in terms of the kinds of transferences evoked, but in terms of outcome as well. Certainly the fact of the mother's femaleness and the father's maleness play a major role early on.

This does not mean that the gender of the therapist either should or should not be chosen on the basis of some preordained concept of what the patient needs; it means only that the therapist's gender will have an effect on the treatment, and that this effect should be considered. The purpose of this chapter is to consider one specific effect that the therapist's femaleness has on the female patient—that of resolving her conflicted identifications.

PSYCHOPATHOLOGY IN TERMS
OF DEVELOPMENTAL DEFICITS

In recent years we have become sensitized to looking at psychopathology in these terms, especially in terms of those developmental deficits associated with the borderline and narcissistic personality disorders. Structural impairment in these cases involves the basic organization of the representational world of self and object in terms of cohesion, differentiation, or integration. But there are other structural issues that are problematic, issues that arise at the end of the separation–individuation process and that come to the fore in the oedipal and postoedipal periods.

These pathologies arise not so much from failures within the mother–child dyad in the first year or two, but from the enmeshment of the individuating child in the pathological relationships within the family as a whole. Whatever basic structure may be laid down in the preoedipal years, there is a further elaboration of this structure as language and meaning begin to play a larger role in the psychic functioning of the child. The integration and consolidation of the self, and of the self in relation to others, cannot fully come about until the developmental tasks of adolescence are completed.

The process of identification and the integration, consolidation, and assimilation of those identifications within the self that emerged from the symbiotic bond with mother are vulnerable to the conflicts of the oedipal period and to the pressures of the family system thereafter. I'm referring specifically to the conflicted identifications of some female patients—not the primary identification with the mother of attachment, symbiosis, and separation and individuation, but identifications with the oedipal and postoedipal mother as well as with the father. In these instances we see how conflict interferes with structures—that is, with the ultimate consolidation of ego and superego identifications. Horowitz (1987) noted how the period of late latency in the processes of identification and superego formation serves either to aid the analytic work or to provide resistance to it. Because there is a cohesive, differentiated, and integrated self representation that can be relied on in the treatment process, these patients cannot be viewed as having character disorders. The work will be largely interpretive, and despite intense transference reactions, there is not likely to be a loss of the observing ego or a serious disruption of the therapeutic alliance. Nevertheless, these situations call for what Grunes (1984) refers to as a therapeutic object relationship in which "parent-like forms of psychic provision . . . ultimately fill in aspects of missing structure" (p. 125). The reparative function of the therapeutic relationship and the importance of the interpretation of conflict are not mutually exclusive, as an artificial schism in clinical theory would have us believe. The therapist will play a significant role in the final consolidation of ego and superego identifications through the work of interpretation *and* as a new model for identification.

THE PROCESS OF IDENTIFICATION

Identification is central to the resolution of three major developmental watersheds: (1) the separation–individuation process; (2)

the Oedipus complex; and (3) the developmental tasks of adolescence, which are a reprise of both of these.

We need to clarify the term *identification* and to distinguish the primary identifications of early object relations development from later identifications. We must also distinguish identification as a process leading to a change in the structure of the ego from the kind of gross identification that serves as an ego defense against object loss or other dangers to the ego. Identification with the aggressor is an example of the latter. The internalizations that allow one to *give up* the object—as happens with the completion of the separation-individuation process and with the resolution of the Oedipus complex—are not the same as the identifications that *defend against* the anxiety and depression of loss. We are often reminded of Freud's (1923) observation that it may be that "identification is the sole condition under which the id can give up its object" (p. 29).

Since identification is a process that is necessary for the resolution of conflicts about separation, individuation, and the Oedipus complex, resolving these conflicts also entails resolving existing conflicts with respect to identification per se. This must be done in such a way that the necessary identifications can be consolidated with the original good-enough objects, who have been restored by virtue of the work of therapy. However, if the original objects cannot be used without serious compromise to the sense of self or to the self-esteem, then new objects must be available to further the identification process.

Identification with the primary caretaker leads to object constancy and the establishment of inner regulating agencies, particularly with respect to anxiety and mood. *Primary* identifications are those that are the outcome of the separation–individuation process, at the end of which identifications with the primary attachment object lead to the intrapsychic autonomy of a fully differentiated self. Through what Kohut (1971) calls "transmuting internalizations," what originally belonged to the object comes to belong to the self. We see this shift in the making in the toddler's relationship with the transitional object (Winnicott 1951). The self comes to be enriched with the assimilation of maternal functions. This assimilation of caretaking activities is an important factor in the structuring and equilibrium of the self representation. The internalization, or identification, is thus a sine qua non for the achievement of intra-psychic autonomy and for increasing autonomy vis-à-vis the object relationships of the oedipal period. That which the other provided vis-à-vis the self now resides within the self. This would include comforting functions and executive modalities (Giovacchini 1979, Tolpin 1971). Identification with the anxiety-reducing object leads to the development of signal anxiety (Horner 1980).

Case Example

The overall developmental process of internalization was tele-scoped in the case of a patient who was preparing herself to deal with my imminent vacation.

> I've been feeling depressed about your being gone. This is the one place that all of me feels real. I don't have to pretend. It'll be a loss. I thought I'd just read your books. Then I thought about doing some creative writing and that felt good.

First she felt the depression of loss. Then she turned to my books as transitional objects. Finally, she identified with me in terms of writing and then felt better.

During this same period, identifications with other important attachment objects, particularly the father, can be noted. Beyond separation and individuation, later identifications continue to mod-ify the self representation throughout life. The identifications with the father and with the later mother of reality (in contrast to the personifications of the object constructed by the infant and toddler in the earliest months), with a loved grandparent, with heroes or heroines, or with other important models, continue throughout the life cycle.

Freud (1923) wrote that with the dissolution of the Oedipus complex there is a father identification as well as a mother identifi-cation. The identification with the parent of the same sex preserves the object relation to the parent of the opposite sex while replac-ing the object relation to the parent of the same sex. Freud noted that the same process takes place in reverse as well. He saw the broad general outcome of this phase as the formation of a precipitate in the ego that consists of these two identifications in some way united with each other. This modification of the ego then "confronts the other contents of the ego as an ego-ideal or superego" (p. 34).

With the final developmental separation from parents that confronts the adolescent as a requirement for adulthood, both ego and superego identifications are essential to the social and emotional autonomy of the young man or woman. Erikson (1950) observed that the failure to integrate and consolidate identifications in adolescence results in what he characterized as "role diffusion."

As described in Chapter 4, a defensive "refusal to identify" (Horner 1984) has two major determinants. The first is the protection of gender identity. The little boy struggles to "disidentify" (Greenson 1968) from the primary attachment figure, the mother, in order to secure his gender identity. This need to disidentify with the mother is a deterrent to the assimilation of those identifications with her that are the basis for object constancy and emotional autonomy.

The little girl's rejection of her identification with her mother tends more to be in the service of her ego ideal. The disparagement of the mother as a model worthy of identification has several of its own determinants. First, the inevitable maternal failures in the earliest years yield a reservoir of resentment. Maternal power is viewed as bad insofar as it was experienced as in opposition to the wishes of the self. Second, just as the little boy must move away from his mother in the service of differentiation and individuation, so must the girl. The deidealization and concomitant disparagement of her mother enable this process. Freud (1931) says that the view of the mother as castrated contributes to the deidealization of her. In addition, mother is also disparaged as a rival for father, and there are typical fantasies of a nicer, more attractive self who will be preferred by father. The oedipally fixated woman characteristically describes her mother as unattractive, sexless, cold, and unloving. The impact of her daughter's rejection may actually bring about maternal hurt, anger, and withdrawal, which is experienced as punishment. Positive feelings toward the mother are generally recovered with the resolution of the Oedipus complex.

The refusal to identify with the disparaged mother protects the developing ego ideal. At the same time, this refusal interferes with the achievement of the assimilations and identifications that are necessary for object constancy and emotional autonomy, leading to emotional dependency and predisposition to depression. Interpretation of these dynamics is essential for the full resolution of both the separation–individuation process and the Oedipus complex with the female patient. It is likely that the competitive issues will emerge in the transference with a female therapist, who may be hard put to tolerate the situation if her own oedipal dynamics are still unresolved. By and large, however, the conflicts with respect to identification in the oedipal patient yield to the analytic work itself. The analyst as model is less important here than in other situations.

Clearly feminine, with a stance of compliance toward a loved and idealized father, oedipally fixated daughters are stuck with the devalued image of the mother, and thus of themselves and of women in general. Consciously rejecting an identification with the devalued mother, they may identify with the idealized father, often through their intellects, while maintaining the sense of femininity that came from the primary identification with the mother of attachment and symbiosis. They may experience the triangle intrapsychically, feeling torn between the conflicting identifications, paralleling feelings of being torn between the two other points of the interpersonal triangle. Analysis of the oedipal conflict should lead to a resolution of the conflict of identifications and to an integration of the feminine and masculine sides of the self. As discussed on page 77, these women—because they devalue other women—tend to choose male therapists; and the transference resistance—namely, the hypervaluing of the male—often remains invisible and unanalyzed, with the collusion of the therapist and his unconscious or preconscious countertransference gratification. Failure to analyze the dynamics of the patient's disparagement of her mother and thus of all women, including herself, will prevent a full resolution of the Oedipus complex. The oedipally fixated woman is more likely to choose a female therapist when the wish for lost maternal nurturance is less repressed. In this situation we see more clearly the overlap of the rapprochement phase of the separation–individuation process and the Oedipus complex. Fears of abandonment or of the loss of mother's love heighten the anxieties of the competitive situation. The oedipal father, and other men in the woman's life, inherit the security- and self-esteem-maintaining function of the mother.

There are certain female patients for whom the need to integrate femininity and power and aggression is especially relevant. In her paper entitled "I Want to Be Daddy" (1987), Rees noted the presence of conflicts about being aggressive and female, with aggression being overly tied to a masculine identification in women with this wish. The little girl's identification with her father evokes conflict insofar as it is a threat to her sense of femininity, although her sense of femaleness, her gender identity, is secure from the start because of the primary identification with the female mother of attachment and symbiosis. To the extent that her aggression is tied to her identification with her father, she is likely to feel the conflict between her sense of being powerful or strong and her femininity. At the same time, she is contemptuous of what she sees as her mother's passivity and weakness. Under no condition does she want to be like her mother.

Over time we have seen how social and cultural changes lead to the emergence of new psychological problems or expose others that have been latent. The woman who has maintained an apparently normal life through a specific role identity in her home town may break down if she leaves her husband and moves to a different city in search of her "full potential" in another role. I have seen some such women as casualties of the women's movement. The split between aggression, or power, and femininity becomes more of a problem with the changing role of women, particularly for those who have entered the business and professional worlds. In rejecting a passive and masochistic position, women are confronted with awareness of the structural conflict that contributed to their staying in that position. They may try to hold on to old ways of relating in a world where those ways do not work. One woman executive described to me how she tried to compete by "out-nicing" others. If the role of the female therapist as a model of the integration of power and femininity is important clinically, might it not also be an important vehicle for the resolution of new conflicts engendered by these social changes? One woman who rejected the solution of being "one of the guys" as a way to advance in her field decided that she would have to find her own path—one that did not require of her what she saw as masculine behavior, yet one that also did not require that she be an adjunct to a powerful man.

THE ROLE-MODEL FUNCTION OF
THE FEMALE THERAPIST

The importance of the female therapist as a role model, one who is perceived by the female patient as both feminine and—in a positive way—powerful—is especially clear in a situation in which neither of the patient's parents offered a suitable model for the healthy and benevolent use of parental power and aggression. Such parents used their power pathologically, malevolently, or sadistically against the child, rather than using it benevolently as a source of security and self-esteem for her. In such cases, power itself comes to be hated and envied. Intense ambivalence motivates a child to inhibit aggression in order to protect the parents from her own rageful sadism, to preserve the good parent, and to maintain the child's own ego ideal that is characterized by goodness. Awareness of their rage and their wish to retaliate suggests to these patients that they are no better than the hated parents and thus have no right to be angry. The child's persistent wish to be good and to be loved, as well as to hold on to the image of the parents as good and to the ability to love them, results in a characteristic victimized and masochistic position vis-à-vis the narcissism or sadism of others throughout the child's life. Such a person's own aggression is deeply repressed, often with reaction formation. Expressing the dilemmas with respect to her feminine identification in such a context, one patient said:

> How am I supposed to identify with my mother? All her aggression went to me, and it was vicious. At times I can identify with you. Your aggression is clean. You don't have to be perfect all the time, and if you do something hurtful, you own it—and you can stand up for yourself too.

This patient was frequently anxious that I might react as her mother did, but she never completely lost sight of her fear as a manifestation of transference. Her view of me as an ideal to be emulated did not have the same reality-denying quality of an idealizing transference. I just had to be good enough. Yet, as Greenberg (1986) says of neutrality, I had to provide an atmosphere of safety that would allow the patient to perceive me as a new object. "Neutrality embodies the goal of establishing an optimal tension between the patient's tendency to see the analyst as an old object and his capacity to experience him as a new one" (p. 97). At times this patient required interventions of reassurance or support from me. Not to have lent myself in these ways would have led to an experience of my power as sadistic, as her mother's had been.

In another case in which a patient's models of power and strength were unacceptable, the physical abuse suffered at the hands of her father and brother was experienced as more hurtful than her mother's more subtle need to maintain a position of superadequacy by projecting her own inadequate self into her daughter, who became the container for it. The overt power of the males was hated and envied, and the patient expressed it in terms of penis envy. She said, "I don't want a penis so I can be superior to someone else. I just want to be equal. If you have a sword, I want one too—not just a shield." Later she observed:

> For me, having to be inadequate is not to have power. I think of the kinds of power I observe in others I like—not like my Dad's histrionic, hysterical, out-of-control power, or my mother's controlling power, her having to be the superadequate one. My brother's power was abusive and victimizing. I've internalized all three of them. I'm searching for a model of woman and power and femininity. I experience your power as calm and centered and nonthreatening. Before, *power* was a dirty word. But a person being nurturant and empathetic is powerful too.

In both family systems, the women had functioned as containers for parental projections of hated aspects of themselves from the oedipal period onward. Because of good-enough mothering in the preoedipal years, the basic structure of the ego remained sound even though the mothering failed as these patients started to individuate. The initial phase of therapy focused on their container role and its impact on their inner and interpersonal worlds. As they separated themselves out from maternal and paternal projections, the issue of identification in its necessary and growth-promoting function came to the fore. The actual parents who had abused or exploited them psychologically were unacceptable models for further ego and superego development, although the primary identification with the good-enough mother of infancy remained as a solid core of a cohesive feminine self. For both patients, the therapist was clearly perceived as separate from the self. As much as an attachment to the therapist enabled their continued growth, rather than functioning as a primitive extension of the self, it served as a basis for safety so that the work of analysis could be done; in addition, it served as a basis for the identifications that would ultimately lead to a healthier integration of both ego and superego.

PART TWO

Character Pathology

7

Early Object Relations and the Concept of Depression

Guntrip (1971) refers to the erroneous application of the term *depression* to schizoid states as well as to the inappropriate treatments that are predicated on that diagnosis. The diagnosis is often made on the basis of a predominant mood that the patient may refer to as depression. The dynamic picture in which this mood becomes evident is by no means a unitary one, and an accurate understanding of the meaning of the mood is critical to treatment.

Jacobson (1971) sees as the essential dynamic in depression a narcissistic injury due to the failure of the loved object to understand the subject, followed by anger at his having failed to do so, and then by a sense of helplessness to do anything about the situation. She sees "constitutional neurophysiological processes" as accounting for the difference between neurotic and psychotic depressions, although she does stress that "such considerations must complement the psychological—i.e., psychoanalytic—assumptions" (p. 183).

THE THEORETICAL VANTAGE POINT
OF OBJECT RELATIONS

However, there is no need to take recourse to any such *deus ex machina* explanations to account for divergent clinical pictures. If one approaches the issue from the theoretical vantage point of object relations, dynamic distinctions become self-evident. It is through an understanding of the developing self in the context of the mother–child matrix, with the associated processes of attachment to, internalization of, and individuation from the object, that various clinical pictures come to make sense.

According to Melanie Klein (Segal 1964), the "depressive position" implies the ability "to enter more fully into whole-object relationships, only to be exposed to guilt and depression over the discovery that he can hurt those he has become capable of loving." This, of course, describes the more or less classical picture of the neurotic depressive in whom anger is turned toward the self in order not to jeopardize the relationship with the needed object. Such a patient has achieved a level of development characterized by whole object relationships—that is, a relationship that is based not solely on the satisfaction of needs—object constancy, and the ability to tolerate ambivalence toward this specific object without regression.

Anna Freud (1968) wrote: "Object constancy means . . . to retain attachment even when the person is unsatisfying." Burgner and Edgcumbe (1972, p. 328) refer to "the capacity for constant relationships" and see this as "a crucial switch point in the development of object relationships." They describe this capacity functionally as "the capacity to recognize and tolerate loving and hostile feelings toward the same object; the capacity to keep feelings centered on a specific object; and the capacity to value an object for attributes other than its function of satisfying needs."

Diagnostic, and thereby therapeutic, difficulties are encountered with the patient who has never achieved this status. And it is with these patients that the usual approach to understanding what appears to be a depressive reaction breaks down. Particularly important to our thinking here is the work of John Bowlby, Anna Freud, and Margaret Mahler.

REACTIONS TO LOSS

Bowlby (1969) describes separation distress, which, while primarily a segment of experience, is most relevant to the developmental processes considered in this chapter. This distress is characterized first by protest, then despair, and finally detachment. Although his conclusions are based on the observation of infants who have suffered a single traumatic separation from the mothering person, we can apply these conclusions in the context of what Khan (1963) refers to as "cumulative trauma." This concept is relevant to the formation of characterological defenses against the repeated experiences of separation distress by the infant. A memory common to many of the patients we are talking about is that of being left crying to the point of exhaustion many, many times over, a memory that often carries with it the sense of despair at ever being responded to. The repeated nonresponsiveness of the mother is experienced as repeated abandonment. Masterson (1972) sees the psychopathology of the sociopath as a manifestation of the use of the defense of detachment to deal with such separation from the mother (p. 228). It is striking to observe the intensity of the underlying despair in such an individual when it momentarily breaks through.

The developmental process itself, in brief, is described as starting with what Freud called primary narcissism and what Mahler refers to as normal autism. From there the infant moves to what Anna Freud calls the need-satisfying object relationship and what Mahler calls symbiosis. Kohut's work (1971) on the narcissistic personality focuses on the patient whose object relations are at this level. Mahler's work (1968) on the vicissitudes of separation and individuation is critical to the understanding of the dynamic of regression to or clinging to the symbiotic bond. As she points out, in the earliest stages of the separation–individuation process, there is a danger of object loss, whereas the "specific danger situation toward the end of the separation–individuation phase, as object constancy is approached, is akin to the danger of *loss of the libidinal object*, although there may still remain some fear of object loss as well" (p. 222). This is an important distinction, as the individual who has achieved object constancy carries the internalized object with him and, despite an interrupted relationship, can maintain a sense of what Winnicott (1965) calls ego-relatedness. Masterson characterizes the borderline personality as being caught in the dilemma of having to choose between the engulfment of symbiosis and the experience of abandonment that is associated with his attempts to individuate. In this instance, one usually finds a mother who withdraws love at the child's first move to define himself as separate from her.

We are talking here, then, about the patient who has not yet achieved what Klein refers to as the depressive position, an individual whose object relations are still at a need-satisfying level and who has not yet achieved full libidinal object constancy.

According to Guntrip, as the mother blocks individuation, the child retreats to symbiosis, and thence further back to schizoid detachment. This does not seem quite accurate, as a retreat from symbiosis takes the person back to autism, for implicit in the concept of regression is the retracing of steps previously progressed. This is the kind of retreat that is likely to be labeled a psychotic depression, and it is usually accompanied by the kinds of vegetative disturbances that Anna Freud (1969) points out result from separation in the very earliest stages of development. The schizoid reaction appears to be more of a flight forward, a premature severing of the symbiotic bond. Since the separation process is, in this instance, so precipitous, it does not allow for the gradual internalization of the libidinal object, which culminates in what is referred to as object constancy.

SCHIZOID DETACHMENT VERSUS PSYCHOPATHIC DETACHMENT

We need to clarify the distinction between schizoid detachment and psychopathic detachment. The schizoid solution to the engulfment–abandonment dilemma is necessitated by the failure of the mother during the process of separation and individuation. The psychopathic solution, on the other hand, represents an even earlier maternal failure, one that takes place during the transition from normal autism to the symbiotic, or need-satisfying, relationship. As such, the attachment process itself is interfered with. Attachment has been achieved with the schizoid individual. However, it is later denied in the effort to escape the engulfment of symbiosis.

We may also see the patient who becomes "sick" for the first time in adult life and who is diagnosed as suffering from psychotic depression. It is likely that this person is, in fact, a borderline personality who has been able to function adequately up to the time of a life crisis in which he experiences pressure toward either pole—that is, toward engulfment or abandonment. Up until that time, a precarious balance between the two may have been maintained in a number of ways. The loss of whatever this support may have been results in a regression to symbiosis, where the further failure of the environment leads to the inevitable feelings of emptiness that are associated with object loss.

Whether we are talking about autistic regression, flight into schizoid detachment, or the despair of abandonment, the common denominator is that of object loss. We might say, then, that the difference between neurotic and psychotic depression is accounted for in terms of the presence or absence of object constancy, and that the experienced difference is that of the loss of the love of the object as contrasted with object-loss proper.

John, a young man of 25, could not be described in terms of schizoid detachment. His experienced feelings were intense. However, his ties to his object (in this case, his therapist) were extremely tenuous, and under the impact of anxiety in the relationship, he would metaphorically curl up and turn his face to the wall. At such times he would call in to cancel his appointment, saying he was too depressed to come in. For him, anger (real or imagined) in the object was equivalent to abandonment. John's early mothering was in the hands of a number of aunts and uncles and assorted adults in a chaotic and unpredictable mode. What we see in John is not the schizoid detachment described by Guntrip, and surely not depression as Klein would view it. His cries for help are feeble at best, and with minimal protest he sinks into despair. The fact that he did not find his way to a less painful detachment may possibly be due to the frequency and duration of the experiences of abandonment. We suggest that the different outcomes of what seem to be qualitatively similar experiences may be due to quantitative factors. One organismic variable in this instance might be the vigor of the infant, the loudness of his cries, and the force he used in making his wants known to the mothering environment. John is strikingly lacking in vigor.

TREATMENT IMPLICATIONS

Implications for treatment are implicit in the dynamic distinctions being made here between various clinical pictures, all of which might be labeled depression.

When the patient is in a state of autistic withdrawal and there is no observing ego available, contact can be made, as it is normally at the very start of life, only by means of what Winnicott calls holding behavior, whether it be literally physical holding or emotional holding. Interpretations and explanations can be made when the time of crisis is past and an observing ego is once again available, and through understanding, future regressive crises can be forestalled.

Naomi, a woman of 30 with a history of hospitalization for depression, would clearly experience object loss whenever the loved object was angry (in reality or imagination). Her inability to maintain object constancy was symbolized by a dream when I was on vacation, a dream about her vacuum cleaner, whose hose had been cut. On several occasions, during the early days of her work with me, she would, during a session, evidence a swift and extreme regression in response to what she assumed to be my anger. She felt herself lost in a grey mist and cried out for someone to help her. At these times my response was one appropriate to the ego level to which she had regressed. I held and rocked her until she felt herself to be in contact once again. Obviously, responding in terms of the understood dynamic may mean departing from classical analytic technique. At the present time in her treatment, Naomi is struggling with the issue of asserting her need to be independent of me, while trying to hold on to a feeling of relatedness with me.

I will, at times of separation, give such a patient something of mine to keep as a transitional object (Winnicott 1965) or suggest she sit down and write to me when the sense of object loss starts to develop. The objective in the treatment is to establish a symbiotic transference with such a patient, from which separation and individuation can then proceed. Naomi strongly resisted this in her therapy, for fear that she would destroy her therapist out of the rage she was sure she would feel as the result of inevitable frustration. Her main defense has been that of acting out with homosexual lovers.

For the patient who has been able to let this kind of intensive relationship develop with the therapist, the separation–individuation phase is a highly critical one. The therapist must be aware of the meaning of emerging negativistic behavior in particular. A nonaccepting attitude on the part of the therapist may well sabotage these tentative steps toward autonomy. If the therapist interprets as resistance a wish to decrease the number of hours, for instance, his response will be read as anger at these attempts at self-assertion, and a loss of therapeutic gains may be the outcome. This puts the therapist in the tricky position of possibly abetting a premature termination of treatment, but sensitive interpretations with positive reinforcement of what the patient is trying to achieve will facilitate further steps toward maturation. As Mahler puts it, the differentiation of self from the symbiotic object can take place only in the normal context of the emotional availability of the mother.

The therapist walks a fine line with the borderline patient, who so readily experiences himself as either engulfed or abandoned. He must assiduously respect the ego boundaries of the patient (Horner 1973), while at the same time being emotionally available to him. With the most skittish of such patients, I will let them set the interval between sessions.

The schizoid individual, on the other hand, will have to undergo a painful regression in order to reconnect with the libidinal object, thence to individuate once again, only this time gradually enough to allow for the development of object constancy. This view makes understandable the schizoid patient's massive resistance to change, since such a move must surely be experienced as a regressive loss of autonomy, which threatens other areas of ego functioning. Without his schizoid defenses, such an individual will more closely resemble the borderline patient, and he will have to experience once again the severe anxiety of this position.

In all the treatment situations described here, a common experience will be that which is designated by the patient as "depression," but which will instead be better understood as object loss. The dynamic considerations presented here point out the limitations of a disease-entity model in the understanding and treatment of the human psyche.

8

Bulimia: A Complex
Compromise Formation

I view bulimia as essentially a manifestation of a failed schizoid defense, a situation in which the pull of the exciting objects— usually the preoedipal mother and the oedipal father—was, and continues to be, too powerful to deny. The obsession with food and weight, like any other obsession, serves to divert and bind anxiety that has its source elsewhere. The symptom is a metaphor for the highly conflicted interpersonal situation. It is for this reason that dealing with the transference and its resistances is central to the treatment of the disorder, inasmuch as the intrapsychic conflicts and the defenses against them will be manifest in the treatment relationship. The bulimic patient cannot be fixed at any definitive level of object relations development but shows evidence of critical issues across borderline, narcissistic, and oedipal spectra.

A psychoanalytic approach to bulimia is likely to fail if it adheres to any singly metapsychological dogma, and an approach to treatment must allow for a creative synthesis of analytic thinking across theoretical lines. Such an approach has technical implications as well.

Bulimia presents us with a veritable potpourri of concepts in action, with the schizoidal defense reminding us of the work of Guntrip, the false self adaptation recalling Winnicott, and the narcissistic positions of idealization and perfection of the self calling up Kohut; also to be considered are the object relational issues with respect to self and object differentiation and pathology of the self representation, and Freudian oedipal dynamics with both obsessional and hysteric features. The therapist who is unwilling to be creatively eclectic will miss important features and make strategic errors. As with all patients with schizoid defenses, establishing an emotional connection in the treatment is of paramount importance; from the patient's point of view, however, this is exactly what is most to be avoided.

CLINICAL FINDINGS

Bulimia is most commonly (but not exclusively) found in females. For this reason, it is discussed here from the female perspective.

The oral fixation, and the use of primitive defenses of somatization, denial, and undoing, as well as the tendency toward concrete and magical thinking that characterize bulimia all speak to the degree of primitiveness that exists side by side with a well-developed social facade and a high intellectual functioning that enable success in the world apart from intimate relationships. Kohut (1977) speaks of the development of compensatory structures that lay atop a primary pathology. The fact that a patient becomes able to relinquish the bulimia and achieve greater success at work, and even to have more social interaction, may indicate a firming up of more adaptive defenses while the incapacity for emotional intimacy remains essentially unchanged. This brings us to the question of what constitutes cure in the bulimic patient.

The symptom is most clearly a metaphor for the highly conflicted and intensely ambivalent interpersonal situation, an expression of the object hunger and the schizoid defense against its dangers. I do not see the bulimic patient as using projective identification as it is employed when there is a persisting developmental split in self and object; rather, there is a denial of the wish for the good mother out of fear of the inevitable disappointment and the intense anger that would ensue, an anger that would render the breach between them irreparable, leading to a loss of the object. Unlike the schizoid personality disorder that develops earlier as a characterological defense against psychosis or borderline pathology, bulimia is a schizoid defense that develops somewhat late in the face of an intolerable conflict at the point at which both rapprochement and oedipal issues are salient.

INTERPERSONAL ISSUES

For each bulimic patient, the symptom must be understood in terms of the unique and specific character pathology in which it is embedded. The intransigence of bulimia as a symptom is largely due to its success as a strikingly complex compromise formation. It allows for the expression of forbidden or dangerous wishes or impulses and their magical undoing. It does this at all levels, condensing preoedipal and oedipal conflicts and defenses, such as the intense wish for and rejection of the primary maternal figure, and the erotic strivings toward the oedipal father and their denial. Thus, bulimia is an unusually rich metaphor for these important interpersonal relationships and their inherent conflicts. A depth psychological approach to its treatment is aimed at untangling the dynamic complexities within the context of the therapeutic relationship so as to allow for healthier relating and a capacity for true intimacy. It does not define cure merely in terms of the removal of the symptom.

NARCISSISTIC ISSUES

In addition to interpersonal issues, narcissistic issues are concretized through the body image. Just as the classic narcissistic personality will defend against the disappointments of dependency needs and the inevitable rage that follows by turning to the defensive structure referred to as the pathological grandiose self, which enables the denial of those needs, the bulimic tries to construct a perfect physical self, again a concretization, that will protect her from a sense of needing narcissistic supplies from the outside. The conflict between impulse and wish and a perfectionistic ego ideal in moral terms may also be particularly intense.

One patient, Miss D., defended against the jealousy and envy evoked by her father's tendency to indulge her mother by feeling superior to the mother, much as she felt superior to her baby brother. She envied the penis that she believed made him more special to the mother. On the other side of the defensive superiority was a deeply felt shame. Although the origin of the shame was her loss of specialness as an adored only child, she now associated it with her fear that someone would discover the shameful secret of her vomiting.

Castration shame is also an affront to the defensive structure, the perfect physical self. Denial of femaleness and the wish to erase its distinguishing features, the fat of the hips and breasts, may be partly in the service of restoring the lost perfection, and the wish for a boy's body may reveal the wish for a penis. Indeed, the hard, lean body toward which she strives may itself be her phallus. The fat, and the femaleness it represents, also constitutes a danger in its sexual-arousal potential for the father and in the anxiety this evokes in the daughter. Of the power struggle with her domineering father, Miss D. noted that she "always lost" because she "didn't have any balls." Whatever her wish to castrate her father, she did not want to topple him or hurt him. She was very aware of his fragile self-esteem, and as much as she wanted to act out her rage toward him, her wish to protect him took precedence. She noted a fantasy of biting off her little brother's penis, a fantasy that was far more syntonic than her wish to act out her rage at her father.

The bulimia both expresses and undoes the sexual and aggressive impulses, expressed in primitive incorporative terms. In this case, the eating and vomiting had previously been associated with cannibalistic fantasies of biting off her baby brother's penis, taking it into her orally, angrily chewing it up, and then spitting it out in disgust. The intense penis envy came from the concretization of what she perceived as the reason for the loss of her mother's total attention and devotion, which she had enjoyed prior to the birth of the brother when she was 2 years old. It is interesting to note that the patient's relationships tended to end after almost exactly two years' duration, and this became a crisis point in our work. Her defenses against a dependent transference were notable, including refusal to agree to more than one session a week, coming late almost every week, and avoidance of eye contact.

The young woman had a dream in which there was a representation of her baby self as a boy who had died. She said that in fact if she were to have a baby, she would want a girl who could be a pretty extension of herself, so that she could reenact the stories of how her mother had treated her like a doll. In this way she could resurrect the lost good mother of infancy. In the dream, she "snatched" the baby, just as her brother had snatched away her babyhood and her idyllic time with her mother.

The anorectic is more successful than the bulimic in the denial of the wish or need for anything from the outside, a denial that necessitates a greater distortion of reality. The bulimic, in this sense, is healthier. However, she feels the need with enormous intensity, and there is fear of the rage that will surely emerge when the needed other fails to respond adequately.

Miss D. spoke of having a craving for emotional intimacy in a relationship, but of experiencing "a sheet of plexiglass" between herself and the other person when she got close. She felt the wish as a set-up for betrayal. When she was disappointed, she would protect herself by insisting that she no longer wanted the relationship, and she was unrelentingly unforgiving. The detachment did not allow for the repair of the relationship. She would pull away and, unable to repair it, would feel the sense of needing to return. She would test the other person in each relationship, including the therapy relationship, saying, in effect, "You have to need me more than I need you." It was far too dangerous to adore anyone. Yet she also wanted me to get her under control, to stop her from acting out, just as she had wished that her mother would stop her when she was having a tantrum.

Another therapist reported that his bulimic patient, Miss A., was concerned that if she got too close to him, she would need

more than he could give her. Behind this concern lies the fear of the
consequent rage and its destructive potential in the face of experienced deprivation or abandonment. In this particular situation, as
he reported it, there seemed to be a construction of a more solid
schizoid defense in which relationships could be maintained as long
as there was some built-in distancing factor: the patient's termination date with her therapist, and the actual geographical distance
between the two people with whom she had ongoing relationships.
Although this patient was enjoying some new-found freedoms as
the result of treatment, her capacity for intimacy and commitment
was still questionable. The ever-lurking dangers of her latent object
greed, her oral rage when disappointed, and her fear of being
devoured by the other person, could be kept at bay with the
firming up of her distancing defenses. There is no doubt in this case
that these defenses were also adaptive, enabling her some degree of
satisfaction, albeit limited, in the interpersonal sphere—as well as
freedom from the tyranny of the bulimia.

In this case, one could observe both the wish to devour and
the fear of being devoured. Both oral incorporation and sexual
penetration, the active and passive aspects of *taking in*, were acted
out, as was the need—out of disgust, guilt, and rage—to get rid of
what was taken in. The object hunger and its denial, the doing and
the undoing, was compulsively acted out through the bulimia until
the time that adequate external support for her setting of boundaries helped her develop more adaptive distancing defenses.

Yet another therapist, reporting on her work with a bulimic
patient, Miss B., noted that no matter how brilliant or accurate her
dynamic formulations and genetic reconstructions, they would
have fallen on deaf ears and would have had no curative value if the
bond between her and the young woman had not been formed.
Because of the availability of the patient's observing ego and the
establishment of a working alliance, the therapist's capacity for
empathy and the continual monitoring of her own countertransference reactions eventually enabled the patient to give up her schizoid
defense and to confront and work through the interpersonal issues.

The first of these two patients, Miss A., had been placed into a
therapy group early in treatment, which diluted the interpersonal
impact and importance of the therapist, aiding and abetting the

patient's resistance to transference in individual treatment and reinforcing her obsessive defenses. The group's support of her "self-assertion," along with the dilution of the transference, led to the consolidation of more adaptive characterological defenses, rendering her bulimia unnecessary. One might wonder whether this aborted the possibliity of what might be considered a complete cure—that is, not only the abatement of the bulimic symptom, but also the development of the capacity for an intimate relationship. Her therapist reported that although group therapy had been discontinued, there remained an unresolved but distanced transference in private treatment and a stance of "good patient."

In contrast, the second patient, Miss B., entered a therapy group after two years of individual work; at that point the relationship with the therapist had already been firmly established and the defensive function of the bulimia was well understood. Her work in group did not interfere with the important emotional attachment to her therapist.

SEXUALITY AND OEDIPAL ISSUES

I wonder whether some therapists may be reluctant to deal directly with sexual and aggressive issues, which I believe play a major role in bulimia. The eating impulse contains in it an expression of sexual and aggressive impulses as well, and, indeed, its very intensity suggests its overdetermination. One is reminded of the concept of upward displacement.

The first of the two patients just described, Miss A., had disclosed to her therapist that whenever her father was angry, he would unzip his pants, an indication of what we may suspect was a readiness to sexualize his anger. He would sometimes come in and hug his daughter in response to his own need and impulse. One might hypothesize that the patient left treatment in part to be sure that the incest issues remained hidden. In the therapy group of one of my colleagues, consisting of female bulimics, every one of them had a history of having been molested. Although the father of the second patient under discussion died when she was 5 years old (Miss B.), it appeared that her mother was grossly seductive in her behavior.

In the case of a third patient, Miss C., the father's obsessive concern about his daughter's physical development—which became symbolized by her weight—suggested incestuous wishes in him that she may have sensed. Her sense of "badness" after engaging in sexual relations and her need to find something wrong with each partner may have represented the use of aggression as a defense against the incestuous impulses of her father and herself. The overstimulation of the daughter in the eroticized atmosphere tends to be traumatic. In female victims of incest, we often find a subsequent promiscuity that represents an attempt to gain active mastery over the sexual trauma by turning passive to active in the seduction of men.

One of my patients observed on a visit to her parents' home how eroticized she found everything about her father. She couldn't even touch anything he had touched, and she avoided eye contact with him. What she wanted most was that he would both leave her alone and would care for her. She had always felt titillated by him, and in addition to being in love with him, had wanted to *be* him. It felt very dangerous to be close to him. She both hated him and was fascinated by him. Even when she hated him she wanted him, and he always seemed to want to be near her. Alongside these powerful feelings toward her father was the intense wish to have her mother all to herself, and the anger she felt at her mother's giving in to her father's insistence that the mother join him instead of participating in "alone time" with her little daughter. She was very upset about the feelings she reported to me, angry that I had "pulled the lid off." She simultaneously did and did not want me to do my work.

Oedipal strivings cannot be metabolized in such a case because of the danger of incest, and there is a yearning to return to the now unavailable good preoedipal mother for comfort and safety. The combination of sexual impingement by father and abandonment by mother evoke a destructive rage. There is no safety in either direction, creating a double approach–avoidance conflict.

In addition to an attempt at self-sufficiency, the drive for perfection is also an attempt to repair the self, to undo the shame that was elicited by the abandonment or rejection by the highly desired parent. In an attempt to repair the devalued self, standards of perfection are set, standards that are unattainable inasmuch as they are only symbols, for what feels damaged or defective is the self. Finding a perfect other and achieving perfection by association is the next best strategy. For my own patient, Miss D., finding a man with a perfect penis temporarily repaired the shame associated with her failure to have what her baby brother had—the maleness she believed to have stolen away her previously devoted mother. The shame of the failure of the self to be worthy of the love of the other, alternates with the rage at the rejecting object, toward whom an intense ambivalence prevails. There is no splitting, but by turning the rage on the self in the form of self-blame and shame, the patient protects the relationship from the annihilating fury. The patient believed that her rage could destroy anyone in her path, and she was afraid that she herself would be unable to ride it out. She also feared that those close to her would not be strong enough to survive her destructiveness. She felt that separateness was inherently disappointing, and observed that she looked only for facsimiles of closeness, inasmuch as passionate attachments were doomed.

The therapeutic relationship must be considered an integral part of the overall treatment program, if not the central factor. Bulimia is, first and foremost, a disorder of *human relationship*. Did the focus on cognitive and behavioral strategies reported by Miss A.'s therapist provide a built-in distancing factor, protecting the therapeutic dyad from the excitement–deprivation–rage pattern that is characteristic of the bulimic relationship? Will that patient also seek facsimiles of closeness now that she is better able to protect her boundaries? In the context of the pretense of closeness, the true schizoid self remains safe and hidden, while the false self negotiates the interpersonal world. As one patient concluded, isolating the self is better; the real self is too vulnerable and too scared.

9

Pathology of
Gender Identity Development

Coates (1989) and Kirkpatrick (1989) note the relevance of object relations development to gender identity development. In my view, the latter becomes subsumed within the former. That is, gender identity becomes an integral aspect of the self representation.

GENDER IDENTITY DEVELOPMENT

The basic character structure, in terms of the inner world of object relations and the integration of ego functions, as well as the integration of instinctual drive and affect within the self representation, is laid down in the earliest years. Later development may be shaped or limited by the underlying structure, and the idiosyncratic picture that ultimately emerges for each individual will be the outcome of complex forces. Nevertheless, the core identity, the sense of self, is

113

laid down before the secondary elaboration of the postindividuation stages of development. For this reason, the tasks of male development are far more formidable than those of female development.

Jacobson (1964) defines identity as that aspect of the self representation that is conscious. In my view, gender identity is an aspect of identity in the broader sense. The cohesion, integration, and object relatedness of that self representation is acquired in part as a consequence of constitutional potential (in particular, the capability of the organism to synthesize and organize), but also largely as a consequence of the organization of the self within the interpersonal matrix of the mother–child dyad. So where does gender identity development fit within the building of the person, starting with biological givens and encompassing the interpersonal matrix that become structured psychically as an enduring representational system? We know that it becomes established in the earliest formative months and years. In my view, gender identity development cannot be considered outside of and apart from the structuring of the self in an overall sense, except for heuristic purposes. Real people do not develop in segments; they develop complexly and intricately, but all of a piece, and that must include gender identity as well.

ORGANIZERS VERSUS ORGANIZATION

In the interest of conceptual clarity and to avoid pseudodisagreements, I want to make clear the distinction between the terms *organizers* and *organization*. For example, it is around experienced affective states—pleasure–displeasure, love–hate—that the cognitive structure of good or bad object and good or bad self representations become organized. The affective state functions as an organizer. In the same way, we should keep clear the concept of organizers, which may differ from child to child and certainly for boys and girls, and the resultant organization that we refer to as gender identity and identity in the wider sense. Coates (1989) notes the importance of biological–morphological factors as critical organizers in male gender identity formation, whereas Kirkpatrick

(1989) notes that these factors are less critical in female gender identity formation. She adds that feminine identity develops from the object relations matrix, and this, in turn, influences how the female genital configuration and sensations will be perceived, rather than the other way around. Coates demonstrates the power of the interpersonal factors, if not to override the biological organizers, then at least to seriously interfere with them.

PATHOLOGICAL DEVELOPMENT

The model constructed by Coates is remarkably comprehensive in both depth and breadth. Essentially, she explores the organizers of disordered gender identity in boys. She notes that extreme boyhood femininity is part of a pervasive disorder and that most of these children meet the criteria for nongender psychopathology. She reports that maternal psychopathology leads to an impairment in the child's negotiation of the separation–individuation process and to the extinction of physical autonomous movement. I find most compelling the notion that the effeminate boy identifies with the mother as a way to regain the lost object, perhaps in the context of intensely ambivalent or need-dominated mothering. This can be seen as a reidentification that reinforces, rather than counteracts, the identification with the primary attachment object, the mother. Perhaps these borderline mothers themselves sought symbiotic merger as an antidote to their own dissolution anxiety. To understand why one boy yields to this kind of envelopment while another protests it from the start, we need to look at constitutional factors.

The work of Escalona (1963) shows the differences between the responses of active and passive 6-month-old babies to the social environment. Certainly the father's readiness to abandon his son to the needy mother will be critical in the overall balance of factors. Perhaps he is only too willing to offer his son up as a sacrifice to his needy, clinging wife in order to free himself from engulfment. This suggests the necessity of looking at the overall family system with respect to what Framo (1965) calls irrational role assignment. Is the boy with certain temperamental predispositions unconsciously selected by a parent or by both parents to be the container for the projection of their disowned or idealized selves, and does this entail the loss of his maleness? Coates does point out that despite the fact that boys with a gender identity disorder have behavior and a fantasy life that is hyperfeminine, they nevertheless do know that they are male.

DIFFERENCES IN MALE AND FEMALE DEVELOPMENT

Kirkpatrick (1989) emphasizes that core feminine identity originates in the primary object relationship matrix. The subsequent course of this core feminine identity, despite affective and attitudinal positions that develop in relation to it, will be relatively uninterrupted once established. Whatever the biological organizers, they will be consistent with and reinforce the primary feminine identity.

However, the course of gender identity development is destined to differ for boys and girls. From the overall object relations perspective, as Greenson (1968) describes, the boy must separate himself from the primary attachment to, and thus identification with, the primary female mothering object. He must disidentify from her and counteridentify with his father to establish and secure his male gender identity. At this point, the biological–morphological factors, as organizers, are probably enlisted in the service of that disidentification. That is, they must override the organization already set down in early object relations development. The developmental sequelae of this critical switch point are more likely than not to resonate throughout the life of the boy and the man he becomes, not only in terms of the relative security or insecurity of his sense of maleness, but also in terms of his capacity for sexual and emotional intimacy with a woman. As Kirkpatrick (1989) notes, interpersonal factors are essential in the development of feminine gender identity. Since the primary identification is already female, the role of biological organizers is less critical in girls than in boys.

I believe that, in theory construction, we must allow for the widest possible inclusion of data, despite the temptation to narrow our investigations to our own particular areas of interest. The object relations perspective enables a theoretical integration of concepts of self psychology, drive theory, and ego psychology, while it also clarifies the link between the family relational system and the intrapsychic makeup of the individual. Gender identity development can best be understood within this wider perspective.

10

Pseudoschizoid Development: The Little Boy's Dilemma

We are familiar with the plaint of the woman who, wanting only to be held by her partner, finds repeatedly that he becomes sexually aroused in the process and wants to make love instead of playing a maternal role. "Why did you have to go and spoil everything?" she asks him.

The little boy, poised equidistant from his preoedipal and oedipal yearnings, finds himself in the same dilemma. At first he responds to his own deeply felt yearning for maternal closeness and tenderness, and then his own sexual nature also responds, confusing him and evoking anxiety. "Why did you have to go and spoil everything?" the preoedipal self asks. On the other hand, if he moves toward his mother in response to his oedipal yearnings, the regressive implications pose a different kind of threat.

These same themes are manifest in the clinical material of the adult male patient. His defense against this untenable position may take the form of a pseudoschizoid emotional detachment, one that allows his male sexuality to survive and develop, but at the cost of nurturant and affectional strivings vis-à-vis his mother and, later, toward women in general.

The true schizoid personality arises much earlier, when the self of the preoedipal child feels chronically endangered by the not-good-enough object and so *denies* the attachment itself. Other areas of ego development are protected by the splitting off from the overly frustrating or threatening object and the traumatic affects engendered by the interpersonal situation. The grandiose self as a pathological, defensive structure develops and takes the place of the human other.

COMPARISON OF SCHIZOID VERSUS PSEUDOSCHIZOID SOLUTIONS

In the case of the pseudoschizoid solution of the little boy described earlier, affectional and nurturant strivings are *repressed*, and although the intellect may become overly cathected, it is not a manifestation of a grandiose self. The resultant obsessive character style may resemble that of the schizoid personality, but the structure of the inner representational world is very different. In the case of the obsessive style, affect is split off from thought and is repressed, while the intellect and reason become the predominant vehicles of expression and interaction.

In the course of psychotherapy, as the defenses of the schizoid personality disorder give way within the context of the therapeutic relationship, we clearly see the emergence of the underlying object relations pathology and the pathology of the structure of the self—that is, the underlying borderline personality disorder (Giovacchini 1979, Horner 1984). On the other hand, as the pseudoschizoid defenses give way in treatment, we do not discover a severe structural pathology. There is a cohesive, differentiated, and integrated self and the capacity for healthy interpersonal relationships. The characteristic dream of the schizoid personality is that of a baby in a coffin; that of the pseudoschizoid is one of a baby being rocked in its mother's arms. The first dream is an existential statement; the second is a wish.

The setting up of the pseudoschizoid defense, with its emotional detachment and intellectualizing style, is overdetermined in the little boy. The most obvious determinant of the denial of feelings toward his mother would be cultural pressures, as manifest within the family, not to be a "mama's boy." His self-esteem appears to require the repression of what are felt to be regressive yearnings, and thus a repression of his feelings. He must not care.

Greenson (1968) writes of the importance for the little boy of disidentifying from his mother in the service of securing his male gender identity. Greenson uses the term *disidentify* in his discussion of the little boy's struggle to free himself from the earlier symbiotic fusion with his mother and its attendant female nature. "The male child's ability to disidentify will determine the success or failure of his later identification with father. These two phenomena, disidentifying with mother and counteridentifying with father, are interdependent and form a complementary series" (p. 306). The repression of nurturant and affectional strivings as well as of regressive, dependent longings enable the move away from his mother and facilitate the process of disidentification.

The several determinants of emotional detachment and overcathexis of the intellect, reason, and logic lead to a clinical picture common in men, whether in the patient or nonpatient populations. In the clinical situation, there is a tendency to see these men as "sicker" than they are. The degree of anxiety evoked by the emergence of repressed affect may lend credence to this impression. Inasmuch as the therapist's interpersonal stance will be affected by the diagnostic formulation, it is important that the structural diagnosis take into account the strengths as well as the areas of vulnerability. It is also important that interpretations address the developmental dilemma. If the emerging dependent, nurturant yearnings are viewed as a regressive defense against oedipal anxieties, the earlier trauma will be repeated. These yearnings were given up prematurely. They need to be acknowledged and integrated *along with the emotionality that was repressed with them*, not once again simply renounced. If the therapist believes that there is a significant pathology of the structure of the self and that her role should be one of a "selfobject," the necessary interpretive work will not be done and the developmentally later conflict will remain unresolved.

The patient, man or woman, who straddles the rapprochement-oedipal periods, unable to move in either direction, presents the clinical picture most likely to lead to an inaccurate diagnosis and will probably be viewed as either too "sick" or too "healthy." Failures of treatment may be the result of such errors in formulation. The pseudoschizoid man is a case in point.

11

The Double Approach–Avoidance Conflict and Obsessive Disorders

In the psychoanalytic treatment of obsessive disorders, I have found the concept of the double approach–avoidance conflict especially useful. An approach–avoidance conflict exists when a person is simultaneously attracted to and repelled by a single goal object (Munn et al. 1972). As the person moves closer to the goal on the basis of the attraction, the strength of the repelling force becomes stronger, reaching a point at which an avoidant turning away from the goal is mobilized. Then, as the individual gets further and further from the goal and anxiety is thus reduced, the attraction, or wish, asserts itself once again, and again the direction of movement is reversed.

A double approach–avoidance conflict exists when the individual has both positive and negative attitudes toward two goals that have come to be felt as mutually exclusive, with the same opposing forces operating in relation to both goals. There is a potential for the emergence of a double approach–avoidance conflict at various levels of early development when the caretaking environment does not facilitate passage through critical phases. At the level of differentiation, the inherent strivings of the self may be accompanied by the threat of object loss and a consequent loss of cohesion of the self, while movement back toward the object may restore a sense of cohesion at the cost of the loss of identity of a separate self. One patient described this by saying, "If I move closer I get lost, and if I move further away I get lost."

An unsuccessful resolution of the rapprochement phase of the separation–individuation process leaves the individual both drawn to and repelled by moving closer to the object and by moving away from the object. The dependent wish is countered by a fear of engulfment or loss of autonomy. The wish for autonomy is countered by fear of object loss, which engenders intense separation anxiety or depression.

The obsessive stasis of the oedipal situation is one in which the wish for mother is countered by the fear of loss of father and the loss of his love and developmental support, or by fear of his anger and punishment. The wish for mother may also be countered by its regressive implications. On the other hand, the wish for father may be countered by the fear of either the loss of mother or the loss of her love. Essentially, to have mother is to lose father, and to have father is to lose mother.

The confluence of the preoedipal and oedipal levels intensifies the double approach–avoidance situation. Any individuation on the part of the little girl may signify emotional abandonment for the mother, while the child's turning to father makes her a treacherous rival as well.

Despite the differences in the underlying character structures, the clinical picture may seem to be the same: the patient is unable to make decisions and ruminates obsessively about the possibility of making the "wrong" one. From the point of view of the double approach–avoidance conflict, *any* decision has an inherent wrongness to it.

In my clinical experience, a stage-appropriate interpretation of the underlying developmental dilemma as it is manifest in current situations as well as in the transference leads to a resolution of the developmental impasse and an abatement of the obsessive symptoms.

12

Creativity and Pathological Solutions

The term *not-me*, which Sullivan (1956) used to denote dissociated aspects of the personality, refers, in fact, to aspects of the self that have been disowned. Sullivan, writing of the dissociative process, said that he was concerned "with the actual dynamic situation . . . by which an important system of the personality is effectively barred from any disturbing influence on personal awareness for a period of years and perhaps for a lifetime" (p. 167). He noted the tendency of these dissociated systems of the personality to reappear in dreams, and he implies that premature interpretation of their meaning will lead to greater repression and "forgetting" of dreams, since the closer the dissociation comes to awareness, the greater the anxiety.

Sullivan's "not-me" concept is the antithesis of the phenomena that I will be describing—pseudoself phenomena that *take the place of* the actual self in one manner or another or that *compensate for* its felt deficiency or absence. Sullivan's "not-me" refers to an important aspect of that actual self that has been denied. There are important distinctions among Winnicott's (1965) "false self," what I have called the "constructed self" (Horner 1988b), the "self-effacing trends" described by Horney (Ingram 1987), the "as-if" personality first described by Deutsch (1942), and the "factitious disorder." All of these can be understood as the outcome of the developing child's use of his creative potential to cope with forces inimical to his healthy development of self.

THE FALSE SELF (WINNICOTT)

As I listen to therapists discuss clinical problems, I find that the term *false self* is often used indiscriminately to signify any and all forms of interpersonal adaptation. When a term becomes too general, it loses its usefulness. It is critical that we understand the structural and dynamic issues with precision so that our interpretations are correct, so that the patient will feel understood, and so that we do not traumatize the patient with an inappropriate therapeutic stance.

The false self, in the purest sense, is in my view basically a relational self that has been shaped in accordance with the unconscious needs and projections of the primary caretakers. When the mother's intercessions are impingements—intrusions into or disruptions of the child's spontaneous experiencing—the child's own self-directed flow of attention and movement becomes reactive instead. When this situation is chronic, rather than the occasional failure of the mother to be "good enough," identity becomes consolidated around the reactions and adaptations to the impinging object. Identity may become consolidated around parental projections of some rejected or idealized aspects of themselves or around projections of their own internalized objects, be they persecutory or idealized. The false self identity takes on the specific shape of the self or object representation that is thus projected. For example, if the mother needs to feel perfect and omnipotent, she may project her flawed and helpless self into the child and treat that child as though he were a personification of the projection. There is a kind of "shaping" that takes place, in operant-conditioning terms, and for all intents and purposes the child "becomes" that personification. Meanwhile, the "true self," which is based on the child's own spontaneous experiencing and will, becomes split off and repressed. Since it cannot evolve, it maintains its relatively primitive qualities.

Although Winnicott (1965) views the function of the false self as essentially that of protecting the true self, it also serves the function of maintaining some connection with the parent. That is, it both enables and maintains the connection, and it protects the hidden true self from impingement or assault. It is because of its critical function of object connecting that the false self is so difficult to relinquish in treatment. A depressed false self, which developed as a way to connect with a depressed mother by joining her mood and by hiding the exuberance of the true self, is not depressed in the usual sense of the word. Giving up the depressed false self may lead to a sense of object loss, which would then evoke a true depressive reaction. Similarly, the prescription of antidepressant medication may constitute a threat to the individual's tie with the internalized object. Such an individual may be surprisingly happy in other arenas of life.

The false self has a specific face. It is not fluid. In fact, the individual evokes an adaptive reaction in the other through projective identification in which the complementary self or object representation of the parent is put upon the recipient and by means of which the false self identity is supported. For example, if the individual has developed a false "inadequate" self that early on helped to maintain the mother's stance of superadequacy, then the superadequate object will be projected outward and the interpersonal dynamic of superadequacy vis-à-vis inadequacy will be played out once more. That is, the false self will be one half of an internalized object relation that becomes reenacted in interpersonal relationships. This is often multigenerational, with the primary caretaker projecting her own unintegrated and unassimilated internalized object representation into the child.

Since the individual with a false self will attempt to replicate this internalized object relation with the therapist, it is critical that the therapist identify the dynamic and structural issues and not inadvertently collude with the pathological object relation set-up. This collusion is more likely to occur when the projection is not dystonic for the therapist—when it fits an aspect of the self that is valued, such as strength and adequacy. Winnicott (1965) notes that

> A principle might be enunciated, that in the False Self area of our analytic practice we make more headway by recognition of the patient's nonexistence than by a long continued working with the patient on the basis of ego-defense mechanisms. [p. 152]

With this kind of patient, the working alliance may be with the false self, and, as a result, the work of therapy is not experienced as real and cannot be integrated or sustained. Winnicott sees this issue as relevant to the interminable analysis. The critical question is, Is there an accessible, core true self that can form the nucleus for the organizing of a true self identity within the therapeutic matrix? The phase of the developmental timetable at which true self development was derailed will determine the structure of the true self with respect to its cohesion, integration, and differentiation. The presence of a false self alerts us to the existence of an underlying structural pathology, but it does not tell us the specific nature of this pathology.

THE CONSTRUCTED SELF (HORNER)

In his paper *Language and Psychoanalysis*, Richardson (1987) describes the horrendous history of a patient named Norma Jean Baker and the creation of Marilyn Monroe. Norma Jean had started well before that time to construct an identity that would bring her a sense of worth and pride based on her fantasies of being rescued by an idealized father and, later, on her immersion in the film world and its stars. Her inquiry, laughingly made to an autograph seeker—"How do you spell Marilyn Monroe?"—was a clear statement of the split between her real and constructed selves.

The constructed self is not a false self in Winnicott's (1965) sense. It evolves as a defense against intolerable shame and self-hatred and is shaped in accord with a fantasied ego ideal. It is not grandiose in the usual sense of the term, but it must be perfect lest the shame erupt once again in full force.

As Winnicott observes, we make little headway unless we work with the true self. Unfortunately, it is easy to collude with the patient in his attempts to fix the constructed self through analysis of it. The most important interpretation with respect to the constructed self is its defensive function. In this work I will generally point out that it is as though there were a sheet of glass laid over the original self, and the new self constructed atop the glass. Although each can see the other, there can be no communication between them. The real self cannot avail itself of the achievements and positive feedback that comes to the constructed self in order to evolve a healthy and realistic self-esteem. The constructed self, on the other hand, cannot avail itself of the sense of authenticity that is attached to the rejected real self.

Unlike a rejection of identification with a mother or father who has lost the respect of the child, this is a manifestation of the rejection of identification with the self and, as such, requires a more violent and complete split between the self who is and the self the child wants to be. In Kohut's (1971) terms, this is a horizontal split.

A Defense Against Shame

The development of a constructed self is often found in women with a history of sexual molestation, although it is not restricted to those who have undergone such trauma. Individuals who are inordinately ashamed of their family of origin may use the same defense. The intensity of the combined shame and guilt, particularly shame, motivate the defense.

One woman in her early forties had been molested by both grandfathers from the age of 3 until she stopped them both when she was 12 years old. She recalled how the grandfather she really loved had warned her that if she told anyone, her father would kill him and then the father would have to go to prison. Needless to say, she never told. She recounted how she had decided at a very young age to be a movie star, and did in fact have minor roles in a number of films. She developed problems that led to her seeking therapy when she began to take lessons in method acting. This technique requires individuals to reach into the deepest recesses of the unconscious in order to access the range of affect required by the role they are to play. This sent her into such a panic that she was never able to act again.

The woman had a variety of unsuccessful treatments, and I was to join the list of failed therapists. I brought up the issue of the constructed self and how I was often drawn into colluding with her wish to perfect it. In fact, she experienced those sessions as not helping. She felt good about sessions in which she got to the buried feelings and cried, but then she would become upset at how the crying affected her appearance and she would refuse to pursue this way of working. She was a beautiful woman with a lovely, seductive little-girl quality.

Early in her treatment she invited me to a large Hollywood party she was giving, with the idea that it would help me build my practice. I thanked her for the invitation, but explained how I would become another in a list of people who exploited her for their own needs if I were to accept. She was not especially pleased at my response, as she clearly wanted to co-opt me and her treatment into her constructed life. She left treatment when she was about to marry a very wealthy man who would enable her to live the life of one of the "beautiful people" (her words). When the defensive constructed self works, there is little or no motivation for analysis.

Dr. Richardson (1987) noted how Marilyn Monroe's analyst would take her home to visit with his family, quite probably with the hope of providing corrective family and home experiences. However, at times the family's excitement at having Marilyn Monroe as a guest at their parties co-opted her therapist into her constructed life. Since the constructed self is most often attractive in a variety of ways, the therapist must resist the gratifications that accompany participation in it. If the therapist acts out in this way, the patient is very likely to get the message that the therapist does prefer the constructed self to the split-off shame- and guilt-ridden identity.

There are similar developmental discontinuities when an individual immigrates to a country where a different language is spoken. Affect is likely to be contained in the mother tongue. There is good reason to believe that treatment will be facilitated if the therapist can speak the patient's original language.

Another woman's constructed self had entailed ridding herself of her Brooklyn accent. Her speech tended to be hesitant, her words measured. With the interpretation of the defensive function of the constructed self and the exploration of the molestation and its aftermath, she began to feel free to let the old language patterns come out. There was a release of affect and spontaneity as well.

It is important to interpret the defensive and compensatory functions of the constructed self as well as to point out the price that is paid for the defense early in treatment. The patient's adherence to this stance is a major resistance, and therapy readily becomes co-opted into it. Of course, the way in which this is done has to take into consideration the patient's vulnerabilities, with due respect for feelings of safety and self-esteem, particularly when there is significant structural pathology of the split-off real self.

SELF-EFFACING TRENDS (HORNEY)

Horney (Ingram 1987) spoke of "self-effacing" trends that are characterized by such tendencies as an inability to say no, inordinate fear of criticism, putting up with unfair treatment and being nice about it, self-deprecation, compliance, and avoidance of self-assertion. The self-effacing trend becomes characterologically embedded in the individual's way of relating to others. Such a stance may cover over the patient's own arrogant demands for consideration and what Horney calls the expansive drives. Underneath the niceness one may find vindictiveness, retaliatory fantasies, and the holding of grudges. The person may come to feel hatred toward others as a result of the self-effacing tendencies.

Horney, like Winnicott, has a concept of a real self, "a nuclear capacity to grow constructively and to progressively engage the world and one's own being" (Ingram 1989). But when things go awry early in life, the person may become alienated from this real self:

This alienation from self means that the person, in order to avoid conflict with the world, must invent a way to be. Depending on the situation, the person will consolidate the various attitudes into what Horney called solutions, becoming in general terms self-effacing or expansive or detached. At the same time, the person relies heavily on idealization and projective defenses to secure this invented position. . . . The self-effacing person responds compliantly under nearly all circumstances, showing symptom formation when this solution won't work. [personal communication]

Meekness, goodness, and loving-kindness are idealized, while feelings and attitudes inconsistent with this posture are externalized. In a sense, an ego ideal is created in accord with a particular view of moral perfection, and the self-effacing trend becomes a structural arrangement in which the individual becomes more or less identified with this pathological ego ideal. While this way of being in the world is supposed to achieve interpersonal security, the insistence on being small, together with the projection of rage and aggression, lead instead to an anxiety-ridden existence and a predisposition to being victimized.

The self-effacing trend probably comes close to what in mainstream psychoanalysis today would be characterized as the masochistic personality disorder. The masochistic personality must secure the illusion of good self at all costs, and the only form of aggression that can be acknowledged is based on righteous indignation.

With her break from Freudian psychoanalysis, Horney anticipated modern psychoanalytic interest in the character disorders, which she called "neurotic solutions." As Horney describes the analysis of self-effacing individuals, it becomes apparent that these individuals project their own potential for narcissistic rage and then do everything possible to avoid it, often by catering to the assumed narcissism of the other. In this case, the interpretation of the self-effacing defenses would have to be made with full consideration of the individual's narcissistic vulnerabilities. One might say that there are two layers of defense against the deeper existential anxiety: first those defenses we find to be characteristic of the narcissistic disorders, and then the self-effacing trends that keep these first layers of defenses safe from attack. Although a "self-effacing trend" refers to a defensive structure, it is not definitive of the underlying structure of the self.

THE "AS-IF" PERSONALITY (DEUTSCH)

Deutsch first described the "as-if" personality in 1942. She noted that such individuals may have a number of imitative relationships and shifting interests and occupations, depending on with whom the individual is connected. She reports a case in which the individual carried this dynamic into the therapeutic relationship, which one would expect to be the case. Deutsch writes (in Meissner 1988):

> The analytic work seemed unusually successful. The patient began to understand many things about herself, and as she did so the eccentric behaviors seemed to fall away. In part, her hidden agenda had been to become an analyst in imitation of Deutsch. When she realized this was impossible, she collapsed into a state of total lack of affect and inner emptiness. She gradually became increasingly negativistic and resistant to the analytic process. [p. 560]

Meissner (1988) also calls attention to the kind of patient who presents a compliant facade in an effort to be a model analysand, believing that there will be some payoff or reward for playing this role. This kind of person adapts various personae and plays roles in many contexts of life. Meissner notes that such an individual may react with hurt, anger, disillusionment, and pained disappointment when the compliance and the conformity to others' wishes do not seem to get what is felt to be desperately needed. Although this may sound like Horney's description of self-effacing trends, what is at issue is the nature of the underlying structure and the dynamic function of the adaptive behavior and how they differ for each of these disorders. In the case of the as-if personality, we find a plasticity of the sense of identity.

Meissner writes that for these individuals, life is often lived as a kind of imitation, an attempt to be like others, but this is carried out without real feeling, significance, or belief. The intensely felt need to meet the expectations of important others, regardless of the cost to oneself, reveals the "despair, uncertainty, and agony they experience when the issue is a question of standing alone on their own feet" (1988, p. 570). The plastic adaptability leaves the individual with little sense of self. There is a chameleon quality to object relationships, and often the individual's sense of identity is determined by the nature of his involvement at the time. Indeed, such individuals may describe themselves as chameleons. One of Meissner's patients told him that she felt she could have a sense of existing only by molding herself to a pattern set by others.

He sets as the issues for treatment the "problems in exploring the underlying motivation for compliant adaptation and in understanding the obstacles to establishing a solid, autonomous, and consistent identity that is authentically the patient's own" (p. 557).

Greenson (1954) notes that Deutsch's patients appeared to be normal, "warm-hearted people, but closer scrutiny indicated they were almost totally lacking in genuine object relationships. They took on other people's affects by means of quick imitations" (p. 86). He concludes that in reality her patients were empty, schizoid personalities.

Greenson describes a man who had been in analysis for a number of years with another analyst. Upon exploration, Greenson concluded that the man did not know what he was supposed to do in the analytic situation. He had been lying down, meekly submitting to what he said the previous analyst had demanded—that is, constant and instant free association. He did not keep silent or think about what his analyst said. He was afraid of blank spaces, which seemed to signify some awful danger. And if he were really to think and disagree with his analyst, his disagreement could be tantamount to killing the analyst. Greenson describes how the passivity and compliance were a form of ingratiation that covered inner emptiness, insatiable infantile hunger, and terrible rage. After six months of treatment it became clear to him that the patient was an as-if character who could not bear the deprivation of classical psychoanalysis. Greenson adds that at this time he helped the patient obtain supportive psychotherapy with a female therapist. Meissner's explication of the therapeutic tasks would lead one to question Greenson's giving up on the as-if patient as essentially untreatable, although one might be sympathetic toward his reluctance to undertake the task.

Giovacchini (1975) calls the as-if personality the "blank self." He too notes that, like the chameleon, these patients blend in with their surroundings. He says that while they seem to adopt the characteristics, style, and even the standards and ideals of others, these are pseudoidentifications, transient and easily exchangeable. Giovacchini makes the important distinction between characteristic behaviors and the underlying character structure. He observes what he calls "pseudo as-if personalities," who actually have a modicum of underlying organization but who incorporate significant external objects as defensive superstructures. The underlying organization is lacking in the true as-if personality.

Giovacchini reports the kind of countertransference that might be evoked by the as-if patient. Describing a new patient, a young woman in her twenties who was brought to treatment by her husband, he writes:

> In spite of her apparent fragility—almost bordering upon dissolution and panic—she was able to give me a surprising amount of information. As the session progressed she seemed to anticipate what I wanted to know, and so I found it unnecessary to ask questions to satisfy my curiosity. At the time, I was aware of an uneasy feeling within me which I could not explain; there was an uncanny quality to what I was experiencing. [1975, p. 81]

Although the patient described herself as shy and withdrawn, she also felt a need to be with people, fearful that her loneliness would swallow her up. "She had difficulty 'anchoring' herself and knowing who and what she was and what the purpose of her existence was." She had no ideas of her own and saw herself as a "sponge," soaking up the personality and identity of any companion. If she was alone, she felt that she did not exist. Others could readily observe her tendency to imitate and incorporate their ideals and mannerisms.

Giovacchini also notes that although there is no obvious transference, these patients develop a unique type of transference that is a specific product of their characterological difficulties. In the instances of the two patients he describes, both of them gradually developed mannerisms that puzzled him until he realized that they were imitating his gestures, inflections, and favorite expressions. Furthermore, they seemed to have no awareness of what they were doing. While they did not project anything into him, they incorporated parts of him. He learned that these seeming identifications disappeared when they left the session, at which time they reverted to their usual behavior.

Unlike Greenson, who referred his patient for supportive therapy, Giovacchini did work analytically with his patients. He writes:

> This patient's vision of me was obviously a projection of her self-representation and the principal aspect of the maternal image. After I pointed out her projection, she brought up material that dealt with her amorphous image of her mother and her mother's amorphous image of her. . . . The patient often described ours as a "tape-recorder" relationship. She was completely blank and she projected "blankness" onto me. The only way she could fill the void was to incorporate others into it, but they could not be "held." This was an extremely interesting phase of her analysis because, as her existential anxiety mounted, she was able to obtain some relief by incorporating me. Then she would ignore me again but, as could be seen, this represented a transference fluctuation rather than a lack of transference. [1975, p. 86]

Giovacchini notes that while some patients may use blankness as a defense, the blankness of the as-if personality is part of the underlying self representation. He notes that the capacity to make genuine identifications is impaired in both the as-if patient and the pseudo as-if patient. "They cannot make clear distinctions between themselves and the outer world; they tend to fuse with external objects instead of making selective identifications" (p. 90). Although, not surprisingly, their superego development was lacking, both his patients were able to withhold their aberrant impulses by conforming to the repressive aspects of the outer world, while their affectlessness was the result of their lack of distinct structuralization.

An important distinction between the false self and the as-if personality is the essential permanence and consistency of the false self identity as contrasted with the plasticity of the as-if personality. In either case, recognition of the underlying structural pathology is critical to the treatment process.

FACTITIOUS DISORDERS (DSM-III-R)

In the *Diagnostic and Statistical Manual of Mental Disorders* (3rd ed., revised [DSM-III-R]), the diagnosis of Factitious Disorder with Psychological Symptoms is described as follows:

> The essential feature of this disorder is intentional production or feigning of psychological (often psychotic) symptoms suggestive of mental disorder. The person's goal is apparently to assume the "patient" role and is not otherwise understandable in light of the person's environmental circumstances (as is the case in Malingering).
>
> This disorder is often recognized by the pan-symptomatic complex of psychological symptoms that are presented and by the fact that the symptoms are worse when the person is aware of being observed. . . . He or she may be extremely suggestible and admit to many additional symptoms the examiner mentions. Conversely, the person may be extremely negativistic and uncooperative when questioned. The psychological symptoms presented usually represent the person's concept of mental disorder, and may not conform to any of the recognized diagnostic categories. [p. 315]

DSM-III-R notes that the presence of factitious psychological symptoms does not preclude the coexistence of true psychological symptoms. I treated one such patient for a long time before I came to suspect that there were factitious symptoms superimposed on a combination of paranoid personality disorder and schizoid personality disorder. From time to time the patient would insist that her problems were all due to her having been abused and that she did not have any kind of mental disorder, that she was absolutely normal. Needless to say, the therapist may be led down many wrong paths in the attempt to understand the patient's pathology in developmental, structural, or dynamic terms. Meanwhile, the patient may react violently to the inevitable failures of the therapist, who is trying to work with information that does not mean what it seems to mean.

This patient apparently created disorders that she believed would be of particular clinical interest to the therapist. It was only in retrospect that I came to understand the significance of her laughingly telling me at the very start of treatment that she had once made a doctor believe that she was schizophrenic so that he would prescribe megavitamins. I took this to indicate the difficulty of making an accurate diagnosis. Putting this episode together with her stories of other therapies in which she had presented still different clinical pictures, I now understand what she said as a statement of conscious and deliberate distortion.

When in treatment at a later time with a male therapist whom she believed to be primarily interested in her sexuality, she engaged in a rather dangerous period of promiscuous acting out, believing that her therapist wanted her to behave that way so that they could both understand her sexuality. For some weeks during the time I worked with her, she presented a particular body of bizarre material. As I attempted to understand it with her, she came up with the idea that I should write a book about her. It would make us both famous, she said, much as the Wolf Man had made Freud famous. When I did not join her in her grandiose fantasy, she became enraged, and when I tried to work further with the material—on content rather than process—she admitted that none of it was even true. With some irritation I commented on the difficulty of working when she wasn't being honest, at which point she became even more enraged at me for impugning her honesty.

In retrospect I understand that she had made up the pathological material in the service of her megalomania, which she had at first projected into me, reclaiming it as her own through a kind of collaborative fusion with me. At our last session, she revealed her conscious distortion of the process in the direction of what she thought I thought had to be analyzed.

Although this phenomenon can be viewed as a variant of the false self insofar as it is a relational self, it does not have the person-to-person consistency of the false self; rather, it varies in accord with the specific interpersonal situation. Although it is an interpersonal adaptation, it is not an enduring structure. Robbins (1989), writing of the primitive personality organization, notes the "*interpersonal* adaptive function served by the destructive repetition" in the treatment situation.

Factitious disorder is not a diagnosis that comes readily to the minds of most therapists, and it is one that is given relatively little attention in the literature, but it is a possibility that should not be overlooked when nothing makes sense from one's usual clinical perspective.

What was probably reenacted in the transference was this patient's confusing and confounding me by pretended bizarre behavior, just as she was confused and confounded by the bizarre behavior of her paranoid–schizophrenic mother and grandmother. And just as she was humiliated by her father's malevolent teasing, she attempted to humiliate me by her sadistic teasing, by trying to make a fool of me as she felt he had made a fool of her. Her parting shot to me was that she no longer had to feel ashamed, as the shame was now mine. It was as though she had drained what had been toxic to her and deposited it in me.

It is quite likely that in addition to engaging me by giving me the kind of material she believed I was interested in, the psychotic behavior, which was readily turned off the moment I said the time was up, may have been the only way she could let me know how it had felt to be her as a child vis-à-vis her psychotic mother. This is not to say that she gained nothing from the therapy. Since any form of engagement led to onslaughts of abuse from her and accusations that I was abusing her, I felt the only possible course of action was to be silent and to attempt to function as a container and metabolizer of her projections. At times it was difficult not to respond to her provocations. Projective identification was prominent in her interpersonal relationships and particularly in the transference, where she projected her abused self as well as the psychotic abusive object. She would not tolerate interpretations, although at one point she herself observed that I was being forced to sit and listen as she had been forced to sit and listen to the outpourings of her mother and grandmother. During these protracted periods of my own silence she did, indeed, remember her early traumatic interpersonal experiences in the family in greater detail and was able to abreact and reframe them in a way that left her feeling better about herself. She was also able to attain a position of ambivalence toward her mother, denying neither the psychotic abuse nor the love she felt for the mother.

In summary, what Winnicott described as the false self both protects the true self from impingement and maintains a connection to the object. The constructed self defends against the shame of a disowned self by constructing one of a number of possible ego ideals and then trying to live up to it. Horney's self-effacing solution both protects a pathological, morally perfect ego ideal and identifies with it, while defensively attempting to manipulate relationships with a variety of compliant and placating behaviors. What Deutsch called the as-if personality defends against the terror of a lack of inner organization and existential anxiety.

The factitious disorder is an adaptation specific to the clinical situation, whereby the patient endeavors either to engage the therapist by being of imagined particular clinical interest or to communicate to the therapist something that may be otherwise inarticulable. The psychotic content is probably best understood in terms of its interpersonal function rather than as a true picture of the patient's structural pathology.

The existence of any of these manifestations of what I am calling not-me phenomena constitutes a major barrier to a successful therapeutic outcome. It is essential that they be addressed early in treatment and appropriately to the patient's capacity to do the work. An accurate diagnosis of both structure and dynamics will guide the work itself.

PART THREE

Treatment of
Character Pathology

13

The Creative Alliance

Lydia Rapoport believed that people need a sense of worth and dignity, a sense of self and an identity, and an opportunity to make choices regarding the direction of their lives in order to achieve a sense of self-realization. There can be no clearer expression of the fundamental goal of treatment, whether it be from the vantage point of social casework or from that of psychoanalysis. Winnicott (1971) wrote that "it is only in being creative that the individual discovers the self." This chapter deals with creativity as a quality intrinsic to the human mind, its role in the treatment process, and the barriers to that creativity on the parts of both patient and therapist.

PRIMARY CREATIVITY

Winnicott speaks of creativity as primary, as an attitude to external reality. There can be no more convincing example of an innate, primary creativity than the creation of the self and object as mental structures by the perceiving, experiencing, synthesizing personal self of the very young child. Infant research (Lichtenberg 1981) confirms the child's innate potential for self-direction. Films of social interaction between mothers and their babies reveal that the child is as much an initiator as a responder in those interactions. Since it is these characteristic interactions along with their characteristic affective quality that are built up in memory in the form of enduring schemas of the self and the other, the infant plays a central role in its own psychic development. The innate synthesizing capabilities of competent brain functioning, which are a sine qua non for the building of psychic structure, are also the contribution of the child to its own developmental process. Through these innate, self-directed synthesizing activities, the child is, in the final analysis, creator of its own self and inner world. That is, the self as the locus of experience and activity creates the self as mental structure. Paradoxically, the product of the child's creativity, the inner representational world, may stand as a barrier to access to the creative self later in life.

Sutherland (1983) characterizes the psychoanalytic image of man in terms of the way he functions as a creator of guiding images for himself that are determined by the properties of the self and its perception of the world. The self, he says, "is surely the heart of the matter regarding the organization and functioning of subjective experience" (p. 539).

Winnicott observes that when we are involved with the analysis of the artist's product—the book or the canvas—we lose sight of the artist's creativity as process, relating this to the therapeutic situation in which we may become so caught up in the patient's material that we forget about the creative process necessary for the individual's discovery of himself or herself. Freud (1908) wrote about the same distinction between product and process when he wrote that "not even the clearest insight into the determinants of [the creative writer's] choice of material and into the nature of the art of creating imaginative form will ever help to make creative writers of *us*" (p. 143).

Balint (1968) describes three areas of the mind. The first, he says, is the oedipal area, where everything happens in a triangular relationship involving the subject and at least two parallel objects.

The oedipal area is inevitably an area of conflict, which is caused by the ambivalences arising in the complexities of the relationship between the subject and these two parallel objects. At the level of the basic fault, in contrast, all events belong to an exclusively two-person relationship. If there is a third person, he is a burden, a source of intolerable strain. The problems associated with the level of the basic fault are caused, writes Balint, not by the conflict of ambivalence, but by a lack of fit between a child and the people who represent its environment.

Balint characterizes the third area as the area of creation. This is a one-person situation. In this area there is no external object present. "The subject is on his own and his main concern is to produce something out of himself." Balint states that since there is no external object in this area, no transference can develop here. Before there is a transference, an organized object has to be created so an interaction can take place at one of the other levels. Thus, he implies that there cannot even be a narcissistic selfobject transference in this state. He notes that we cannot be with the patient during those moments—only just before and just after them.

Elsewhere (1979, 1984) I have written that there are three states of being in the developmental stage of what Mahler (1968) refers to as that of normal symbiosis. "There are the good self-object constellation based upon pleasurable experiences in social interaction, the bad self-object based upon dysphoric experiences in social interaction, and the core self-without-object" (p. 81). The latter is based upon the parallel and even simultaneous organization of self-experiences that consolidate around the emerging autonomous functions, particularly perception and motor development. In the healthy organism, organization goes on with or without the object.

This core self-without-object corresponds to what Balint calls the area of creation. Even with the failure of human attachment, there is a clear ability to organize nonhuman reality competently. This ego state can be seen as the *anlage* of defensive detachment and is analogous to what Guntrip (1969) refers to as the schizoid core. When the object world actively interferes with the child's creative process, overwhelming it with intrusion, impingement, or even with assault, the cognitively competent child may be able to continue to organize itself creatively and actually function at a higher level when alone, or when emotional detachment can be maintained, as in the case of the schizoid solution. But the creative, integrative process can be partial only if the data of interpersonal experience must be excluded, split off, and repressed with the dangerous representational world created by the child earlier out of its interpersonal situation. In patients with a psychotic or paranoid core, where there is no salient early positive selfobject representation to draw upon for basic trust, the creative process may have to be circumscribed in the service of sanity. Kohut (1977) saw this situation as indicating the necessity of building compensatory structures atop repressed pathology. There are some, like R. D. Laing (1967), who would enable the psychosis to emerge, putting total trust in the patient's primary creativity and ability to recreate the self.

SILENCE AND CREATIVITY

Speaking on behalf of silence in the therapeutic hour, Balint notes that it may be more of a running toward something than a running away. It may be a state in which the individual feels relatively safe and can do something about what is troubling her. Balint adds that we should not see silence as a resistance. Winnicott agrees indirectly, saying that the therapist should allow the patient to be creative in the analytic work, adding that "a patient's creativity can be stolen by a therapist who knows too much" (p. 57). Without negating the validity of Balint's comments about the value of silence in the treatment situation, I must stress the importance of being able to discriminate between productive silence and that which is, indeed, defensive, as in the case of the patient who screens out material he believes will evoke the therapist's disapproval.

Freud (1908), and later, Winnicott (1971), drew a parallel between play and the creative process. Both the creative writer and the child at play create a world of fantasy which they take very seriously, while at the same time separating it sharply from reality.

Winnicott (1971) writes that psychotherapy is done in the overlap of the play areas of the patient and the therapist—that is, in the areas of creativity. Both must suspend rigid belief systems, whether it be those associated with the patient's neurosis or those associated with the therapist's theoretical assumptions. He states forcefully that "if the therapist cannot play, then he is not suitable for the work. If the patient cannot play, then something needs to be done to enable the patient to become able to play, after which psychotherapy may begin" (p. 54). Through creative play, the individual will then discover the self.

Bromberg (1983) reminds us that Winnicott is offering "play" as a metaphor, and not as a substitute for interpretation. "It is a climate in which the timely and creative use of interpretation can flourish so as to maximize the patient's own creative use of the analytic experience" (p. 377).

RESISTANCE AND CREATIVITY

Sharing with humanistic psychologists the philosophical goal of "self-realization," Balint, Winnicott, and the self psychologists tell us that if the therapist can suspend belief and empathically join the patient in the transitional area of play and creativity, the patient will essentially cure himself. But some things are more readily said than done, and the major work of therapy may be to address those very barriers to the capacity to play in the Winnicott sense, barriers to the area of creation. In classical terms, the major part of the treatment process may well be the analysis of resistance. The newer brief psychoanalytically oriented psychotherapies (Davanloo 1980, Sifneos 1979) focus specifically on the resistance aspects of the problem, leaving the major part of the creative working-through to the patient to carry on after the end of treatment. More often than not, in long-term treatment, it is only after a laborious plodding through a minefield of psychic dangers that the patient is able to run freely with the creative process that will lead to the creation of a whole and integrated self. While the earlier stage of treatment may be predominantly analytic, the later phase may be predominantly creative and integrative, although from the very start there will be some degree of overlap of the two processes. If our obsessional or hysteric patient is cut off from feeling or knowing, there can only be a partial integration unless libidinal and destructive affect, impulse, and ideation can also be assimilated. The resistances to knowing and feeling must be dealt with before the individual can let herself even be aware of the basic data that are to be processed and transformed via the creative process. I think Winnicott is too narrow in his view of what is curative when he tells us that it is only when it is possible for the patient to play that psychotherapy can begin. The analysis of the resistances is as much a part of psychotherapy as is the creative, integrative phase of the process.

Although the child may have been the creator of his own inner representational world, those very products of the creative self may now be projected outward, coloring the adult's perceptions, expectations, and meaning and belief systems. Whereas this inner world was originally based upon interpersonal experience, the inner world now plays a determining role in shaping current experience. The fear of an envious and rageful inner object may inhibit the creative process. Preoedipal pathology may lead to a generalized defensive ego construction that interferes with the synthetic function itself. And, as Balint notes, intense conflicts at the oedipal level may inhibit the creative process. The competitive strivings associated with the Oedipus complex may generate an inhibiting anxiety about potential punishment for those strivings or an inhibiting guilt over the wish to defeat the rival. Defenses against these anxieties may constitute a subtle but powerful transference resistance that will require resolution before the patient is truly free to use her creativity in the service of the growth of the self. Balint believes that ultimately, it is the structure of the area of creation that really matters. Nevertheless, the individual must first have the sense of freedom and safety to enter into it.

Just as the therapist may, at times, have to function as an auxiliary ego for the patient when the individual's own ego fails and he is endangered by that failure, so, at times, the therapist may have to act as a stand-in for the patient's blocked capacity to be creative. "Listening with the third ear" (Reik 1949), we allow the patient's associations to wash over us. Keeping in mind as an organizing principle what we already know about this person, and with our own unhampered capacity to listen creatively, we may have to offer the creative constructions which the patient's unconscious defenses still disallow. Needless to say, not only the accuracy but also the timeliness of such offerings are critical lest they traumatize or confuse patients, or leave them feeling untouched and hopeless.

Case Example

Early in treatment, in response to a number of obvious transference allusions, one therapist made what seemed to be gentle inquiry into their possible relevance for the treatment situation. The patient, through his creative unconscious, was able to say that these offerings were premature. He brought in a dream about a house under construction. While he was outside working on the foundation, someone was on the inside doing the wiring before the foundation was ready. He was puzzled as to the meaning of the dream, still blocked from the conscious creativity lost to him under early pressures to conform and perform. The therapist made the interpretation: "Perhaps you are telling me that I am making connections before you are ready for them, before a foundation has been laid down here." The patient reacted very positively and with affect to the interpretation, and the issue of trust emerged, the foundation that was just starting to be built. In making this interpretation, the therapist's creativity stood as proxy for that of the patient, who was blocked by anxiety and the defenses against that anxiety. The accuracy and timeliness of the interpretation enabled the patient to connect with it at a feeling level, furthering the very development of a foundation of trust. It was a transference interpretation of conflict both intrapsychic and interpersonal, but one that was felt to be empathically correct.

Balint's opinion that the patient may need the safety of silence to enter the area of creation was borne out by this same man's ability to work hard, and with affect, between sessions, only to be blocked in the wish to share the full process with the therapist. He could bring in only the cognitive product, divorced from the affect experienced in the original discovery. He agonized over this block.

The therapist responded empathically to the felt intensity of the wish to share his feelings, and the patient was able to see that, although trust was growing, he still needed the safety of "playing" alone. Although this saddened him, the release of integrated thought and affect between sessions offered him a sense of hope. His dreams continued to provide information about his resistance to "playing" in the presence of the therapist and about the dangers he feared would emerge. In analytic terms, the analysis of resistance was paving the way for the potential creative discovery of the whole self. The unconscious creativity persevered in his dream life, while the defensive detachment still blocked the process in the treatment hour.

Freud (1908) reminds us that the opposite of play is not what is serious but what is real (p. 143). The term *play* tends to be misleading because of its cultural connotation, and for this reason I don't like to use it. Sometimes the "play" may lead to frightening and shameful discovery. Nevertheless, in the service of the integration of the self, these discoveries provide the basic material for the creation of a more whole and real self. The fear of what may be discovered about the self, its departure from the ego ideal and the possibility of shame, or its potential danger to an important relationship and the possibility of guilt or depression, stand as barriers to the individual's creativity, to his capacity to "play" in the therapeutic space, barriers that themselves need to be understood and worked through.

BARRIERS TO THE THERAPIST'S CREATIVITY

This brings us to Winnicott's dictum, "If the therapist cannot play, then he is unsuitable for the work." Dealing with our countertransference resistances, characterological or otherwise, is indeed an essential component of our preparation to function as dynamic psychotherapists. In contrast to the induced countertransference reaction, which informs us of what is going on with the patient, the personal and idiosyncratic barriers to therapeutic creativity that are the contribution of the therapist do indeed need to be analyzed and resolved.

I especially want to pay attention to the therapist's theoretical orientation as a potential and substantial barrier to her capacity to work creatively in the therapeutic situation. At the risk of being accused of presenting an argument ad hominem, I will nevertheless state my impression that a rigid adherence to one particular analytic theory may be a manifestation of countertransference resistance. The self psychologist who always presents himself or herself as a mirroring selfobject may possibly be avoiding conflict or denying his own narcissistic and competitive strivings. The rigid Freudian, on the other hand, who maintains an attitude of authority and who denies the subtleties of the interpersonal process in the therapeutic situation, may be defending against the experience of existential annihilation or helplessness experienced earlier vis-à-vis a narcissistic or engulfing mother, or against other dangers of interpersonal encounter. Even more subtly, a particular theoretical emphasis may have the feel of experienced truth when it fits our own particular character structure or dynamics. If we universalize from this experienced truth to an egocentric approach to understanding others, we are likely to do our patients a disservice, for their truth, indeed, may not be the same as our own.

A doctrinaire attitude toward theory may spring from the therapist's need to preserve a particular image of self, perhaps a need to protect an identification with an idealized figure, be it the originator of the theory or an admired teacher or mentor. Greenson (1962) writes that "possessing" an idealized object brings with it a feeling of being joined with the object, and that this feeling of being joined to some idealized object is typical for states of elation (pp. 174–175). The identification with the idealized figure may provide an identity for the therapist and/or a source of pride and self-esteem. To challenge the theory is to question the perfection of the idealized object and thus to call into question the perfection of the self that is identified with the object. Unlike the developmental identifications that lead to change in the self representation, defensive identifications may compensate for felt deficiencies in that self. However, the self cannot grow and become its own source of esteem under these circumstances. One's achievements belong to the defensive identification, reinforcing it overtly while unconsciously also reinforcing the imperfection of the self for which it must compensate. Also, there is always the danger that the emergence of envy and thus of hate of the idealized model may constitute an inner source of its destruction, making it necessary to redouble efforts consciously only to affirm the perfection of the idealized other by protecting the theory.

TOWARD AN INTEGRATION OF PSYCHOANALYTIC THEORY

In his last paper Kohut (1982) wrote that empathy *informs* the mother or the therapist of what is needed by the child or by the patient. Empathy is an instrument of observation and an informer of action, which in therapeutic analysis is called interpretation. Leaving aside the sustaining effect of the empathic response per se, and following Kohut's premise that the introspective–empathic stance is the basis on which analysis rests, providing the data base for the work of treatment, we still need an organizing principle that will enable us and the patient to understand the meaning to the patient of the raw data. For this we turn to theory.

Theory is a tool that helps us give shape to our perceptions, in and out of the clinical situation. Each of us carries our own personal belief system, or theory, about ourselves, about others, about the world, and about God or fate or whatever gives us some sense of predictability about life. So does our patient. In science, when a theory fails to account for new data, we do not discard the data—we amend the theory. Our way of understanding each unique patient, what we call a diagnosis, is a theory about that person. It will be useful only insofar as it advances the work of treatment. It will interfere with our creativity and constitute an impingement for the patient when we discard or ignore or only selectively perceive the patient's data in order to protect our theory. Every approach to psychoanalytic theory is based upon a particular body of data derived from clinical observation. Lest we join the folly of the blind men and the elephant, it behooves us to synthesize our observations in a manner that broadens the scope of our understanding, enabling us to work unencumbered by dogma.

Greenson (1969), in pondering the origin and fate of new ideas in psychoanalysis, wrote of Freud that no preconceived idea precluded the development of new ones, but new discoveries did not lead automatically to the elimination of old ideas. "Creativity," he writes, "is not the antithesis of conservation" (p. 343).

Greenson (1969) observes that innovators in psychoanalysis are not awed by tradition nor are they conformists. They are able to risk being wrong, to expose themselves to the attacks of colleagues. But, he notes, there is an aggressive component in putting forth a new idea. He writes that "the creative psychoanalyst whose aggression is not under control may use his innovations to destroy the old and traditional ideas. He will discard them as valueless" (p. 346). In contrast, the analysts who do not destroy the old theories when they conceive of a new idea are able to "conserve the parts of the old they consider useful, add their innovations, and try to integrate them into a cohesive framework which is not closed off from further elaboration and emendation" (p. 348).

Finally, Greenson says that if he tries to imagine an analytic session with a "true believer" analyst repeating the catechism of his school, "it is hard to see this as a living creative experience for either the patient or the therapist" (p. 354).

Anna Freud (1981) regretted the losses in psychoanalytic theory that take place under the name of progress. She apologetically described her shifting back and forth from a topographical theory—where consciousness is the point of reference—to structural theory, with its focus on the conflicts and balance between the id, the ego, and the superego, as a "bad habit." Kris (1983) recommends this kind of eclecticism as essential if the analyst is to have the conceptual freedom to be able to listen to the patient's associations and translate observation into understanding and useful intervention. He cautions us not to permit theory to co-opt the method of psychoanalytic observation and deprive it of its independence. "Errors due to imposition of theory on data," he says, "are even harder to detect once the analytic method, itself, is defined according to a theory" (p. 408). He notes that the imposition of theory can be avoided by moving *from* the associations *to* the formulation, rather than by searching for data to match the predetermined theoretical organizing framework.

Hurwitz (1983), addressing the issue of the integration of various approaches to psychoanalytic theory, observes that object relations theorists as well as self theorists have to reckon in some way with instinct theory. He writes that he subscribes to their views that instincts and affects have to be conceptualized within a framework of the internalized selfobject relationship, agreeing that the search for objects or persons may well be a more basic motivating force than the gratification of drives. I agree with him when he adds that he also feels the roles of libido and aggression have to be reckoned with as significant motives although they are influenced by the matrix of internal relationships and relationship needs. Hurwitz says that he sees the problem of the integration of instinct theory and self theory as one of the exciting challenges for psychoanalysis.

Elsewhere (1979, 1984) I have written that if there is a failure to structure drive or affect or both within the matrix of the self and its relationship with the other, the experience of such drive or affect will evoke a sense of disorganization. In accord with Hurwitz, I believe that the defenses against aggression, either because of the inability of the ego to bind it within the internalized structures or because aggression may endanger a valued relationship, need to be analyzed on their own terms, and not only in terms of an empathic response to the experiences that evoke them.

Kohut (1971) made a major contribution to the understanding of psychic development, particularly that which occurs at the switch point where the child's illusion of omnipotence and perfection is lost and is replaced with a more realistic sense of the exquisite dependency of the self on the object, who is now perceived as the locus of power and esteem. His concept of transmuting internalization, consistent with Winnicott's (1951) elaboration of the function of the transitional object, sets the stage for the child's move forward from idealization of the object to those identifications with the object that lead to what Mahler and colleagues (1975) refer to as object constancy, and to Freud's (1933) observations on the structuralization of the superego, particularly the ego ideal.

Kohut's contribution, if integrated with the work of others like Freud, Bowlby, Winnicott, Guntrip, Melanie Klein, Mahler,

Sullivan, Piaget, and others, enriches our understanding of normal development as well as that of pathology and its clinical implications. The historical buildup of psychoanalytic theory, and its continuing elaboration by numerous contributors to the literature, provides a rich tapestry of understanding and a powerful tool for our clinical work.

The fragmentation of psychoanalysis, theoretically and politically, robs us of that richness and threatens the integrity of our work. Commitment to any single school of psychoanalysis leads to perceptual distortion, skewed emphasis, and clinical work that is designed to lend support to a theory, rather than theory functioning as the servant of our clinical work.

Within the context of a self theory, I may respond to the patient's struggle to individuate and to his feelings of being trapped in relationships. But then, in the context of a conflict model, I may use an interpretation with respect to guilt and anxiety at the aggression experienced as part and parcel of the individuation process. Within one session there will have been an integration of concepts from both self and instinct theory, and the therapist will have both mirrored the self and its wish to individuate, and interpreted conflict around aggression and the defenses used to mitigate the guilt and anxiety. Unlike an eclecticism that jumps from one conceptual system to another in a way that confuses the patient and that comes from a kind of trial and error approach by the therapist, there is an integration of various conceptual systems that allows for a fuller creative synthesis of the patient's experience.

Bromberg (1983) refers to Sullivan's (1953) observations that the analyst must be responsive to where the patient is on a gradient of anxiety, trying to maintain it at an optimally minimal level—low enough so that the patient's defenses do not foreclose analytic inquiry, but high enough so that the defensive structure itself can be identified and explored. Bromberg writes of the maintenance of the optimal balance between empathy and anxiety as an approach to treatment that is independent of the analyst's personal metapsychology. It is an approach that allows for the integration of the concept of the self psychologists concerning the analyst's selfobject function, with the concepts of conflict and defense and their analysis in the Freudian sense.

Case Example

A man who was anguishing over the feelings his little son would have if the father left home could not move from the pain of his identification with the hurt child, nor could he use this identification productively. It was not until this identification could be understood as a defense against the guilt of his taking independent action that movement could be made. He also struggled against the identification with his own father, who had failed to protect him in important ways, and to create a good father by becoming one in his relationship with his child. Technically there was a shift away from the empathy end of the gradient to the anxiety end, from an empathic response to his feelings as a child to an interpretation of the conflict between his wishes and his ideal of the good parent, a conflict intrinsic to his important relationships.

In summary, by starting with empathic attending as an instrument of observation and an informer of therapeutic action, maintaining an optimal balance on the empathy–anxiety gradient, and using an expanded and enriched theory as our organizing principle, we can participate in a creative alliance with our patients as they struggle to resolve the conflicts that stand as a barrier to the creation of a whole and integrated self.

14

Ego Boundaries
and Resistance

Most therapists have had some experience with what might be called "hard-core" patients. These are individuals who have been in therapy for many years, but who cling tenaciously to the defenses and resistances that preclude resolution of barriers to what they say they want most in life, an intimate relationship.

THE FUNCTION OF UNSHAKABLE RESISTANCE

What is this person who appears refractive to all therapy so zealously guarding? Angry, frustrated therapists conclude that his secret agenda is to defeat the therapist. Perhaps so. But what gain is there for him in doing so? Why is defeating the therapist so important to him?

With many such patients the answer would be that he must, at all costs, protect his very existence. The "ontologically insecure person is preoccupied with preserving rather than gratifying himself," for unlike the ontologically secure person, he does not have a "centrally firm sense of his own and other people's reality and identity" (Laing 1962, p. 41).

Such a condition is not unique to persons we would call psychotic. It can be seen to a greater or lesser degree in patients who present a variety of diagnostic pictures. There are patients who appear to be functioning at a fairly high level of ego integration, but whose interpersonal relationships seem predicated on the avoidance of intimacy, whether the mechanism be schizoid withdrawal, provocative hostility, or the setting up of chronic power struggles. What may appear to be a power issue originating at the anal stage of development may instead have its roots in a preexisting issue for the young child of preserving himself against invasive mothering. This is concretized in the terror of the child who believes that with the bowel movement he is in fact losing a physical part of himself. Ultimately, in therapy, this loss of self will become an issue with such patients.

Guntrip (1969) speaks of the need–fear dilemma of the schizoid individual. "His need to achieve relations with real people is countered by his intense fear of this, so that after oscillating with great anxiety between 'in' and 'out' situations, he is driven to retreat into detachment and mental isolation." The feared loss of self in close relationship is variously described as "the dread of being 'smothered,' 'stifled,' 'suffocated' . . ." Guntrip describes how the patient's struggle to save himself forms the resistance to therapy. R. D. Laing (1962) refers to the negative therapeutic reaction to correct interpretations that are experienced as impingement, or what might also be called a violation of ego boundaries.

EGO BOUNDARIES

The question of ego boundaries has been dealt with extensively in the literature of ego psychology and existential psychology. Federn (1952), with whom the term originated, says that it "should be understood in its literal sense to mean that we feel how far the ego extends, or more correctly, the point beyond which the ego does not extend" (p. 331).

"Existentialism holds that authenticity—the condition of real-ness and full-functioning, of expanding sensitivity and awareness, of absorbed involvement in issues and work and people, of joy and of love—is based on a proud *awareness of oneself as a living, choos-ing, self-determining,* unique individual" (Button 1969, p. 11; italics added).

Perls and colleagues (1951) conceive of the boundary as limit-ing, containing, and protecting the organism, while at the same time being the organ of contact with the environment. They describe the conditions in which the boundary does not adequately define what is the organism and what is outside it.

Developmentally, the definition of self as separate from non-self starts within the early months of life. Searles (1965) says that the 3-month-old infant's ability to distinguish and react to the mother's face marks the developmental step of differentiating the "I" "from the 'non-I,' in which the infant becomes aware of the 'otherness' of the surround" (p. 645). Winnicott (1965) views the development of an awareness of "I am, I exist" and "I am seen or understood to exist by someone" as a process closely linked with holding. When mothering is hostile and nonresponsive to the child's overall state of being, it can be experienced as an impinge-ment. "It is indeed possible to gratify an oral drive and by so doing to violate the infant's ego-function, or *that which will later on be jealously guarded as the self, the core of the personality*" (p. 57; italics added). "The use of defenses, especially that of a successful false self, enables many children to seem to give good promise, but eventually a breakdown reveals the fact of the true self's absence from the scene" (p. 58).

Watzlawick and colleagues (1967) describe more blatant ex-amples of impingement found later in life in pathological commu-nication of severely disturbed families. They refer to "disconfirma-tion," in which concern is "no longer with the truth or falsity—if there be such criteria—of P's definition of himself, but rather negates the reality of P as the source of such a definition" (p. 86). How often does a therapist, or a member of a therapy group, similarly disconfirm an individual by telling him what he "really" feels or "really" thinks. The quip has it that a sweater is what a little boy puts on when his mother is cold. This ceases to amuse when we consider how the consistent bombardment by this kind of parental attitude methodically destroys whatever remnants there might be of a consciously sensing, valuing, and choosing self.

That the establishment of a sense of self and the defensive need to protect that self in the face of a hostile and impinging environment occur so early in life explains why it is often beyond conscious awareness, or why it is so vague and unarticulated and so is not brought up by the patient as a therapy issue. If this is so, it would seem to be the responsibility of the therapist who has reason to suspect that the motivating force behind the resistance is this preservation of the core self to define the dilemma, to help the patient establish contact with the core self, and to lend support to it. As long as therapy is experienced as still another impingement, it and the therapist will be fought off in one way or another.

COUNTERTRANSFERENCE

Countertransference reactions to this kind of patient may be intense. It is essential that the therapist not be dependent upon his patients as a source of his own self-esteem. Whatever doubts the therapist may have of his own adequacy will be stirred up. Neither his love nor his cleverness nor his authenticity will make a dent in the resistance. His feelings of impotence are likely to lead to an eruption of rage. He will castigate the patient for his wish to be sick. The patient's techniques of thwarting him will be interpreted as a displacement of the wish to have vengeance on the offending parent, usually the mother. The therapist's intense reactions will not be totally in error. However, unless he can see and go beyond the resistance to its significance in the preservation of the self, he will continue to get nowhere with his patient and will be stuck with his own impotent rage. When the therapist accuses the patient of choosing to stay sick or helpless, he implies a deliberate, conscious will to defeat whoever tries to help him. However, it is just this inability to experience himself as the center of volition or choice that is the patient's problem.

May (1969) concerns himself with disturbances of will:

> Protesting is partially constructive, since it preserves some semblance of will by asserting it negatively. . . . But if will remains protest, it stays dependent on that which it is protesting against. . . . [and] it borrows its impetus from the enemy. . . . Sooner or later your will becomes hollow, and may then be forced back to the next line of defense (which is) projection of blame. . . . The self-righteous security that is achieved by means of this blaming of the other gives one a temporary satisfaction [but] . . . we have tacitly given the power of decision over to our adversary. Blaming the enemy implies that the enemy has the freedom to choose and act, not ourselves, and we can only react to him. This assumption, in turn, destroys our own security. [pp. 192–193]

This becomes the malignant progression of events in therapy. The patient must protest, resist, and blame the therapist, and in so doing, he further undercuts his own potential as a willing and choosing human being.

Case Examples

Nancy, a young woman of 27, attractive, professionally successful, first presented herself to her therapy group as hostile, provocative, and challenging. Her relationships with her family and her boyfriend were in this same competitive and provocative mode, with which she managed to alienate people. After a short time, the defensive nature of this behavior having been analyzed and acknowledged, she seemed to be relating at a more positive level, although still at considerable distance. However, she soon started to come to sessions late, completely avoiding the leaderless presession. As this was explored she said she did not want to talk about her boyfriend, as she experienced the group as pressuring her to give him up. I commented on what seemed to be her inability to protect her own boundaries, to say what she chose or did not choose to discuss with the group, and her subsequent avoidance of contact with the group. She responded, "I don't know who I am or what I am."

A short time later, Nancy participated in a weekend marathon group. A middle-aged man persisted in telling her that she really did not mean what she was saying or that she really did not feel what she said she was feeling. Although this act of disconfirmation was pointed out, she became increasingly anxious and attempted to stay away from him. He continued to move close to her, appearing to be affectionate and caring. She finally exploded, screaming at him to get away from her and leave her alone. His affection had the same associated injunction of "don't be you" heard long ago from her father. She remembered him as outwardly affectionate, but had a frightened sense that he did not want her to exist. She recalled turning herself off to love at the age of 5 in her frantic effort to preserve her core self. The therapist helped her regain contact with who she was and what she was experiencing, and supported her ability and right to maintain her own boundaries against such impingement.

A professional woman of 34 has been in therapy for 17 years. She is also a professional "patient" who clings to a relationship with her "doctor," a relationship that takes the place of real intimacy. Therapy of many years has been focused on her unwillingness to let go of her mother, to relinquish a stance of dependency. As soon as she would start to "get better" in the past, and termination of therapy became a possibility, she would relapse. The therapeutic goal with her present therapist has been, from the start of their work together, to pry her loose from the patient role. A firm and unalterable date of termination was set for one year hence. As she had to face the threat to her pseudointimacy with her doctor, her fear of real intimacy became exposed. She expressed her fear of being "swallowed up." Her hatred and fear of men had in the past been interpreted as transferential in nature. Now its defensive value in protecting her from the threatening intimacy with men became evident. Her "sick" self is the false self on which her relationship with her mother was predicated. As long as she had something wrong with her body that mother could minister to, a relationship of sorts was maintained, while at the same time her core self was protected from her mother's incredible invasiveness. But while her core self was being preserved, she also lost conscious access to it. She reports unbearable anxiety when she is alone, as though she will somehow stop existing. In the absence of pseudo-relating, authentic being is unavailable to her. She was given instructions to deal with this anxiety by making contact with her self at the body-ego level, by focusing on her body, differentiating where it left off and nonbody started, to get in touch with her own physical self as the center of her world and thus of her existence.

During a weekend marathon therapy group, hostility directed at her led to an explosive reaction in which she felt herself "going all over the room." On her own instigation, she was able to regain her sense of self and to distinguish it from the self of the other person. She was then able to renegotiate her relationship with the woman involved.

May (1969) writes that the "growing awareness of one's body, wishes, and desires—processes which are obviously related to the experiencing of identity—normally also bring heightened appreciation of one's self as a being" (p. 263). This awareness of one's self as a being is essential to friendship and love, which he points out requires "that we participate in the meaning-matrix of the other but without surrendering our own" (p. 262). When the boundaries or content of one's own meaning-matrix are uncertain and are easily surrendered to the other or contaminated by the other, friendship and love evoke anxiety rather than gratification or fulfillment and, though deeply longed for, lead to terror and flight.

15

A Characterological Contraindication for Group Psychotherapy

Group psychotherapy is especially indicated when the patient's character defenses constitute a source of resistance in individual psychotherapy. These defenses may or may not be evident in the one-to-one situation. The therapist may know they are there, but their manifestation and ego syntonicity may make them particularly difficult to get at. In a group situation they will stand out with greater salience; and the patient, when confronted with his defensive maneuvers, will be less able to deny them and less free to act them out in treatment.

An example of such a defense would be compliance as a characteristic way of warding off anger or criticism, originally that of the parent and now, transferentially, that of the therapist. The compliance may be manifested as "good patient" behavior, and indeed may be so well carried off that therapeutic work appears to be progressing when, in fact, it is not. The therapeutic alliance is with the conforming child, and no real inner change takes place.

It is not my purpose to trace the difficulties of therapeutic work with the narcissistic personality disorder, but rather to point out the issue of character diagnosis in assigning patients to group. I suspect it is the difficulty and often downright unpleasantness of working with such a patient, with his archaic demands and ready rage, that leads many therapists to assign him to a group, where the therapist will not get the full force of the transference. This kind of patient is certainly not every therapist's cup of tea, and any given therapist can tolerate only so many such cases. But although referral to group may be the easy out for the therapist, it will be a solution that, in the long run, may prove detrimental to both his group and the patient.

CHARACTER DEFENSES VERSUS CHARACTER STRUCTURE

At this point it is necessary to make a distinction that is often overlooked in the selection of patients for group. This is the distinction between character *defenses* and character *structure*. It is because they are often equated that patients are sometimes erroneously referred for group psychotherapy.

A character defense is a behavior (overt or covert) that may have a number of aims: to ward off anger or disapproval, to win love or to get pity, to protect the individual from conscious awareness of aspects of himself for which he would feel guilty or ashamed, or to help keep controlled certain impulses that he fears might get out of control and that would then bring guilt, punishment, or retaliation. Each of these is made evident and analyzable in the group context.

When we speak of character structure, however, we are dealing with the very fiber of the personality, and confrontation may not only not help, but, unless handled carefully within the context of the transference, may make matters worse.

In examining character structure, we consider the functions of the ego in general, and the level of object relations development in particular. Elsewhere (Horner 1975) I describe this developmental sequence as the

> negotiation of the process of attachment, and then of separation and individuation, with the achievement of the psychological status of a separate individual who has a firm sense of self and other, who is able to relate to others as whole persons rather than as need-gratifiers, who can tolerate ambivalence rather than maintaining a split into good and bad objects, and who can sustain his narcissistic equilibrium from resources within the self which are the outcome of the achievement of object constancy. [p. 95]

To some extent, these are issues of relevance for most of our patients. For others they are central, and constitute the core of their problem.

THE NARCISSISTIC PERSONALITY AND GROUP THERAPY

I will focus here on an example of the narcissistic personality disorder as delineated by Kohut (1971). This kind of patient is frequently referred for group on the basis of his need to be confronted with his behavior and the unrealistic nature of his prevailing attitudes. The outcome, in my experience, has been nonproductive for the patient at best, and destructive for both the patient and the group at worst.

A critical aspect of this disorder is the incapacity to experience others as people in their own right. It is assumed that their needs, feelings, and motivations are the same as those of the self, and failure to keep in perfect harmony is experienced as an assault. Others exist to meet the needs of these individuals, to gratify and validate them. The failure of the world to grant them these "entitlements" is reacted to with infantile rage. They alternately idealize others or treat them with base contempt. All this is characteristically acted out in the transference.

Countertransference

The kinds of countertransference reactions induced by the narcissistic transferences are severe discomfort at being idealized, discomfort and anger at the readiness of this patient to point out realistic human failings when the idealization fails, and the experience of a quasi-annihilation that goes with not being recognized as a person. Kohut (1971) describes this as "the specifically frightening implication of feeling drawn into an anonymous existence in the narcissistic web of another person's psychological organization" (p. 276). He says of the analyst who works with this kind of patient, "He must, furthermore, be aware of the potential interference of his own narcissistic demands which rebel against a chronic situation in which he is neither experienced as himself by the patient nor even confused with an object of the patient's past. And finally, in specific instances, the analyst must be free of the active interference by archaic fears of dissolution through merger" (p. 294).

In the group, other members will be related to on the same transferential basis and subjected to the same dangers previously described. It is a difficult enough task for the therapist to negotiate the demands of treating the narcissistic personality disorder. It is unreasonable, and sometimes toxic, for members of a therapy group to have to negotiate them as well.

As one might predict, these demands will elicit intense, angry reactions from other members. However, the patient in question will not be able to make therapeutic use of these confrontations. They will be experienced as serious narcissistic assaults and will pose a threat to existence itself. Because of the inadequately defined ego boundaries, there may be little or no observing ego available, particularly under stress. They cannot, by edict, go forward developmentally, and instead they are likely to experience the disruptive panic that goes with the threat of annihilation. Under these circumstances they become intensely paranoid. As one patient expressed it, because the group was unwilling to validate her existence by listening to her endlessly, it meant they did not want her to exist.

This she translated into their wish to kill her. The panic-induced regression that followed brought her to the point of fragmentation, and an hour's work with her alone was necessary to bring her back to the preexisting level of integration.

Narcissistic patients may defend against these dangers with superficially compliant behavior, such as suppressing their demands or acting as though they are interested in others. In such instances, however, no real therapeutic work is accomplished and there is no real change.

In addition, the group situation facilitates object splitting, which is characteristic of the narcissistic patient. In the one-to-one therapy setting, the inability to tolerate ambivalence and the extreme libidinal swings with respect to the therapist are clear and can be worked with. In a group, the group is often used to maintain the split, representing either the good or bad object, with the therapist defined as its counterpart. The work of integrating the good and bad mother into a single object representation is interfered with as a result.

DEVELOPMENTAL ISSUES

In the normal course of development, the child cannot relinquish his narcissistic stance unless there is predictable, good-enough mothering (Winnicott 1965) to sustain him through this stage of increased vulnerability to object loss and anxiety. Gradually, through a series of "transmuting internalizations" (Tolpin 1971), maternal functions are taken over by the self, with the consequent achievement of object constancy and a diminished need for others as need-satisfying objects alone.

The narcissistic personality disorder represents a developmental failure at the early end of the separation–individuation process, a failure to differentiate fully as a psychological entity out of the earlier symbiotic attachment to the mother. This differentiation carries with it the danger of object loss, with consequent depression, and the danger of a sudden loss of omnipotence and subsequent helplessness, with its consequent anxiety.

In the treatment of the individual who is fixated at a position of narcissism and narcissistic entitlement, there must be a predictable, good-enough mothering relationship with the therapist to sustain the patient if he is to relinquish this position without the concomitant experiences of either unbearable depression or unbearable anxiety.

Although group therapy may be effective in the confrontation of the narcissism, it does not provide what is needed for a true structural shift from this point of developmental fixation—that is, the intensity and the predictability of the good-enough one-to-one relationship with the therapist.

Furthermore, because of his behavior, this individual is likely to become the focus of the negative transferences of other group members, representing all their demanding, manipulative, and guilt-inducing mothers rolled into one. He then becomes scapegoated by the group. Because their anger appears to be so reasonable—his demands do deny and invalidate them as persons—this can become a source of group resistance that is group ego-syntonic. The therapist may aid and abet this in her relief at getting the patient off her back, as well as in an unconscious acting out of her own rage at the patient. As far as the patient is concerned, the scapegoating plays into his paranoid fears and further aggravates the situation for him.

It is often not until the narcissistic patient has left the group that the degree to which he has limited the group becomes evident. Other members who were previously united against his demands now become increasingly aware of their impact on one another. Issues that were previously obscured as members dealt with their reactions to the narcissistic patient begin to emerge. The group no longer has to struggle, week after week, against being ground down by the unremitting rage, envy, paranoia, and self-pity of the narcissistic member. They may have learned how to cope with this kind of person and thus to deal with some of their own narcissistic issues, but have been prevented from pursuing other ones.

As with any clinical decision, assignment of the patient to a therapy group must be carried out with a clear understanding of both dynamic and structural issues. It is a decision that should take into account the potential effects on both the individual and the other group members; and a decision that should be based on the therapist's concern for the well-being of and therapeutic advantage for everyone who might be affected.

16

Object Relations, the Self, and the Therapeutic Matrix

In *Object Relations and the Developing Ego in Therapy* (1979) I brought together attachment theory, cognitive theory that deals with mental structures, and object relations theory. The major focus is on the evolution of a cohesive, reality-related, object-related self. This self develops within the context of the maternal matrix, and the primary mothering person is viewed as the mediator of organization. Analogously, psychotherapy (or psychoanalysis) is conceptualized as a therapeutic matrix within which the therapist is similarly seen as the mediator of organization. My approach can be understood as a theory of the self. The shift from classical psychoanalytic drive theory to object relations or self theory is completed with the position that instinctual drive is only one aspect of experience, which must be integrated within the self-representation along with other aspects of experience, whether they be of internal or environmental origin.

In this chapter I first present an overview of early development and its consequences with respect of character structure. Following this, I will address the issue of the psychoanalytic treatment of

171

patients with character disorders, with defects or deficits in the structure of the self.

THE OBJECT RELATIONS FRAMEWORK

The development of object relations has become increasingly central to present-day psychoanalytic theory. The work of Margaret Mahler (Mahler 1968, Mahler et al. 1975) on the separation–individuation process in particular has played a major role in this shift in emphasis. The term *object relations* refers to the structural and psychodynamic interrelationships between self and object representations. The object, of course, refers to the image derived from the primary mothering person or persons in the environment of the infant and the very young child.

In review, the developmental sequence begins with what Mahler calls the stage of normal autism. Kohut (1971, 1977), who thinks in terms of the evolution of a cohesive self, calls this same stage that of the fragmented self. That is, while Mahler's term reflects her object relations orientation, Kohut's term conveys his concern with the structure of the self. Freud (1910) referred to this same period as that of autoerotism, which, of course, is consistent with a drive theory point of view.

Through the process of attachment, the child comes to the stage of normal symbiosis in which self and object representations have been organized but not differentiated. The undifferentiated mental representation of symbiosis is referred to as the selfobject.

From this point the child faces the developmental tasks of the separation–individuation process. This process is subdivided first, into the substage of hatching, the stage of physical differentiation of the self from the object, who is still not psychologically differentiated. This substage is characterized by the achievement of object permanence, the capacity to remember the object even when out of sight, and a corresponding sense of its absence.

Next comes the practicing period, the time of the rapid unfolding of the autonomous functions and the peak of narcissism. The omnipotence of this substage is the developmental anlage of the grandiose self.

This is followed by the rapprochement substage, which is ushered in by the rapprochement crisis, the child's recognition of mother's total separateness, the loss of omnipotence, and the experience of shame and helplessness and dependency on the now idealized object. The good and bad self and object representations of symbiosis become integrated with the achievement of representational intelligence. The concepts of "Baby" and "Mama" bring diverse experiences into a single idea.

The end of the rapprochement period is characterized by the internalization of maternal functions and qualities into the self, a process which ideally culminates in a firm sense of identity and object constancy. At this point, the child—and thus the adult he will become—has a firm sense of self and differentiated other. He is able to relate to others as whole persons and not just as need satisfiers, and he can tolerate ambivalence without having to maintain a split between good and bad self and object representations. He now has the ability to sustain his narcissistic equilibrium, or good self feeling, from resources within the self as a consequence of the transmuting internalizations (Giovacchini 1979, Tolpin 1971) into the self. At the same time, the internalization of parental functions and modes of interaction in what Schecter (1979) has characterized as "the imperative mode" results in the structuring of the superego.

This object relational view of development, although powerful in explanatory potential, must be examined with a higher-power microscope, as it were, if we are to understand more precisely what sometimes goes wrong with this process and what we can do about it in treatment. Sullivan (1953) remarked that if, from birth onward, "we go with almost microscopic care over how everybody comes to be what he is at chronological adulthood, . . . we [may] learn a good deal of what is highly probable about him and his difficulties in living" (p. 4).

ORGANIZING PROCESSES AND THE GENESIS OF THE SELF

The evolution of the self and the object as mental structures comes about as the result of processes of organization that take place from the very start of life. The neonate begins life in a state of mental and psychological nonorganization and nonintegration. With the mental equipment with which it is born, it must organize its entire universe of experience. There is a readiness from the start to perceive and respond to patterns in the environment. That is, organizing tendencies and capabilities are intrinsic to the organism. These mental activities take place as a consequence of the synthesizing function of the central nervous system, which is the physiologic substrate of what we call the synthetic function of the ego. This inborn, autonomous biological function can be interfered with by an inherent inadequacy of the organism, by failure of the environment, or by a combination of the two. This failure may be relative and occur only in certain areas of psychological functioning. For instance, schizoid defenses may enable the individual to organize the nonpersonal world of reality effectively enough to carry out intellectual and work-related tasks. However, the failure of the schizoid detachment in an intense interpersonal situation may reveal the pathology in the organization of the self and object representations.

During the height of the organizing processes of the stage of symbiosis, we should consider that there are *three* states of being that become organized. Eventually, these three states must become integrated within a single self representation. There is the good selfobject constellation, based upon pleasurable experiences in social interaction; the bad selfobject, based upon dysphoric experiences in social interaction; and the core *self-without-object*. The latter is based upon the parallel organization of self experiences that consolidates around the emerging autonomous functions. That is, *in the healthy organism, organization goes on with or without the object.* This self organization is connected with external reality—nonhuman reality (the cradle gym, the rattle), the child's own wiggling fingers, and what it perceives in the physical surroundings—although it is the reality of the nonpersonal world. In cases of failure of attachment in an organically competent infant, we see quite clearly the ability to organize nonhuman reality. (An example of this is the affectionless psychopath.) This early ego state can be seen as the developmental anlage of the state of detachment, be it a pervasive characterological detachment or a state that is used as a defense later on under conditions of interpersonal stress. It is what Guntrip (1971) refers to as the schizoid core (p. 118). In general, the child does not need to invent its defenses actively; there are developmental anlagen to which memory has access.

Piaget (1936) investigated the processes of organization that go into the formation of what he called *schemas*. A representation, as used in object relations theory, is a schema. A schema is defined as an enduring organization or structure within the mind that is the outcome of the various processes involved in organization. These include assimilation, accommodation, generalization, differentiation, and integration. Piaget's definition of a schema brings to mind Sullivan's (1953) definition of a dynamism as "the relatively enduring patterns of energy transformations which recurrently characterize the interpersonal relations" (p. 103). The term *object relations* refers to self and object representations as enduring structures and the dynamic interplay between them.

At the very start of life the infant's world consists of a variety of sensorimotor, physiological, and somatic experiences. Feelings are global—either distress or nondistress. As they become refined and specific to a stimulus in the form of pleasure, anger, or anxiety, these feelings also become part of the world of experience to be organized and integrated. In this manner, the predominant affect, whether the rage of frustration, the anxiety of uncertainty or overwhelming distress, or the positive feelings that go with basic trust (Erikson 1950), becomes an integral aspect of the self.

When the environment fails in its need-fulfillment and tension-reducing functions, the child's rage may be organized within the bad selfobject representation characteristic of the narcissistic personality disorder. In some instances, however, rage and anxiety may be severe enough to disrupt the organization and patterning of the self, leading to a more serious psychopathology. When there is a failure of integration of affect in the symbiotic stage of development, evocation of this same affect later on will have a disorganizing impact upon the self organization and it will have to be defended against rigidly. Sullivan viewed dissociation as the central theme in psychosis, noting that in schizophrenia, the "not-me" processes were present in awareness. With integration, affect and impulse become subject to ego control. One of the tasks of treatment of such a patient will be the facilitation of such integration, the facilitation of the structuring of the self.

Also to be organized and integrated are impulses, which are the felt precursors of motor activity. Of particular importance are self-initiated, assertive, and eventually goal-directed actions and their associated aggressive impulses. From this point of view, aggressive impulses are neither hostile nor destructive in themselves, but only become so when fused with negative affect. The infant reaching for his rattle is demonstrating nonhostile aggressive behavior. Often in the clinical situation, healthy aggression becomes available for goal-directed behavior only after it has been teased apart from the infantile rage with which it became bound in the early stages of psychological development.

Thus, the fragments of the child's own somatic, sensory, motor, and affective and impulse experiences come into interaction with that which is experienced vis-à-vis the mothering person. The consistent and predictable presence of this individual throughout the early months of life serves to tie the infant's experiences together in a particular way. It is through her that the body, impulse, feeling, action, and eventually thought become integrated not only with each other, but with external reality of which she is a representative. That is, she is a bridge between the child's inner world and the outer world of reality.

Winnicott (1965) views the false self identity as the consequence of the failure of the mother to bridge these two worlds adequately. In this instance, a serious and consistent failure of empathy on her part may lead to a situation in which her mothering efforts are not in harmony with the child's bodily needs and experiences and, later on, not appropriately responsive to his feelings and goal-directed behaviors.

When this happens, efforts at mothering become impingements toward which the child can only react. There may be a defensive withdrawal, which will interfere with the attachment process itself and with the establishment of object relations at the most fundamental level. The child may react with a degree of rage, which repeatedly disrupts the budding ego organization and thereby interferes with the establishment of cohesion of the self.

In the instance of the false self identity described by Winnicott, the pseudoidentity is consolidated around reactions to the impinging mother, while the core self remains shut away from both reality- and human-relatedness. This core self may become the nucleus for delusional thinking, as in the situation of the woman who was hospitalized with the delusion that she was pregnant with the Messiah. The Messiah she carried within her was the mad, omnipotent self of which she was aware as the most real part of her, even though it had never become related with the external world or anyone in it. The first major goal of her treatment was to enhance the object-relatedness of that core self and eventually for the therapist to become the bridge between it and external reality, as does the good-enough mother of early infancy.

The mothering person not only mediates the process of organization and reality-relatedness, but her image is part of that which is organized. The internalization of her image in all its aspects—her maternal functions as well as the quality of the interaction—eventually yields the object representation that emerges with increasing differentiation and integration. Sullivan's (1953) term *personification* seems relevant here—that is, the pattern of the mother's participation in recurrent situations related to need satisfaction (pp. 111–112). When, for some reason, this internalization does not take place or is interrupted, the child fails to develop the capacity for human-relatedness upon which is based, in normal development, the achievement of object constancy, emotional autonomy, healthy self-esteem, and the structuring of the superego.

There may be a disruption of developing object-relatedness in the situation of premature ego development described by Blanck and Blanck (1974). With a superior child who is cut off from maternal support during the practicing period and at the start of the rapprochement period, we have a situation in which the maturing autonomous functions—particularly motility and thought—develop outside the sphere of object-relatedness. This may result in an individual who seems to function well, who appears to have a cohesive self, but who complains of chronic depression, emptiness, and the inability to be productive. The kind of character detachment that comes about either in response to emotional abandonment or as a defense against an impinging environment also has serious repercussions with respect to the development of healthy self-esteem, inasmuch as the developing autonomous functions are assimilated into the grandiose self, which is intrinsic to the practicing period. The now pathological structure protects the child from the shame and anxiety of helplessness. Since the child turns to its own ego in lieu of the lost object, there is a side-tracking of object relations development in a way that prevents the achievement of object constancy.

In summary then, the mother functions as the mediator of organization and of reality-relatedness, and her internalized image becomes the cornerstone for human object-relatedness and for the eventual internalization of maternal functions that produces intrapsychic autonomy.

Failure of each of the processes of organization that are part and parcel of object relations development and the structuring of the self and object representations—that is, failure of cohesion, failure of reality-relatedness, or failure of object-relatedness—has its specific consequences in terms of character pathology, symptomatology, and implications for treatment. The earlier the interference with the processes involved in object relations development and in the structuring of the self, the more serious the pathology. The character structure of our adult patient as it is manifest in the symptoms, disturbances in interpersonal relationships or in the transference, will be directly related to the relative successes or failures of early development. Our developmental diagnosis, treatment plan, and strategies will be consistent with our structural diagnosis and will take into consideration the quality of cohesiveness, reality-relatedness, and object-relatedness. When we have determined that there has been a failure of or defect in the organization of the self in these major dimensions, we can view the most important function of a therapist to be parallel or analogous to that of the primary mothering person of infancy—that is, as the mediator of organization.

THE THERAPEUTIC MATRIX

If you look at the diagram in Chapter 1, you will see that I have related the various diagnostic categories to specific kinds of failures along the developmental continuum. Each failure will have its counterpart in therapeutic terms. For example, if there is a failure of differentiation, boundary structuring will be an important aspect of the therapeutic process. Everything we say or do, as well as what we don't say or do, contributes to the total milieu within which the repair of structure will take place.

Mullahy (1949) wrote that "fixed biological needs and drives and their frustrations do not provide the locus of mental illness . . . instead the social order itself is the ultimate matrix of functional mental disorder" (p. xxxi).

Chrzanowski (1978) points out that "Sullivan's major contribution consists in viewing the self as rooted in a network of relatedness to one's fellow human beings" (p. 38). He goes on to state that the therapist "functions more in the role of instrument than as his particular interpersonal self" (p. 42).

A modern interpersonal view might be synthesized to read that the social order of the therapeutic relationship is the ultimate matrix for the *treatment* of mental disorders, but that this matrix is based more upon what the therapist *does* than who he *is*.

The therapeutic matrix, the analogue of the good-enough mother of infancy and of separation and individuation, sets the stage for the repair of the defects of the character structure. It facilitates organization and integration of the various aspects of the self, some of which may have been cut off, denied, or repressed, and some of which may have a disorganizing impact when experienced. The therapeutic matrix facilitates the attachment process that will eventually provide the basis for the internalization of maternal–therapist functions, as well as for the further integration of the self within a context of human relatedness. The therapeutic matrix facilitates differentiation, the structuring of ego boundaries, and the achievement of identity coupled with the achievement of object constancy and the structuring of the superego.

There is still no general consensus as to what is curative in the therapeutic situation. There is an increasing agreement that psychoanalysis is a highly interpersonal affair. Langs (1976) writes of the "bipersonal field" and notes that every communication from the patient is influenced to a greater or lesser degree by the analyst and vice versa.

Sullivan (1953) writes that skill in the person-to-person psychiatric interview is of fundamental importance. It is "the development of an exquisitely complex pattern of field processes which *imply* important conclusions about the people concerned" (p. 381).

Giovacchini (1972) comments on the organizing function of the therapist as like that of the mother who comforts the child in such a manner that his affective state does not become traumatically overwhelming. Still, his emphasis is on interpretation as the specific and major contribution to the patient's improvement. I would emphasize the importance of interpretations directed at structural issues per se. An example of such an interpretation would be, "You need to keep me nonexistent to protect your sense of separateness, to protect the existence of your self."

Our interventions, although falling within the traditional frame of interpretation, may have either an organizing or a fragmenting impact. The so-called negative therapeutic reaction may well be related to accurate interpretation that, nevertheless, has a destructive impact upon the structure of the self.

THE THERAPIST AS GUARDIAN OF THE SELF

Psychoanalytic teaching has always emphasized the importance of the analyst as the guardian of autonomy. I would add that it is critical that the therapist also bear the responsibility of being the guardian of the self in the treatment of the character disorders.

I believe that the single most critical and powerful message that one can communicate to the borderline patient—or indeed to any patient with a character disorder—is one's concern for and dedication to the survival of the self. The therapeutic alliance depends ultimately upon this fundamental trust. Khan (1974) cautions us that we must not be omnipotently curative at the cost of the person of the patient (p. 128). I will often comment of the character defenses that they were adaptive at one time and are an indication of the person's determination to survive. This recognition enhances the self-esteem, which is bruised by the awareness of the pathology of the self.

Patients with characterological problems are acutely sensitive to what goes on in their interpersonal relationships, and are particularly sensitive to intrusion. When the observing ego is primarily a defensive ego, it is not available for analytic work. Such patients have a stance of vigilance (Giovacchini 1979, p. 439). If, in treatment, it becomes clear that here the self will not be impinged upon or humiliated, nor will autonomy be abrogated, the observing ego will be released from its defensive vigilance and will become available to the working alliance.

An intrusive interaction consists of someone's imposing something of himself upon another individual. For some patients, anything short of total mirroring constitutes an impingement. The reaction to impingement may, in the narcissistic personality, be anger at the therapist's failure to mirror and the threat to the patient's need for omnipotent control of the needed object. There may be a paranoid reaction, viewing the impingement as an assault by the bad object who wishes to destroy him. The reaction to impingement with a borderline patient, in whom the self is more tenuously organized, may be more traumatic and experienced as annihilating of the self.

The reaction of the narcissistic personality can be interpreted generally. That of the borderline who reacts with acute anxiety, even bordering on panic, may have to be handled instead. *Handling* refers to any means other than interpretation used by the therapist to promote a therapeutically desirable state of affairs. Most often this translates into a restoration of the observing ego. Handling the transference in a patient with a character disorder is a manifestation of the restoration of an appropriate therapeutic matrix—one which has as its goal the facilitating of the various processes subsumed under the general category of organization that are aimed at the structuralization of the self.

The following case material is an example of an impingement, a therapeutic error, and the restoration of the therapeutic matrix, the observing ego, and the working alliance.

Case Example

The following session with Miss R. explores her experience of visual imagery that she is coming to understand as a function of cognitive style and not as an aberration. With the mobilization of my intellectual curiosity and my need to know, I forgot for a moment that the visual images were equated with the very vulnerable, isolated core self. I asked her if she had ever put any of her images down in art form—a complete departure from my meticulous respect for her boundaries and autonomy. She replied:

> They're very abstract. I'd be afraid they would disappear. (You mean, if you put them outside yourself?) (Cries.) They won't exist for me. I didn't want to tell Jerry any more about the images when he asked. I didn't want to go into it. Maybe I *don't* think in images. (Are you afraid that I'm going to take them away from you?) I'm afraid they're not there. I have a sense that talking about it is wrong.

At this point I have not yet become fully aware that she is reacting to my inquiry per se. She goes on:

> I would neutralize the importance, to get control because spontaneity is so frightening. Today I have an image that I'm like the Pillsbury dough-boy, being pinched and poked—not letting me move forward, stifling me, taking my wind away. I feel like I'm treading water right now—thinking of a capsized rowboat. (Do you feel in danger right now?) I feel very frightened. (When did it start?) When you talked about painting. (You became frightened when I invaded your inner world with my question, when I broke through your boundary. It must have felt like you would lose the sense of your very self as existing.) I think of my early image of no inner core. I'm aware of going from a cylinder and of a core with particles going through the core, to a more spherical shape. The idea of thinking in pictures gives substance to that sphere. (I am truly sorry that I said anything that you experienced as so hurtful. What I said must have stirred up the fear that if I were to break through the sphere, there would be nothing to contain the pictures.) Yes.

At this point she is clearly no longer anxious and returned to her concerns about being different. Her visual images throughout treatment had reflected the changes in the self-image in a startlingly and stirringly graphic manner. Changes in her associations, affect, and way of relating were always in harmony with the changes in imagery. As spontaneous experiences of her mind, these images were the most directly experienced manifestation of her core, real self. When, in my need to know, I violated the boundaries of that core self, she became very frightened of the potential for the dissolution of the self. My apology was genuinely felt and, I believe, clinically indicated and necessary for the reestablishment of trust and the therapeutic alliance. It was a way of saying, "I am not perfect in my understanding of you, but my imperfection is not malevolent." Because of the solidity of both therapeutic and working alliances, she recovered quickly from the effects of my unfortunate error. Fortunately this young woman was an unusually fine observer and reporter of her own mental processes. In another situation, such a therapeutic error might instead have led to acting out or to a sudden breaking off of treatment.

THE ANALYTIC SETTING AND
THE STRUCTURING OF EGO BOUNDARIES

Giovacchini (1979) emphasizes the importance of defining the analytic setting in our work with patients with primitive mental states. The aim of the definition is to clarify the function of the analyst and the motivation for his analytic behavior. The content of the definition will vary, depending upon the dominant material and affect. The analyst in some way makes it clear that he reacts to the patient's feelings as intrapsychic phenomena that are interesting and worthy of understanding. He has an observational frame of reference in which he feels neither elated, nor despairing, nor seduced, nor threatened by what he observes. He maintains an analytic attitude, and by defining the analytic setting, he is conveying this attitude to the patient.

I have just begun using the couch with a 40-year-old woman who has had many therapists over many years. For her, therapy was an arena for acting out a merger of helpless self with omnipotent object. I defined the situation in a recent session saying, "Here you and I will be separate. We will not merge." She responded, "That's remarkable. I haven't merged with you. Your personality doesn't lend itself. You're too passive." As the therapist on the receiving end of the projective identification of the idealized, omnipotent object, I am not seduced into playing out this role as were her previous therapists, nor am I "conned" by her protestations of helplessness. A few moments later she said, "You just said not to merge with you and I put you inside me." She describes the phenomenon of "swallowing" people whole. As we explored this example of this kind of experience, I made the interpretation that perhaps my refusal to merge with her had frightened her and that this was a way to regain control of me. She thought it was a rebellion against the process as well as a way to restore her sense of well-being. I chose to address the issue of rebellion as *her* attempt to be separate and not under my control, to reinforce the healthy drive toward the individuation of the self.

Patients with primitive mental states often try to create a setting where their projections need not be viewed as projections. That is, they attempt to induce in the therapist feelings and behaviors that are consistent with their view of themselves and of the interpersonal environment. Because the analytic setting and the therapist's analytic attitude do not blend with these distortions of reality, the patient is helped to consolidate his ego boundaries and to see himself as a separate and discrete individual.

The analytic setting is an instrument par excellence for the mediation of organization. The consistent, reliable, empathic, and nonintrusive presence of the therapist mediates such organization.

Winnicott (1965) defines the "holding environment" as one which conveys to the patient that the therapist knows and understands "the deepest anxiety that is being experienced or that is waiting to be experienced" (p. 240). With some patients he sees holding as like the task of the mother in infant care. It acknowledges tacitly the tendency of the patient to disintegrate, to cease to exist, to fall forever.

Winnicott distinguishes "holding" from "living with," noting that the term "living with" implies an object relationship. As soon as the infant is able to perceive that he and mother are separate, she appropriately changes her attitude and waits for the child to give a signal as to its needs. Applying this concept to treatment, he notes that, except when the patient is very regressed, the therapist should not know the answers except insofar as the patient gives the clues. This limitation of the analyst's power is important to the patient.

One young woman whose material tended to be very vague often referred to the fact that things were "understood" in interpersonal situations, especially in her family. I commented that she would probably have to deal here with my shortcoming that I am not a mindreader. In effect, I defined the situation as one in which I would not merge with her on my part. It was a statement of boundaries. The definition of the setting is itself an interpretation that promotes structuralization.

Just as the holding environment provides the matrix within which organization can take place, so the "living with" environment provides the matrix within which differentiation of self from object can take place. The therapist must be attuned to the patient, as the mother is to the child, so as to respond appropriately to the stage of development and its attendant tasks.

The fact that the treatment setting does not blend with the pathology of the patient emphasizes his separateness and the boundaries of the self. This aspect of work with the patient with a primitive and pathological organization of the self and the object world can be difficult to maintain in the face of projective identification, a defense common in these patients.

Melanie Klein (Klein et al. 1952) described projective identification as a mechanism in which parts of the self are projected into the object. Projective identification is distinguished from projection in that a self representation or an unassimilated maternal introject are projected, whereas in simple projection, a trait or attribute of the self is thus externalized.

Bion (1959) notes what happens to the therapist who is on the receiving end of the projective identification of the patient. There is a particular countertransference experience that is characteristic of this situation. "The analyst feels he is being manipulated so as to be playing a part . . . in somebody else's phantasy" (p. 149). There is usually a temporary loss of insight on the part of the therapist as he experiences strong feelings that seem justified by the objective situation. He feels that he has actually become the kind of person with whom he is identified. Bion comments that "the ability to shake oneself out of the numbing feeling of reality that is a concomitant of this state is a prime requisite of the analyst" (p. 149).

Even if the therapist does become the "container" and participates in what Langs (1975) calls the therapeutic misalliance, it is possible to recover and to make use of the event for further analytic work. In the case of projective identification, the definition of the setting is manifest in the therapist's refusal to participate in the situation. Maintenance of the analytic attitude also defines the boundary between the psyche of the patient and that of the therapist.

RESISTANCE AS AN ALLY IN THE SERVICE OF STRUCTURALIZATION

Giovacchini (1972) reminds us that the concept of resistance "as something to be overcome creates an atmosphere, a moral tone, that is antithetical to the analysis of many patients. . . . Analysis of resistance . . . is not the same as overcoming resistance" (p. 291). The analysis of resistance must not become an exhortative struggle to make the patient give up something in the interest of analysis.

Defenses against the development of transference can be viewed as a serious resistance from the point of view that working within the transference is the most important focus of our interventions. When there is a danger of a psychotic transference, it may be deliberately avoided in planning therapeutic strategies, limiting the treatment to a more circumscribed area of concern. Resistance to developing a transference is also seen with borderline patients. There are some patients for whom the transference interpretation will constitute an impingement, an insistence on the part of the therapist that the patient acknowledge his existence when the patient prefers, for important defensive reasons, not to acknowledge it. Yes, this is resistance. But as a defense is it, at the moment, protecting the survival of the self? And if it is, should we interfere with this defense at this point of treatment? The work with Miss R., who needed a wall for others to come up against so they (and she) would know she existed, is a good example of going along with the defense and working outside relatedness issues. She commented in her one hundred and thirty-sixth session, now experiencing the solidity of a cohesive and integrated self,

> What I don't understand is that you haven't existed very long, and all I've read about transference. Now it seems that it was very important that there was none—whether because I refused to allow it, or the essence of my problem precluded considering you as a person. I want an intellectual answer for that more than I need an answer emotionally. I'm curious about how transference is important.

I explained that there had indeed been transference, at the start of our work, when she expressed the feeling that I had put up a certain picture just to draw a reaction from her, that she had experienced me as the intruding and impinging mother. I explained that the transference was manifest negatively, in its absence, by what its absence protected her from.

With the structuralization that took place in this context, she was now able to let herself experience me as a person and to deal with transference issues at this more evolved level. With the achievement of cohesion and integration, rapprochement issues emerged. A dream suggested that she feared my anger at her wish to reduce the number of her sessions from three times a week to twice. She acknowledged that she had a "lingering fear" relative to that issue. Will this mother abandon her with emotional withdrawal as punishment for asserting her separateness and growing autonomy?

The therapeutic alliance is directly related to the attachment to the therapist. Even when the patient is detached as in the situation with Miss R., the obvious presence of the alliance is an indication, in my opinion, that there is also an attachment, albeit denied. Easy rupture of the therapeutic alliance mitigates against the establishment of the attachment, through which the therapist becomes the mediator of organization and the eventual source of those internalizations and identifications that promote autonomy. A rupture of the therapeutic alliance, once there has been an attachment, will evoke the experience of object loss and its attendant anxieties and defenses.

Miss R.'s continued elation at the experience of realness and wholeness as her treatment continued was expressed as follows:

> At this point I'm more conscious of you as a person. I don't want this, but I suspect it's a necessary next step. I want to say no, that's enough. . . . I was thinking that I was born this April thirteenth. The last two days I have felt more mellow here. I hear a difference in my voice. It sounds more self-assured. . . . I've been thinking about my dreams and what we said Tuesday about them. The greatest enterprise seemed to be to think about thinking. To understand the thought processes was an endeavor that was pleasing and worthwhile. . . . I like thinking about how excited I was about my own thoughts, a fascination and real affection for my mind. . . . I'm conscious of being very close to tears. I don't understand that. (When you talk about your thinking, you are also talking about your real, core self. Perhaps the tears have something to do with the feelings you have about the "birth" of your self.)

Therapists who view their role as that of the mediator of organization within the therapeutic matrix will sometimes have the opportunity of sharing with the patient the joy of the emergence of the self out of the darkness of existential despair.

17

Innovative Techniques in Work with Character Disorders

When we consider the use of innovative techniques in psychotherapy with patients with character disorders, it is critical that we consider such techniques in terms of their potential to inflict damage as well as their potential to cure. My own observations of psychotic breakdowns, as well as the body of research on encounter-group casualties, have led me to a stance of caution.

Elsewhere (Horner 1968) I noted my growing discomfort with the "anything goes" approach to a variety of psychotherapies on the West Coast during the 1960s. Many of these involved physical contact, and I wondered when touching gratified the patient's need in a manner that held out false promise for more, and when touching served as a "corrective emotional experience."[1] I was also concerned about situations in which the gratification of the thera-

---

1. In 1987 I addressed similar concerns in an article that has been reprinted in this book; see Chapter 19.

pist subtly took precedence over the therapeutic needs of the patient. Cornelius Beukenkamp's response to my concerns was this: "The significant questions are 'With which people?' 'At what time?' and 'With what authentic emotions do we relate?'" (1968, p. 28). He concludes that the antithesis of rigidity is not flexibility; it is wisdom. And wisdom is what must guide us in our search for innovative techniques in psychoanalytic treatment.

What is called for is a reasoned creativity—that is, a creativity that has a specific outcome goal. MacKinnon (1961) compared artistic and scientific creativity. He notes that the products of artistic creativity are expressions of the creator's inner states, needs, perceptions, or motivations. In other words, the artist externalizes something of himself and puts it into the public field. The products of scientific creativity, however, are unrelated to the creator as a person, because the scientist, in his or her creative work, acts largely as a mediator between externally defined needs and goals. MacKinnon sees the architect as a combination of artist and scientist: he expresses *himself* through his creativity, with an artistic product, but in a manner that must also meet the needs of the external world.

It seems to me that the creativity of the therapist is similar in some ways to that of the architect. To the extent that therapists, like artists, externalize our own inner worlds in our work, we may impinge upon our patients with potentially damaging consequences. Before bringing creativity and innovation into the treatment situation, we must define the relevant goals in the patient's terms and not our own.

TREATMENT PLANS AND THERAPEUTIC STRATEGIES

The treatment plan and therapeutic strategies should be determined by the diagnosis in structural terms, and by the goals for treatment. In my supervision of group therapy, I encourage student therapists to be creative, to be inventive. By this I am not suggesting that they engage in some kind of arbitrary activity. Rather, there should first be some thought about the immediate goal. What does the therapist hope to accomplish? If it is to facilitate interaction, one can invent an interaction that will move things in that direction, always, however, taking into account the effect that that decision will have on each member of the group as well as on the group as a whole. The same principles will hold true for innovation in individual treatment. We are certainly not talking about "wild analysis" (Freud 1910b), which refers to the inappropriate application of theoretical principles with a concomitant disregard of their impact.

In his discussion of Franz Alexander, Greenson (1964b) cautions against the use of techniques that are essentially manipulative and antianalytic. When such techniques are used, "the patient does not learn to recognize and understand his resistances, there is no premium on insight as a means of overcoming resistances, there is no attempt to change the ego structure" (p. 136). Although other approaches may constitute effective symptomatic psychotherapy, Greenson says that they are not psychoanalysis. He notes that what he refers to as "antianalytic" procedures block or lessen the patient's capacity for insight and understanding. "Any measure which *diminishes* the ego's function or capacity for observing, remembering, and judging would fall into this category. Unnecessary transference gratification would be a typical example" (p. 366; italics added). Any time we deviate from standard technique to make what we deem a creative interpretation, we must be sure that although our behavior may be nonanalytic, it is not antianalytic.

Myerson (1981) helps us make this determination with his distinction between need and desire. Putting these concepts into the developmental context, he asks, "When does a child's need *from* a parent become or not become a desire *for* the parent?" (p. 614). The "from" reflects a passive attitude, whereas the "for" reflects a more active one. Needs that may be age-appropriate at one stage of development will be regressive at a later stage. Myerson notes that "the shift from *needs from* to *desire for* is indicative of biological maturation, but the quality and the character of the shift is influenced in a significant way by how the child's various needs are met by his parents" (p. 616). He views the shift from the passive mode to the active mode as an important criterion for judging whether or not this shift has taken place. Inappropriate parental response to this shift may lead to the child's continuing in a passive state of neediness rather than developing an active sense of himself as a desiring and responsibly aggressive person. That is, such a manner of parenting will be analogous to the therapist's antianalytic behavior. Will our innovative technique diminish the ego's functions or capacities rather than contribute to its strength? Will our active response to the patient's passively felt need enhance the ego, or will it infantilize by reinforcing passivity and by giving credence to unrealistic wishes and fantasies?

In effect, when we meet a need as it is defined by Myerson, we act as an auxiliary ego at a moment when the patient's ego is overwhelmed by anxiety or when developmental failure leaves him ill-equipped for the psychological task at hand. When we provide a holding environment (Winnicott 1965) or mirror in Kohut's (1971) sense, we are responding to a developmental need. As treatment progresses and structuralization takes place, the need should give way to the wish, and a more traditional approach becomes possible. At times we may use our creativity in the service of promoting the growth of the patient. First we must ask, Is this innovation clinically necessary? Then we should ask, Is it clinically appropriate?

The concept of innovation goes beyond that of the "parameter," which Eissler (1953) defines as "the deviation, both quantitative and qualitative, from the basic model technique, . . . which requires interpretation as the exclusive tool" (p. 110). Parameters are aimed at removing obstacles to the analytic process. Innovation also has a more positive aim of facilitating the desired structural change directly, through itself, rather than merely removing the obstacles to such change. To the extent that our innovative technique is successful in achieving its desired aim of structuralization, it should automatically phase itself out and become unnecessary and unproductive. Carried beyond this point it will become antianalytic.

Case Examples

The problem may be one of the moment, or it may be an ongoing one. Our innovative technique may be aimed at restoring the observing ego, or at handling a resistance that is not yet able to be relinquished, in a manner that allows for other important work to proceed. Or it may be aimed at promoting structure, at facilitating the achievement of any one of a number of previously failed developmental tasks. We may wish to promote cohesion of the self representation, integration of various split self and object representations, differentiation of self from object, or the securing of object constancy. Innovation may be called for when the patient is unable to tolerate or make use of a straightforward interpretation. An accurate assessment of the ego's capacities and defenses is essential lest we infantilize the patient by responding to him as though he were more impaired than he really is.

The technique of enlisting the patient as a consultant in his own case may be effective in the promotion of the observing ego when acting out in the transference does not yield to interpretation. I used a variation of this with a patient who was himself a therapist:

> A middle-aged man, he was emotionally involved with a woman with borderline personality disorder. Her projections and extreme vacillations of feeling and intent evoked rage and anxiety and a loss of his observing ego in the context of the relationship. The parallels in his relationship with his mother were clear, but no amount of interpretive work touched him. He lost his sense of his own separateness and autonomy, and his separation anxiety bordered on panic. He was fearful of making a full commitment to treatment, lest the same situation develop there. In order to mobilize his observing ego, I asked him to describe the woman as though he were referring her to me as a patient. This he did with notable clarity and understanding. Then, on his own, he extended the task to his mother, to what he would say if he were referring her as a patient also.

Although some might object to the use of such an intellectual device, I would like to point out that affect without a cognitive content is sometimes likely to traumatize and overwhelm the ego (Horner 1980), as was happening to this man. With the integrative work done cognitively, and with the restoration of a reality perspective, he reexperienced long-lost feelings of love for his mother. A defensive splitting had aborted the development of the capacity for ambivalence and the achievement of object constancy. And his making real the lover's projections interfered with his reality testing.

One can also use innovative techniques in the promotion of object constancy. If the analyst is to be used as an object for structuralization, for the internalizations and identifications that will lead to intrapsychic integrity and emotional autonomy, the achievement and securing of the capacity to tolerate ambivalence is essential. As long as there is a defensive splitting, this will not take place. Splitting is used as a defense only after sufficient developmental integration has occurred or after the work of treatment has adequately healed the original developmental split. With the capacity for ambivalence, separation does not induce rage and the loss of the good object so much as it evokes a missing of the one who is loved and needed and feelings of guilt over anger toward the loved other. At this point, in Myerson's terms, the need for the other becomes a wish for the other.

The following material is from thus-far unsuccessful work in a training situation in a hospital setting. Both in- and outpatient work are involved.

The patient is a woman in her early thirties with a long history of drug abuse. She lives in a homosexual marriage, the two women having run away together at the age of 15. The patient has a 13-year-old daughter. As a result of suicide attempts by overdosing, the patient has been hospitalized.

For some time the supervisory work focused on the issue of a false self alliance, with a compliant good self being brought to treatment. This was the patient's major transference resistance, and as a result, no progress had been made in treatment with various hospital personnel over a number of years. The therapist's failures of empathy with the patient's secret real self, and the therapist's cancellations, changes of schedule, or vacations, were usually met by the patient with missing sessions and returning to drug use, although there was always a denial of anger.

The dynamics were those of a clinging rapprochement child who is afraid that she will be abandoned if she does not meet the narcissistic needs of the important other. The way to maintain the attachment with the good object is to meet those needs. But then there is an annihilation of the real self. Furthermore, the sacrifice does not pay off, and she is enraged. Then she feels that she is bad, and when this is projected, she becomes fearful. There is a *wish* to have the total love and devotion of the important other. There is a *belief* that the way to do this is to meet the needs of the other. The *reality* is that no matter how hard she tries, the other is still separate and has a life apart from her. The *consequences* are that she is angry and bad and feels that she has failed and that she is inadequate. At this point there would be a defensive splitting. As long as the core transference and character resistance is not interpreted, everything the therapist says is taken in by the false good self, and is experienced as something else she has to do right if she is not to be abandoned.

It was finally agreed that only extended work would have a chance of saving this woman's life. This was arranged after one of her suicide attempts, and she was kept as an inpatient for six weeks, during which the core issues could be more readily addressed. She was seen five times a week, and with supervisory prodding, the trainee addressed the issue of the false self alliance. For the first time there seemed to be a genuine working alliance.

In the hospital she reported the following dream:

I was in the hospital. My mother and stepfather and brother and sisters were chasing me. Something happened that caused my mother to die. It was my fault because she was chasing me. Everyone blamed me, and I blamed myself. At the funeral my stepfather gave me money to feed my brother and sisters, as though he had forgiven me.

She said she had had other dreams in which her mother died and it was her fault. She said that she felt bad about all she had put her mother through. The object loss as represented by the death of her mother is the consequence of the defensive splitting and the resulting loss of both the good object and the good self. It was also a statement of what was going on in the transference. The inability to hold on to the sense of connection with the good object interferes with the achievement of object constancy.

With sufficient positive affect maintained as a result of the daily visits with the therapist and the support of the environment, the repressed positive feelings toward the mother were also experienced, and the patient reported sadness at missing her and guilt at the acting-out behavior, with its underlying hostility. With the restoration of the good object, there is a concomitant restoration of the good self and the possibility of forgiveness.

Unfortunately, as the patient's six weeks of hospitalization were coming to a close, her therapist was to be away for a week on vacation. When the patient was asked about her feelings at the coming separation, she cried and said, "I'll miss you." In supervision we discussed the importance of her maintaining the positive memory of the therapist during the separation in order to abort the splitting and its usual sequelae.

I have found that the active promotion of positive emotional connectedness with the therapist, during separations beyond those of the normal treatment schedule, has brought positive results. I define the task to my patients quite specifically, saying that although there is anger or disappointment at my going away, it will be important to hold on to the good feelings as well. A therapist can suggest that the patient write to him or her in a journal during the usual hours of therapy or at other times when the wish for the connection is felt. Writing or talking into a tape recorder allows the patient to reestablish the connection in an active, participatory manner, analogous to the young child's use of the transitional object for self-comforting in the absence of the mother or the mother's love. In one case in which I felt that visual contact was particularly important, I gave the patient my picture to sustain the positive memory and sense of connection over extended vacations. This is a more passive device, but combined with some activity on the part of the patient, it was successful in maintaining the capacity for ambivalence and the developmental thrust toward object constancy. Giving one's picture to a more evolved patient who has no real developmental, structural need, but rather a desire for special-ness, would inappropriately reinforce infantile fantasy and impede progress.

Unfortunately, the technique did not work with the patient under discussion, inasmuch as she made a suicide attempt the day after her release from the hospital. It was hoped that with the acknowledgment of the wish for the important albeit imperfect other, and with the relinquishing of the defensive splitting and false self defense, there would be a chance for the development of an inner structure that would sustain her in such separations, and a chance that she would cease to turn to drugs as a way both to express her rage and to make herself feel better at the same time.

RESPECTING THE RESISTANCE

There are times when we need to respect and bear with certain resistances when they are essential to the patient's functioning or ability to tolerate the treatment situation. The schizoid defenses of the borderline patient may fall into this category.

In one such instance I used my patient's stories about her young daughter to promote relatedness in the treatment situation. At the start of treatment, schizoid defenses and a grandiose self enabled the patient to function at a high intellectual level, although they interfered with her capacity for emotional intimacy and with her reaching the level of professional achievement of which she was capable.[2]

> Our work began when the patient's daughter was a few months old, and it had taken us into the child's fourth year. From time to time at the end of the session, as she sat up from the couch, she would tell me stories about the little girl, usually of a delightful nature and obviously with love and pride. Rejecting the principle of avoidance of extra-analytic contact, I found

2. This case is discussed in further detail in the following chapter.

myself responding somewhat like an appreciative grandma, and over time, although I never met the child, I came to feel a sense of loving her. She was obviously very much like her mother, or like her mother would have been as a child had her own mother been more adequate and less engulfing.

We worked for a long time on the transference reactions of daily life—on projection, boundary-structuring, the defensive grandiosity, and her struggle against her identification with the hated mother. In her relationship with her husband, she was extremely vulnerable to his bad-mother projections into her, and she would become confused and frantic when he did this. After long and hard work on these issues, and with structuralization increasingly apparent, she started to come to sessions on time.

The treatment of this patient seems to be a standard analytic treatment. But I believe that the extra-analytic contacts around the daughter played a significant role in the patient's progress. It is my conviction that my positive response served two functions. For one, it actively affirmed her as a good mother, which she definitely is, helping her to further structure the boundary between herself and her own mother. It also connected the bright, loving child self that was buried in the unconscious with a real object, her therapist, making dependence on the grandiose self increasingly unnecessary. The fact that my response was to her daughter and not directly to her allowed it to be there without being a danger to her boundaries, and without evoking or reinforcing infantile fantasies and wishes. With this connection, internalization and identification with the therapist could begin to build toward object constancy in terms of both affect and the executive reality-testing function.

Although I did not actively set out to use this as an innovative technique, I intuitively felt all along that it was an absolutely correct response. Only in retrospect have I been able to observe and come to understand its impact. The hope is that we will use innovative techniques with a consciously formulated rationale, lest we act out something of our own that might feel right but not be so in fact. I suspect that there was some of my own business in this instance as well, but in questioning myself about it, I still felt that it was clinically appropriate. Our creativity must be closer to that of the scientist rather than to that of the artist; that is, it must meet the needs of the patient and not those of the therapist. However, it may not always be possible to be so deliberate in these undertakings. It is incumbent upon us to monitor our responses, our behavior, to be sure that we are appropriately meeting a legitimate growth need and not participating in a misalliance based on a mutual acting out of unconscious wishes or defenses.

In the context of this discussion, we should wonder whether the term *technique* is even appropriate. A technique is a standardized intervention that can be directly taught. There is a difference between a draftsman, who has mastered a technique, and an architect, who uses that technique as a vehicle for his creativity. What happens when an innovation born out of the creative process becomes rigidified as a technique?

In the case just discussed, my response to the patient's stories about her daughter came out of my spontaneous and genuinely felt reactions. My decision to express these reactions as I did was first based on intuition. With intuition subjected to understanding, I had a rationale for my clinical behavior. I may then try to translate all of this into a technique that someone else can learn and apply under similar circumstances. However, if the genuine feelings are not there, will the technique have the desired effect?

I am sure that there is much creative and innovative work being done by intuitive therapists that is perhaps not being labeled as such. These therapists may even be embarrassed at their deviation from standard technique and therefore do not report it. Perhaps, in the final analysis, we cannot teach others innovative techniques; all we can teach is an attitude of openness to their use.

18

Will, Transcendence, and Change

Otto Rank (1945) wrote, "It is in the act of willing that the human creature becomes creator, both of himself and of those products of his efforts" (p. 44).

Will is the taken-for-granted thrust for life that we see in the baby who, just learning to walk, falls, gets up gleefully, and falls again, and who, unable to manage his way to mother fast enough in this fashion, drops to his knees and scurries to her side. Rapprochement refueling is also an act of will.

From the earliest years of life, the developing individual attempts to master challenges. The sense of mastery is closely related to individuation and autonomy. The child who builds and rebuilds his precariously balanced tower of blocks exhibits will in action, and the joy of mastery is his reward. Mastery says, "I can do it!" Will is the energy and determination that does it. Autonomy says, "I can do it all by myself," and is an expression of the child's individuation and of his pleasure in his awareness of that process. It is a pleasure that is closely tied to the exercise of will and the achievement of mastery.

We see manifestations of will in incredible places and under incredible circumstances, often in acts of heroism. The will to live can sometimes make the difference between actual life or death. Will can also be perverted. We see it in the bag lady whose fierce independence, which we ascribe to her paranoia, leads to her freezing to death in the cardboard house she built for herself on the streets of New York City.

The clinical relevance of will should not be underestimated. The terms *aggression* and *libido* refer to innate energies that are genetic givens. *Motivation* refers to the structured manifestations of aggression or libido, and involves a wish, a goal, and an aim. Will stands somewhere between the two and is an attribute of a self that is determined to assert its being. Just as identity is the conscious component of the partly conscious, partly unconscious mental structure, the self representation (Jacobson 1964), so will is the consciously experienced, goal-oriented component of instinctual aggression. It is aggression that is bound and structured within the self representation and experienced consciously as part of the self and as supplying the motive force for expression of that self.

Plato divides the soul into three parts: reason, which is the faculty of thought and knowledge, and spirit and appetite, which are principles of action. Without spirit—or what we call will—even wisdom must fail to influence conduct.

Many of the later philosophers conceive of will as a faculty of desire or activity founded upon reason. Kant says that "the freedom of the act of volitional choice is its independence of being determined by sensuous impulses or stimuli" (*Great Books* 1952, p. 1073). Hegel says that only man stands above his impulses and may make them his own—that he puts them into himself as his own. He tells us that "an impulse is something natural, but to put it into my ego depends on my will" (*Great Books* 1952, p. 1073). I would say that will is impulse structured within the self, or the ego.

For Freud (1916), who does not use the word *will*, the overthrow of the pleasure principle by the reality principle perhaps comes closest to a concern with will as a psychological factor, and he stands clearly in the camp of those philosophers who view will as founded upon reason. He says that "the deeply rooted belief in psychic freedom and choice" must be given up because it "is quite unscientific. . . . It must give way before the claims of a determinism which governs even mental life" (p. 106).

Dr. Johnson tells us that although all theory is against the freedom of the will, all experience is for it (*Great Books* 1952, p. 1078). And William James says of the issue of will that "Doubt of this particular truth will . . . probably be open to us to the end of time, and the utmost that a believer in free will can *ever* do will be to show that the deterministic arguments are not coercive. That they are seductive, I am the last to deny, nor do I deny that efforts may be needed to keep the faith in freedom, when they press upon it, upright in the mind" (*Great Books* 1952, p. 1079). In his 1919 foreword to *Women in Love*, D. H. Lawrence wrote, "The creative, spontaneous soul sends forth its promptings of desire and aspiration in us. These promptings are our true fate, which it is our business to fulfill. A fate dictated from outside, from theory or circumstance, is a false fate" (pp. ix–x).

Rank (1945) protests the causality principle, saying that it "means a denial of the will principle since it makes the thinking, feeling, acting of the individual dependent on forces outside himself and thus frees him from responsibility and guilt" (p. 44).

Somewhere in this age-old controversy lies a paradox, probably because will itself is an aspect of mind that is subject to forces that operate upon it in a modifying, if not deterministic, fashion. The mental activity of the self of the newborn leads to the mental structure we also call the self. In the same convoluted way in which the self creates the self, will is both undetermined and determined. The capacity to transcend the limits of body, mind, and soul depends upon the continuing freedom of a will that is inherently free. Will must be looked at quite independently, not as tied to reason or impulse, although, functionally, will may be the executor of both.

When Rank says that the will derives its energy from the life force and is present in every individual in varying degrees from the beginning of life, he identifies will as an autonomous function of the organism. I am not saying "autonomous function of the ego" to avoid the controversy over whether or not there is an ego at birth. Nevertheless, as with other autonomous functions, under certain circumstances will may lose its conflict-free status and, caught up in conflict, may become inhibited or distorted in its expression. This inhibition or distortion may take place at any stage of development—in the separation–individuation process, as well as in the competitive strivings of the oedipal period.

In his attempt to draw clear and definitive distinctions between self psychology and psychoanalysis, Goldberg (1981) says:

> If conflict theory is allowed to equal any sort of opposition that one experiences including that of a conflict over developing further because of the lack of sufficient structure, then it probably can embrace just about everything and thus runs the risk of trivializing its original meaning. [p. 631]

He believes that "heroic stretching" of classical theory is necessary if one is to see conflict as relevant to developmental deficit.

Goldberg holds to the classical definitions of conflict as relating to the instinctual wishes of childhood, or conflict between the child and his environment, between the ego and the superego, and between drives and affects of opposite quality (Brenner 1979, A. Freud 1965). He argues that the concept of conflict is not relevant to confronting developmental tasks and offers as an example the toddler's moves away from mother alternating with his returns to her for "refueling." He notes that since this is not a true clashing of forces in the psychoanalytic sense, there is no conflict. I agree with him up to that point. He is describing conflict-free autonomous development. But he misses the point that conflict-free functioning can become caught up in conflict. In healthy development the child feels free to follow up on his felt needs and wishes as they alternate vis-à-vis his mother. When there is indeed conflict around these issues, we are likely to see anxious clinging on one hand or anxious avoidance on the other. The conflicts may come out of the vulnerability induced by structural deficit as well as by a more traditional conflict between clashing libidinal and aggressive impulses.

WILL AND CONFLICT

It seems to me that Goldberg's denial of the importance of the conflict that may be inherent in the developmental process and that is clearly a factor in the clinical situation with patients with structural deficit is in the service of keeping self theory as separate and apart from the rest of psychoanalysis. There is indeed a "clashing of forces" which is evident in the intensity of object seeking based on the need due to structural deficit, which opposes the intensity of the will toward individuation. Although the impossibility of resolving the conflict may be due to an ego deficit that is the result of developmental failures, there is nonetheless a conflict. And whatever the therapist's function as a "selfobject," in my experience the interpretation of that conflict and the defenses against it, along with an empathic recognition of the pain inherent in the dilemma, is experienced by the patient in a most positive way as being understood and as having both of the opposing strivings valued and accepted. It mitigates the shame of what is seen as weakness and supports the affirmation of will, which is experienced guiltily as *against* the parental objects. As one young man put it:

> I have to use my strength against my parents to be a man. (*Against them?*) To make an independent decision. They lose control of my life. I'm not an outgrowth of them. (*It sounds like you feel guilty over your own development.*) Yes, I do. . . . When I expressed my own feelings as a child I was put down. Now a war has to be fought to get my feelings out. I'm impressed with some of the things I get done. My power blows me away. The excitement seems to be a product of the powerlessness. (*The juxtaposition of your sense of power with your sense of powerlessness highlights both of them, just as we were talking about how the juxtaposition of the sense of being one with someone and the sense of being separate highlights them. That very juxtaposition highlights your awareness and heightens your tension and anxiety.*) I was just now aware of the juxtaposition to power. I thought I was a free agent. I'm creating my own character. I'm very insecure, but I see it will be less so.

Expression of will is experienced as an act against the other, particularly when will is suffused with anger. Elsewhere (Horner 1979) I said that I use the word *aggression* to refer to the energy of the organism that is used to reach a goal. In this sense, there is nothing inherently bad in aggression. Only with the addition of anger that is evoked by frustration does aggression become a hostile act. I was using aggression in that context much as I use the term *will* here. The expression of will must inevitably come into conflict with the environment. Any mother who lent herself totally as a selfobject would fail in the most fundamental way, not only to civilize her child, but to function as the bearer of reality. As one patient said, "I need something to come up against to know I am there." When I think I am appropriately providing the mirroring matrix with another, he becomes puzzled by his felt need to fight me. Despite his need for a selfobject, he must also define his separateness, and can only do so by opposing me. He needs his aggression and his will to affirm his identity, but that same will and aggression endangers the object needed to maintain the stability of his self.

The developmental dilemma of the patient creates a parallel dilemma for the therapist. It's a damned-if-you-do-and-damned-if-you-don't situation. The way out of the bind, as with all double binds, is to comment upon it—that is, to interpret the conflict. Even though the therapist may be able to contain the tension of the contradiction, the patient is made frantic by it.

Goldberg's statement that we need "a new way of conceptualizing normal growth and development . . . in order to comprehend the existence of lasting and mature selfobjects," is itself an example of what he laments as the overextension of a useful concept, to the point of its trivialization. Stolorow and Lachmann (1980) write that the selfobject is viewed as substituting for a missing part of the psychic structure, and that its function is to maintain the cohesion, stability, and positive affective coloring of the self representation. From its very definition, it seems to me that the idea of a mature selfobject is a contradiction in terms.

Will must be inhibited if we are to maintain the other as a selfobject, for one's will inevitably must come up against the will of the other, and in that juxtaposition we are confronted with our separateness and with our existential aloneness. At that point, although we no longer have a need for a selfobject in the sense of its being a substitute for a missing part of the psyche, there may indeed be a powerful wish for such a partner.

Myerson (1981)[1] points out the distinction between need and desire, or wish. In terms of treatment, we have to ask whether our active response to the patient's passively felt need will enhance the ego through our function as a selfobject, or whether it will infantilize him by reinforcing passivity and by giving credence to unrealistic wishes and fantasies? And in so doing, do we inadvertently stand in opposition to his will?

What happens developmentally and experientially either to encourage, facilitate, or support the exercise of will, or to paralyze it or, more likely, to distort its expression? Beginning work with patients who present a history and picture of passivity and compliance and an apparent renunciation of will, I may inquire as to whether they can recall a single rebellious act in childhood or adolescence. They usually can and, interestingly, with a degree of pleasure. I heave a sigh of relief and say "thank goodness" to myself, for the will inherent in the rebellious behavior will be the nucleus of the working alliance and will be the basis for the impetus to change. I may say "thank goodness" aloud, to communicate to the person not only my acceptance of his will, but my valuing it. The survival of the real self, in the Winnicott sense, is inseparably tied to the survival of will. Rank notes that the acceptance rather than the condemnation of the will toward individuation is the essence of the therapeutic intervention. Such uncritical acceptance conveys the therapist's belief in the patient's ability to progress beyond his current neurotic encumbrances. And Rank adds that the patient's perception of this acceptance and belief enables him to accept his own individual act of willing without guilt.

Just as the expression of will is experienced as against the other in the context of the separation–individuation process, so are the competitive strivings associated with the oedipal period. But again, and paradoxically, the resolution of the Oedipus complex is not without guilt either.

1. See Myerson 1981, pp. 614–616, which was discussed in the previous chapter.

Loewald (1979) notes that the essence of the superego as an internal agency involves owning up to one's needs and impulses as one's own. It means "granting them actively that existence which they have in any event with or without our permission" (p. 761). He comments that this involves facing and bearing guilt for acts we consider criminal, even if these acts exist only in fantasy. The crimes to which he refers are not only the incestuous fantasies of the Oedipus complex, but also what he views as a form of parricide: the murder of parental authority and the assumption of responsibility for one's own life that take place with the severing of the emotional ties with parents. That is, incest is the "crime" associated with oedipal wishes, and parricide is the "crime" associated with the resolution of the Oedipus complex. "Not only parental authority is destroyed by wresting authority from the parents and taking it over, but the parents, if the process were thoroughly carried out, are being destroyed as libidinal objects as well" (p. 757). In this situation, the exercise of will is inhibited by guilt. Loewald does note that if things go well, what will be left is tenderness, mutual trust, and respect—the signs of equality.

The inhibition of will may also function to protect the ego ideal, particularly when will is equated with power. I find in many instances that a woman's continued stance of dependency and her denial of her identification with her mother is a direct consequence of her rejection of maternal power, which is experienced as bad, since it was experienced as in opposition to the wishes and will of the self. In addition, the good, nonpowerful self will be preferred by Daddy, so that compliance and the inhibition of will at one level, are in the service of the will manifest in the attempt to win the oedipal object.

THERAPY IN THE SERVICE
OF THE CREATIVE WILL

Noting that the free and secure expression of an independent will is central to the process of individuation, Rank conceived of therapy as the facilitation of the growth of the patient's creative will. This raises the frequently asked question, "What is curative in the therapeutic process?'' What leads to change in the patient? Is it conflict resolution, with the achievement of insight? Is it structuralization? Is it the internalization of the therapist? Or is it the release of will that is associated with all of these, a will that is free to operate again as it did early in life without neurotic inhibition or characterological distortion, and in the service once again of the expression of the spontaneous and true self?

We see our patients start to change in significant ways well before the end of treatment. At this point it is clear that they are indeed transcending their pathology, transcending the limits imposed by the forces of history and the mark that these forces have left upon the character. I will describe the progress made by a patient in her mid-thirties from a session in her fourth year of treatment with me.

Case Example

At the start of treatment, schizoid defenses and a grandiose self enabled this patient to function at a high intellectual level, although they interfered with her capacity for emotional intimacy and with her reaching the level of achievement in her career which she wanted and of which she was clearly capable. The inhibition of will in the work area was significant.

> For a long time she needed to make believe that I was not there as a real person. She said that she didn't even want to look around the waiting room, as it might tell her too much about me. She was fearful that she would discover imperfections in me that would make it impossible for her to go on working with me. She could tolerate "a 3 or 4 percentage-point failure" on my part—that is, she could still work with me if I fell from total perfection to a 96 or 97 but not much lower. She habitually came to sessions 15 minutes late, and our work made it clear that this had nothing to do with anger but was essential to the protection of the boundaries of her self. If she came at the time I wanted her to be there, or just expected her to be there, it would make us too similar, and there would be a loss of her separate identity. She needed that 15-minute hiatus

to make that boundary very clear. However, her half-hour sessions were extremely productive. Other than this major transference resistance, which clearly could not be relinquished at this time, she associated freely and there was an active working alliance. (Here I take issue with Stolorow and Lachmann [1980], who state that "the establishment of the analyst as a 'realistically' perceived object is one of the developmental prerequisites for a therapeutic alliance.")

Not challenging her need to make me not be, we worked for a long time on the transference reactions of daily life—on projection, boundary structuring, the defensive grandiosity, and her struggle against her identification with her hated mother. In her relationship with her husband, she was extremely vulnerable to his bad-mother projections into her, and she would become confused and frantic when he did this. That is, his projection onto her of his bad-mother representation at times when she failed to function as a selfobject for him resonated with the bad object representation of her own split representational world. At such times she would become confused as to whether she was herself or whether she had, indeed, become her own bad mother. She would fight to eject his projection, to get it out of her as it were, but in the fighting gave validity to his accusations. After long and hard work on these issues, and with some greater degree of structuralization, she was more able to come on time, or closer to it. The following material is from a session around the time of this shift.

> **Patient:** I had the vision of you not minding when I canceled, of your not feeling personally rebuffed. For the first time I recognized the degree to which this arrangement is mine officially. I habitually see that if I don't come to your party you'll be upset. I fail in my obligation to you, and I see you as *really* hurt. It's like, "Mommy, I don't want to play with you." It occurred to me, here especially and in the world at large, that I operate as though there's a bunch of feelings at the end of the tele-

phone. More often it's not so. Even if it were so it shouldn't determine what happens. (Laughs) I can't injure you by not coming. Is it true? Have I gone too far? You won't be injured, hurt, crippled. You will survive to lead your full life. I'm laughing but I'm almost crying. (Begins to cry) The enormity of the idea! It's not that people don't have feelings, but they're not crippling. I have to turn the situation into one in which I and the other do not feel anything—neutered.

Therapist: Not dangerous.

Patient: I know! I dove one hundred feet and wonder if I did it! It's the counterpoint of not being special. As I gradually learn I have no greater rights by virtue of being born a goddess princess, I also have no greater power to destroy.

As structure-building proceeded, she could look at the frightening fantasies behind the transference resistance and subject them to reality testing. Her need to hate her mother as a way to protect the separateness of her boundaries was eased, and she began to experience feelings of compassion toward her. The grandiose self, which had also come under the scrutiny of our analytic work, gave way to a more realistic self-esteem, which allowed her to take active steps toward making very significant changes in her career. The freeing of will that came with the ability to let go of the grandiose-self defense led to a spurt of energy and activity on all fronts, including her relationship with her husband. Can we assume that the core structural borderline pathology was "cured"? Consider this material from a session about a year later.

Early in the session she conveys what we might characterize as transcendence in action. She is speaking of her work.

Patient: Even with the interpersonal turmoil, I can get into something so important to me that the interpersonal turmoil doesn't matter. It's an area of fulfillment, and the fulfillment takes over. The other anxieties of who I am, me or my mother, sane or insane, good or bad—I become sane because those considerations are not important. I become me in my work. There is no identity problem, and the obsessive quality is all in the background.

Therapist: Mhm . . .

Patient: When Bob asked why I was so involved here when they don't appreciate me, I told him I can't not do it because it *is* me. I am comfortable and I know who I am. It's not a conscious decision. . . . I get very absorbed in what I'm doing and not absorbed in my own dynamics. It's a great relief. I'm not inhibited from my thinking to the fullest.

Therapist: It's an area free of conflict for you.

Patient: It's an area of achievement, a situation not equalled by anything else. There's a feeling of great confidence.

Therapist: Your sense of yourself is heightened.

Patient: Yes, and it's almost the same when I talk about it.

During the session there was more expression of the positive changes that have taken place. She referred to what she called her "born-again experience" of the previous year, saying that it comes and goes. She shifted to a comparison of these positive feelings to the other side of the picture.

Patient: I'm still scared by how deeply I can sink into the morass of being not me and being such a lost soul. Only I know how bad it can be for me.

Therapist: Sure.

Patient: I know the depths, when bad is bad, partly because it's so conscious, and I don't deny it. It's a level of anxiety that can't be overcome without more awareness than I have now.

Therapist: Mhm . . .

Patient: I walk there floundering, trying to decide what I should say or feel or do next. There's such a contrast with the one who can not only feel confidence but inspire it in others. I go from being the worst case in the institution to being the director of it.

It should be noted that this sense of confidence is firmly rooted in reality and is quite unlike that which was attributable to her grandiosity. It comes from the sense of mastery that accompanied the freeing up of her will. In the rest of this session and the next, she struggles with her difficulties that can be directly linked to the persisting pathological representational world.

> **Patient:** There is something negative in each of us that makes a system fall apart. The system is riddled with negative quotient. I feel overwhelmed by it. I can't find a way to accept it.
>
> **Therapist:** Is this related to your disillusionment with your father?
>
> **Patient:** I never absorbed that. I never found a place to put it.
>
> **Therapist:** It must also be related to your not wanting to know about me lest you find the imperfections there.
>
> **Patient:** It's basic. I can't deal with negative qualities. It's better not to be aware of it. It becomes unabsorbable. I don't have what I need in my metabolism that would allow me to absorb it.

With the freeing up of her will from its pathological binding within a belief system in which her striving for individuation would probably kill her engulfing mother and thus annihilate her self, she has been able to transcend the still-existing limits of her psyche and to change in a way that she herself characterizes as being "born again."

19

The "Real" Relationship and Analytic Neutrality

One unfortunate outcome of orthodoxy is that it both stifles discovery and stands in the way of professional honesty. By and large I believe we are afraid to expose our work with the kind of clinical material that may render us vulnerable to criticism or, even worse, to public analysis of our character. Do we not, in such an atmosphere, keep our most important clinical insights to ourselves?

WHAT IS THE "REAL" RELATIONSHIP?

Surely the concept of the "real" relationship, how we view it and how we see its role in the analytic process, is one that may well open us to the criticism of our colleagues. Greenson (1971) notes the view of the more "conservative" classical analysts that "all the patient's meaningful reactions to the person of the analyst are transference manifestations and the only important interventions are transference interpretations" (p. 425).

In this statement Greenson notes the contrast to those who see the total object relationship as relevant to the treatment process. I speak from this point of view and agree in part with Friedman (1984), who tells us that "the forces that determine the outcome of the treatment relationship are inevitably interpersonal" (p. 172). The cognitive changes that result from interpretation and understanding must also be part of the process, in my view.

Greenson (1967) describes two aspects of what is real in the real relationship. It may mean "realistic, reality oriented or undistorted as contrasted to the term 'transference,' which connotes unrealistic, distorted, and inappropriate. The word may also refer to genuine, authentic, and true in contrast to artificial, synthetic or assumed" (p. 169). The transference relationship may feel genuine, but it will not be realistic. On the other hand, the working alliance is realistic, but it may not feel genuine. Greenson uses the term "real relationship" in reference to that aspect which is both genuine *and* real. He sees the capacity to form a real relationship to the analyst as a prerequisite for analyzability. The empathic response will be experienced as genuine, although what it is in response *to* may not be realistic. Perhaps it is the genuineness of empathic mirroring that is most significant, inasmuch as it reinforces the patient's sense of genuineness. At some point, however, what is genuine must join with what is realistic if there is to be a capacity for a real relationship in or out of therapy.

Any behavior is a manifestation not only of motivation, conscious or unconscious, but of the conflict-free autonomous functions as well—of thought, of the synthetic function, and of language as communication. To think, to create, and to communicate are what the human animal does as part of its essential nature. The quality and style of the basic elements of social behavior in terms of autonomous ego functioning along with affective predispositions come out of a combination of innate temperamental predispositions and the personality as it evolves in the original social milieu. Although it is certainly true that our cognitive and affective styles may elicit a transference response from the patient, these are, nevertheless, ways in which we show our realness to him even when countertransference factors are least in operation. They are also ways in which the patient shows his realness to us, although his autonomous functions may be caught up in conflict and inhibited or distorted in their expression, and his affect is, in much larger part, determined by the past.

Patients often suffer from the consequences of having had parents react transferentially to their realness, with negative labels being assigned to their basic nature—to their innate temperamental predispositions, to their spontaneity, to their motility, to their sexuality, and to their will. We have to be careful not to do with interpretation what parents did with labeling—not to pathologize the patient's healthy and intrinsic nature, but to distinguish it from his pathology and to affirm its fundamental value. Rank (1945) wrote, "It is in the act of willing that the human creature becomes creator, both of himself and of those products of his efforts."

WHAT IS NEUTRALITY?

The other side of my title, "analytic neutrality," has been discussed a great deal in the recent literature as a manifestation of the struggle within psychoanalysis to allow for what is referred to as its wider scope without sacrificing certain wisdoms well established and validated in clinical practice.

Held-Weiss (1986) writes:

> For an analysis to have vitality, the innermost regions of the person must be explored. At best the analyst is open and receptive to the direct and profound person-to-person contact with the patient. This creates a history together, experienced as relevant engagement, and characterized by wholeness and complexity. Such encounters do not result from prearranged roles or institutionalized technically correct behaviors. [p. 3]

Where is the line between what Held-Weiss calls spontaneity in the analyst and the analyst's acting out of his own needs and desires? The therapist who values realness between himself and his patient is under greater pressure to monitor this potential danger. It is probably easier, at some level, to adhere to more rigid, classical rules, although at times it is self-deceiving to believe that counter-transference reactions will not become manifest, however subtly, and be perceived by the patient. Acknowledgment of the interpersonal process prevents the attribution of the patient's reaction entirely to what is contained within his psyche, the kind of interpretation that may be experienced by the patient as crazy-making.

Shapiro (1984), speaking from the orthodox point of view, believes that newer models of genetic reconstruction using data of the early preoedipal mother–child relationship have, "in some hands," diminished the insistence on the need for neutrality. He states that "the crucial aim of psychoanalysis remains the uncovering of the unconscious." He adds that, as he understands it, "that is the *sine qua non* of the Science. If it is not the aim of analysis, then neutrality is no longer necessary and we can dispense with it" (p. 280).

With this posture he evades the challenge of bringing wider aims, such as the repair of structural deficit, into harmony with useful analytic principles.

Poland (1984) defines true neutrality as originating "in genuine respect for the patient's individuality . . . [a] fundamental regard for the essential otherness of the patient, for the uniqueness of the patient's self in its own right" (pp. 285–286).

Wachtel (1986), discussing the limits of therapeutic neutrality, reminds us that "the stance of neutrality is designed to assure that we do not muddy the waters of transference." But he also speaks to the inevitability of our influencing the process even as we observe it. "We are always observing something in relation to us, and not just to us as screens or phantoms, but to us as specific flesh and blood human beings sitting in the consultation room" (p. 61).

Greenberg (1986) believes that neutrality is "a way of affirming our own commitment to exploration and self knowledge in contrast to other therapeutic aims" (p. 82). He provides us with a creative and clinically useful definition of neutrality that allows for its application in a manner specific and appropriate to the uniqueness of any given patient. He agrees with Schafer (1983) that there is an intimate connection between the analyst's neutrality and the patient's experience of safety, without which he would continue to "feel injured, betrayed, threatened, seduced, or otherwise interfered with or traumatized" (p. 32). In terms of a relational model of psychoanalysis (as contrasted to a drive model), Greenberg (1986) notes that "the atmosphere of safety would depend on the analyst's ability to create conditions in which the patient perceives him as a new object" (p. 95). However, he adds, if the situation is too safe, there is no room for transference and for confronting the threatening feelings that are part of an archaic relationship.

Greenberg (1986) arrives at a new definition of neutrality from the perspective of the relational model: "Neutrality embodies the goal of establishing an optimal tension between the patient's tendency to see the analyst as an old object and his capacity to experience him as a new one" (p. 97). His rationale for this definition is this:

> The patient can become aware that he is assimilating the analyst into his world of archaic internal objects only when he has already become aware that there is an alternative possibility. . . . If the analyst cannot be experienced as a new object, analysis never gets under way; if he cannot be experienced as an old one, it never ends. [p. 98]

Greenberg (1986) notes that "the activity of the neutral analyst is always dependent upon the quality of the patient's relationship with others. . . . Neutrality is thus not to be measured by the analyst's behaviors at any moment but by the particular patient's ability to become aware of and to tolerate his transference" (p. 97).

The idea of a continuum along which the patient moves and of our responding according to where he is on that continuum frees us from the constraints of predetermined theoretical positions. Bromberg (1983) refers to Sullivan's (1954) observations that the analyst must be responsive to where the patient is on a gradient of anxiety, trying to maintain it at an optimally minimal level—low enough so that the patient's defenses do not foreclose analytic inquiry, but high enough so that the defensive structure itself can be identified and explored. Bromberg writes of the maintenance of the optimal balance between empathy and anxiety as an approach to treatment that is independent of the analyst's personal metapsychology.

THE DELICATE BALANCE BETWEEN
REALNESS AND NEUTRALITY

Perhaps we can use the concept of the patient's place along a continuum to come to grips with the delicate balance between realness and neutrality. We might reformulate Freud's (1933) statement, "Where id is, there ego shall be," not in terms of making the unconscious conscious, but in terms of freeing interpersonal relationships as much as possible from the deleterious effects of transference.

How can the patient gradually move in this direction if we do not in some way respond to and thus reinforce his realness when he shows it to us? Obviously there may be transference elements embedded in his realness, in his genuine and realistic behaviors, but it is my opinion that we do no damage if we postpone its interpretation until a clearer context presents itself. I believe that we do indeed do harm if we interpret the transference at critical moments of attempted realness, which the patient then experiences as our pathologizing what he most values about his intrinsic and spontaneous nature. Of course, we must not collude with the kind of resistance to transference that takes the form of attempts to make the therapeutic relationship a social one. Schafer (1983) tells us that "there is always room in analytic work for courtesy, cordiality, gentleness, sincere empathic participation and comment, and other personal, although not socially intimate, modes of relationship" as well as a "respectful affirmative attitude" and an attitude of "appreciation."

How can we stand as a new object if we do not offer the alternative of a real relationship as a possibility to the patient whose relationship to us is predominantly shaped by transference?

Grunes (1984) articulates this stance, calling it the "therapeutic object relationship," which he distinguishes from the real relationship. He cites its relevance to problems of structural impairment, which, "combined with the depleted and archaic functioning of external and internal object relations, creates a relationship demand factor in treatment which cannot be met by interpretation alone" (p. 123). And he asks: "Could the analyst's developmentally informed input, as at least a semi-real figure, reverse serious structural distortions, or even develop parent-like forms of psychic provision which would ultimately fill in aspects of missing structure?" (p. 125).

He argues (Grunes 1984) for the legitimacy of such techniques as reassurance, self-revelation by the analyst, and suggestion, noting that this broader view of treatment differs from the parameter approach, "the critical difference being that the psychotherapeutic action does not necessarily have to be analyzed, since it is considered to be organically related to the analytic treatment in the first place" (p. 128).

Grunes (1984) views the therapeutic object relationship as "a situation of primal intimacy between patient and analyst which contains both an illusional (transference) and real aspect" (p. 131). He clarifies this concept by explaining that the "analyst and patient are not pausing for a detour into a *real relationship* and then getting back to the serious business of analytic treatment. They are ipso facto in a special illusional and real relationship which is part of the very process of analysis itself" (p. 136).

A single patient's analytic work had focused on her role as the container of parental projective identifications and the distortions of identity that ensued from this situation, on parental paradoxical injunctions and mystification, as well as on the oedipal issues inherent in her mother's standing as a barrier between the patient and her father. For the first time she came to feel that she might have a mind, body, and life of her own, and a man of her own. She came into treatment with me after several years of a Kleinian analysis, where interpretations were experienced as something being put into her just as were parental projective identifications. She had become more and more frightened by that analytic work. Reporting an upcoming weekend away with a man she had recently met, she experienced severe anxiety. This was explored and interpreted in terms of the family and oedipal dynamics as well as in terms of how they were manifest in the transference. With this work she felt much better and left telling me how much she looked forward to the weekend. On the way out I smiled and said, "Enjoy." Her eyes teared and she commented on how much that meant to her.

I am sure that some would view this as an error. In the strictest of terms it was indeed a departure from neutrality and could be viewed as my siding with the id. It could also be seen as encouraging a regressive and dependent stance of needing permission, and this, in her case, might have some validity. Grunes warns us of setting up an addictive relationship that may lead to an interminable therapy, and I agree with him fully. If these issues do exist, they will show themselves in other ways and will then be open to interpretation. On the other hand, if we think of the process of individuation as requiring parental mirroring and support in order to establish object constancy, the internalization of the good mother of rapprochement and the good oedipal mother as well, is it not possible that my blessing, so to speak, would contribute to the development of that object constancy as well as to what Schafer (1960) refers to as the loving superego? What can be the basis of such a development if not a loving relationship, or at least one that is experienced as such?

If we think of the therapist as a new object who will inevitably be internalized as part of both ego and superego, who we are and how we are with the patient will surely play as important a role in structural change as do our constructions and interpretations. Although the patient's wish to be like the therapist may be part of an idealizing transference, it is also the basis for new superego identifications.

Grunes speaks of the analyst as a semireal figure and of the combination of the illusory and the real.

Working with a 32-year-old successful businessman who had originally presented as a schizoid personality with a grandiose self-defensive structure, an emotional contact was finally made with the cut-off, anguished true self. It was only in this state of profound "sadness" that he felt real, and it was only through my empathic response to him in this particular affect state that a true connection could be experienced. Once these feelings emerged, my failure to respond quickly and appropriately to that level would lead to a malignant regression, first to a paranoid state, followed by further retreat to an autistic isolation that carried with it perceptual distortion in which he could no longer see me.

While in the regressed, but real, ego state of sadness, he would sob convulsively. At these times I would move next to him and pat his shoulder, speaking in a calm voice, and recalling how terrible it must have been to be such a tiny boy and to have his mother go away to work every day and leave him with someone who didn't talk to him or touch him or play with him. Had I been unwilling to allow the physical contact, I could not have reached him. I would have replicated the original trauma of the distant and unreachable caretaker, and clearly this would have been far from neutral from his perspective. Myerson (1981) reminds us of the distinction between need and desire. If we respond to desire, we gratify inappropriately. But if we do not respond to need, we traumatize the ego.

On one hand, I participated in an illusory relationship, inasmuch as he was not actually a little boy and I was not actually his mother. Yet, despite the illusion, at an affective level, the experience was genuine for him and for me as well. Creating an "as-if" situation in which at the nonverbal level I responded as if the relationship were a real one between mother and child, at the same time I made a genetic construction in a language appropriate to the patient's regressed state. These parallel responses, one genuine and the other realistic, enabled an integration of verbal and preverbal levels of experience, leading to gradually more enduring structural changes and to his relating in an increasingly differentiated manner without recourse to withdrawal or other distancing mechanisms.

To participate in this kind of illusory interaction, one must look to one's own potential regressive wishes and their gratification, especially those that join mother and child affectively. What Grunes calls the therapeutic object relationship entails a combination of empathic and cognitive understanding, with the first drawing us into the patient's affective world, and the second anchoring us in here and now reality. It is my experience that a willingness and freedom to be a semireal object in this manner for some patients makes the difference between a failure of treatment and a structure-building attachment.

A turning point came during such an interaction when a memory emerged, a detailed picture of himself as a tiny child, standing by the window and watching his mother drive away. At this point the overwhelming unstructured sadness that became his identity, who he was, the totality of his real being, became structured as grief for the lost mother. My participation as a real, albeit as-if, object enabled the emergence of memory and the structuralization of affect.

Subsequent to this development, an empathic error on my part threatened to evoke, once again, a regression to the paranoid state. However, the firming up of an internal good object enabled us to weather this situation. I acknowledged my insensitivity, but further commented on his detachment as a way to avoid the anger he felt toward me. This was the first time that interpretation was effective while he was in the regressed state. He was able to acknowledge the anger and struggled not to lose the positive connection. Here we can see the beginning of healing of the split and further structuralization of affect—in this case, anger.

The patient saw my willingness to "go after him" and to join him in the morass of sadness as critical to the establishment of the positive bond and the relinquishing of schizoid defenses. He commented that if he had to go back to that way of living, he would kill himself. The patient needed an object with whom to attach before he could make use of interpretation. The participation in the semireal relationship steers the more neutral path when a failure to do so destroys the patient's experience of safety.

In his discussion of illusion and narcissism, Mitchell (1986) notes that the analyst's participation in illusion is essential to the establishment of the narcissistic integration, while "the analyst's questioning is essential to its dissolution and the establishment of a richer form of relation" (p. 130). Whatever the degree of illusion in the therapeutic object relationship, its genuine quality should not be underestimated.

I cannot help but wonder if this same process does not take place much more subtly in the interpersonal situation of analyst vis-à-vis the more structurally evolved patient. To what degree does the realness experienced by both analyst and patient provide a context within which both ego and superego identifications inevitably take place? Indeed, I pose the question: Does this aspect of treatment constitute the context within which the interpretation of transference and resistance becomes effective? Does it not go beyond the therapeutic alliance, the "nonobjectionable transference"? How does who we are in the treatment situation cast its shadow on the final outcome of treatment just as powerfully as what we do?

CONCLUSION

An accurate structural diagnosis in terms of the inner representational world and its deficits and resources (Horner 1984) enables us to formulate treatment goals and to anticipate problems in the treatment process. The ability to conceptualize what is happening at any given moment in structural and dynamic terms, along with our empathic intuiting, informs us where we need to be on the empathy-anxiety gradient and what is needed from us to maintain an optimal tension between the patient's view of us as an old object and experience of us as a new one, along with an appropriate balance between the illusory and the real.

We need to incorporate into our clinical theory the structuralizing effects of our standing as a new object for the structurally impaired patient. The notion (Alexander and French 1946) of the corrective emotional experience is too vague, too nonspecific, to accrue any real respectability within psychoanalysis. Self psychology's view of the function of the analyst as a selfobject is equally incomplete and unsatisfactory in my view. Structural change within the treatment process must be documented with hard clinical data, not only theorized about in metapsychological terms. In order to do this we will have to expose our work in a less sanitized manner and take our chances with our analytic colleagues.

20

Object Relations and Transference Resistance

Transference resistance can be usefully defined as a way of managing the therapist and the therapy relationship so as to bring about a wished-for interaction and/or to prevent a feared one.

If we make a careful structural diagnosis and understand both the defensive and gratification functions of the transference resistance, we can make a measured decision with respect to its management, handling, and eventual interpretation.

The more central object relational issues (i.e., pathology of the character structure) are to the patient's problems, the more they will be expressed transferentially and the more they will stand as a source of significant resistance.

The concept of *acting out* in the transference, rather than *remembering*, is especially relevant to the treatment of the patient whose early object relations situation is still dominant in the inner representational world and is played out with the therapist.

227

The psychic dangers and the infantile wishes associated with this representational world will be experienced in treatment and will be either played out or defended against in the transference. To the extent that this acting out is not analyzed, it will constitute a major resistance to change. However, the timing of such interpretation is critical in the face of significant structural psychopathology.

Freud (1914b) reminds us that we must treat illness, "not as an event of the past, but as a present-day force" (p. 151). This is especially relevant to the treatment of the patient with structural pathology. It is the here and now of the treatment relationship and what it tells us of the patient's here and now character structure, of his still active early representational world, that is a major force in treatment. Interpretations that have a genetic focus are likely to bring an intellectual defense into action, or lead to a disillusioned "So what?" What is being experienced now in the transference is experienced as real. The capacity to maintain the observing ego and the working alliance in the face of the activation of this prototypical interpersonal situation is not to be counted on with such patients, especially in the earlier stages of treatment. Only while working in the here and now, on the structural as well as on dynamic issues that are manifest in the transference, can we expect that some connection with the past will probably take place. However, even here, the route to the past will have to be through the present, through the analysis of the individual's here-and-now way of relating with significant others as well as with the therapist. He must come to understand both the structural and dynamic importance of rigidly maintaining these patterns of interaction.

Freud (1912) tells us that in analysis there is a tendency toward the activation of unconscious fantasy and that this process is a regressive one and revives the subject's infantile imagos (p. 102). It is this regression and this reactivation that will at times confuse us with respect to the character diagnosis. Are these the emergent repressed imagos of a well-differentiated individual; or are they the imagos, the self and object representations, that are still central to the character organization and pathology of object relations that constitute, not memory, but experienced reality?

Freud also notes that when a person's need for love is not entirely satisfied by reality, he tends to approach every new person he meets with anticipatory ideas, and that these are directed toward the analyst. He comments that "this cathexis will have recourse to prototypes, will attach itself to one of the stereotype plates which are present in the subject" (1912, p. 100).

The analogy of stereotype plates lends itself well to the concept of self and object representations as structure, and the manner in which these representations are played out in the treatment situation. To the extent that the patient must cling to this stereotypical manner of relating for one reason or another, the transference will be a powerful source of resistance.

STRUCTURE AND TRANSFERENCE RESISTANCE

What are the organizational desiderata of a mature self representation? In my view they are cohesion, reality-relatedness, and object-relatedness.

The cohesive self is characterized by an adequate integration of affect, impulse, perception, and cognition; it is not subject to fragmentation or disorganization. Deficits of cohesion, in my view, characterize the borderline personality. In a more evolved character structure, under the impact of intrapsychic conflict, integrated feelings, wishes, or thoughts may become subject to repression. However, their reemergence into consciousness will result in guilt or anxiety and not in disorganization. The borderline's deficits in cohesion are the basis for the excessive dependency upon the object. The sense of connection with the object has an integrating effect; that is, the object serves as an intrapsychic prosthesis for a structurally vulnerable self. It is because of this excessive dependency that differentiation and object loss are traumatizing for the borderline patient; that is, they result in the dissolution of the self.

Because of severe separation anxiety and the potential panic that goes with loss, the borderline patient will have to protect his connection with the analyst. This situation can lead to a pervasive transference resistance that has, as its motive, the sense that survival depends upon maintaining the optimal status quo. Obviously, managing, handling, and interpreting this resistance will take tact, skill, patience, and much preparatory work.

A reality-related self not only has adequate reality testing, but also has a firm sense of a real self in contact with the external world, and particularly with the interpersonal environment. In the false self organization described by Winnicott (1965) there is a deficit in the reality-relatedness of the true self. The false self identity is consolidated around the child's *reactions to* the other, who may be either abandoning or impinging. The false self may also be consolidated around parental projections. The true self identity is consolidated around that which originates from within and to which the object responds empathically. Thus, the responding other is a bridge between the inner world of experience and the outer world of reality. A self representation that is cut off from reality-relatedness and is in autistic isolation is potentially a delusional self.

When the false self is brought into the therapeutic alliance, what appears to be a therapeutic process is, in fact, an acting out. To the extent that the therapist participates in the alliance with the false self, he is either consciously or unconsciously in collusion with the resistance. The positive transference may be at one and the same time both an aspect of the alliance and a manifestation of transference resistance. When the therapist is seduced into playing out the role of helper, rescuer, or encourager, for instance, he is probably participating in the acting out. The false self, in such instances, may be that which has been consolidated around the maternal projection of her inadequate self, allowing the mother to realize her idealized, perfect, mother-self in her interaction with her child. Later, as a patient, this child brings the inadequate self into the treatment relationship and often quite subtly manipulates the therapist into playing out the corresponding superadequate object role.

The object-related self is characterized by internalizations and identifications that, in optimum development, lead to libidinal object constancy, to a well-secured identity with the capacity to regulate one's narcissistic equilibrium from resources within the self, to the capacity for signal anxiety (Horner 1980), and, finally, to the structuring of the superego.

Failure of object-relatedness characterizes autism in the extreme, as well as schizoid detachment in which a pathological self and its corresponding pathological object are split off and repressed early in development. With pathological detachment there can be no achievement of object constancy and its desired correlates. Since the individual who uses these character defenses is thrown back into a state of excessive emotional reliance upon an essentially impoverished self, the pathological grandiose self takes on important defensive and compensatory functions.

Detachment and denial of the significance of the therapist as a person also constitute a transference resistance. When what is being defended against is the severe object relational pathology, the loss of a separate self, and the dangers of overwhelming negative affect, the management of the resistance is quite critical. I have written (1984) of resistance as an ally in the service of structuralization. Working directly on structural issues hopefully brings about a greater degree of ego strength, which then makes it possible to move toward the dangers that have been defended against with the detachment in the therapy relationship.

What happens to the early object representations? To the extent that they are essentially a composite constructed by the very young child out of preverbal experience and with immature cognitive abilities, they may bear only a slight resemblance to reality. We have to keep this in mind and not assume that we are being presented with a true picture of the real mothering person: it is the mother as perceived and personified by the very young child. In healthy development, the early, primitive object representations become subject to repression, but may be manifest later in dreams, fantasy, and regression with developmental or situational stress or in the analytic situation. They will be replaced in consciousness by the specific images of the specific mother and father, and by more closely reality-dominated perceptions and memories of others.

With the more evolved character, interpersonal issues and transference issues will spring largely from relationships with the real mother (the mother of reality), with a father who is clearly differentiated from the mother, with siblings who are differentiated from others, and so on.

When the object representation has not been fully differentiated from the self representation, it remains as part of the ego—as an unassimilated introject (Giovacchini 1979). It will later be projected in the interpersonal situation with a considerable distortion of reality. This, of course, will become evident in the transference. To the extent that self and other come together from the start of life in characteristic kinds of interaction, the early representations are derived from these interactions and bear the imprint of their characteristic quality. Later, we find that a particular self representation tends to be associated with a particular object representation, along with characteristic affect, impulse, and later ideational elaboration. To the extent that the patient has an emotional investment in a particular experience of self, he will need the other—the therapist—to be the embodiment of the corresponding object so as to enable that self to be realized. This situation will be one that stands as a formidable resistance. Interpretation made precipitously will be experienced as a danger to the loved self.

These transference reactions emerge rapidly at the start of treatment when there is significant pathology of object relations. With a more mature character structure, although the early situation is still present in the unconscious and manifest in dreams and fantasies, it is not likely to emerge in the transference until later in treatment (with the regression inherent in the analytic process), if at all.

In general, object relational issues—remembering that object relations refers to the structures we call the self and object representations—will be evident, and manifest in the transference, with patients who have failed to negotiate the early attachment process and the subsequent separation and individuation processes satisfactorily. The inner representational world will still be characterized by failures to organize certain affects and impulses within the self, by a lack of full differentiation of self from object, and by the failure to integrate disparate self and object images. The immature representational world will be externalized in the transference and will generate certain resistances that can be characterized as transference resistance. There may be massive defenses against the dangers to the survival of the valued self, to the identity that is the conscious experience of a positive self representation. The dangers are particularly those experienced in the affectively colored interpersonal situation.

THE THREAT TO THE SELF

The dangers facing the self in the interpersonal situation will be directly related to the specific nature of the developmental pathology. When affect or impulse have not been structured within the self representation, their activation will pose the ever-present threat of disorganization. In a more evolved character, where ego and superego structuralization has taken place, the threat may be to the sense of consonance and internal harmony of that structure—the structural and dynamic basis of neurotic conflict. Basch (1976) comments: "Emotions are subjectively experienced states and always related to a concept of self vis-à-vis some particular situation" (p. 768). When that situation is an interpersonal one, affect will be related to the self in interaction with the other.

We need to distinguish the traumatic state from signal anxiety. Krystal (1978) describes psychic trauma as the outcome of being confronted with overwhelming affect: that is, the ego is overwhelmed. With signal anxiety, adequate defenses can be mobilized and trauma prevented.

Khan (1963) attributes what he calls cumulative trauma to the failure of the mother to function adequately as a protective shield for the child. This may be due to lack of empathy, or it may be due to illness and pain in the child that she is powerless to alleviate. The child is then subjected to repeated traumatic states that interrupt and interfere with the budding organization of the ego and the synthesizing of a cohesive self representation.

Krystal notes that in adult life, the fear of affect may represent a dread of the return to the infantile type of trauma. There is not only a dread of the return to the traumatic state; there is an *expectation* that it will occur (p. 98). Winnicott (1974) views the fear of breakdown in a similar way. The fear of death may represent the fear of nonbeing that is experienced when this breakdown occurs.

How does this relate to transference and resistance? When fear and rage carry the threat to disorganize the self and lead to a state of psychic death, they will have to be warded off in the interpersonal situation, and particularly vis-à-vis the therapist. This may be carried out by an assiduous clinging to a positive attitude, along with detachment when that attitude cannot be maintained. As always, we must deal with the danger behind the defenses before the defenses can be relinquished. Inexperienced therapists will often push for the anger in a confrontational manner. The outcome too often is an overriding of the ego and an emergence of the traumatic state once again. The indiscriminate "going for affect" before the structural deficits are tended to is the basis for many unfavorable reactions to treatment.

When differentiation of self from object is not secure, the danger to the boundaries of the self will be experienced in the transference. Whatever the therapist says or does may have to be rejected to safeguard those boundaries.

Case Example

A 28-year-old married professional woman, with predominant schizoid defenses and complaints of severe death anxiety, was experiencing disgust and revulsion associated with her sexual response to a seductive colleague. As her therapist attempted to explore further, she said she did not want to tell her thoughts. She was certain the therapist wanted her to think something in a particular way. "I don't want to say anything to make you think you're right." She accused the therapist of having some preconceived notion, and felt she had to carve room for herself either with silence and withholding, or by not letting herself have the feelings or thoughts she believed the therapist was demanding.

The revulsion was experienced not only in a sexual context, but in a cognitive one as well, and was a reaction to felt impingement and demand for sameness. There was generally a wish element in all these situations that the patient described, and they were experienced primarily with her mother, father, brother, and the therapist, who was a woman. The wish for oneness, sexual or nonsexual, led to the same annihilation anxiety. Revulsion—a reaction formation—defended against the danger of sexual attraction and physical annihilation, while silence defended against the danger of cognitive annihilation.

Referring to her "crush" on her colleague, she said, "When he reacts as though we think the same it drives me nuts!"

Although the interpersonal and intrapsychic dangers of the oedipal situation were clearly operative, the more fundamental danger to the boundaries of the tenuously differentiated self was the major determinant of her resistance in the transference. It was manifest in the transference, and in her need to maintain her sense of differentiation vis-à-vis the therapist through silence and withholding.

It is in this kind of clinical material that we can see so clearly how object relational issues are central, and how sexual and aggressive impulses are experienced, expressed, or defended against in a manner that is determined by the structural, object relational situation. In this instance, the patient's oedipal strivings threatened her psychic survival, and this danger played a major role in her retreat from them. She could not understand her pull to her mother, but when we see the importance of the mother as the external and primary internal organizing object, this begins to make sense. With differentiation comes a further danger, that of the rapprochement crisis. At this point in a child's development, at about 18 months of age, the illusion of infantile omnipotence is lost and the self is experienced as weak, dependent and helpless, and generally devalued vis-à-vis the now-idealized object. The shared omnipotence of the symbiotic period now clearly belongs to the other. With this awareness of psychic as well as physical separateness that is central to the rapprochement crisis comes the emotional dangers of anxiety and shame.

This patient continued to struggle with the conflict between her wishes for closeness and her drive toward individuation. The wish for closeness carried the danger of the annihilation of the separate self. The wish for individuation carried the danger of object loss. She continued to express her discomfort about discussing her feelings with her therapist. If Dr. M. did not mirror her—that is, if she defined herself as separate from the patient—the patient felt stupid and dismissed; that is, she once again felt the shame and anxiety of the rapprochement crisis with its painful confrontation of the realities of separateness. "But it's no good if we *are* the same!" she emphasizes. Withholding and silence were her reactions to this danger. She said she no longer brought up her crushes, which were associated with the revulsion, because she felt her therapist was not interested in hearing about them. A denial of sameness—that is, that they are *both* interested—protects separateness and further embellishes the rationale for acting out the transference resistance by withholding.

At the same time, she noted the fear of nothingness, and the ever-present underlying panic continued to haunt her. Object loss carried the threat of the dissolution of the self, of a terrifying level of nonbeing. Structurally, the failure to develop a cohesive self representation made her intrapsychically dependent upon the internalized object, which was still part of the undifferentiated self. The internalized object served as a psychic prosthesis for the tenuously organized self. The crush, for her, was a manifestation of the sexualized wish for the idealized other. It was experienced in her oedipal strivings for her father, but the interpersonal dangers vis-à-vis an angry mother were there, made even more lethal because of the object relational situation. The anxiety then led to further retreat and regression.

In her work with this woman, Dr. M. became caught up in the issues of power and control, a focus that did not go anywhere. In general, it is my view that the pathology of structure (the object relational issues) must be tended to before the dynamic interpretations can take hold. As long as there is a structural danger inherent in the therapy relationship, the interpretive work must be focused here.

Elsewhere (Horner 1984) I have reported on my work with another patient with similar object relational pathology. Her detachment was understood and interpreted as a way to maintain her sense of separateness and her psychic survival. She spoke of her detachment in her relationship with her boyfriend as follows: "With Carl it's a wall that he would come up against and would have to acknowledge. It would force him to do something. It would make him aware of me." The relevance of the wall to the transference came up when we talked about her need to screen out any reaction to me. I suggested, "Perhaps you want a wall for me to come up against." She replied, "I guess there's that and also the sense that having a more personal involvement would mean opening up and the more precious elements would run out." She continued as she began to cry, "I'm not sure there would be anything left when I wanted to close."

Over time there was an ongoing focus on the structure of the self representation—on issues of boundaries, integration of various aspects of herself, and on the defenses that protected her from the dangers to her psychic survival. During this time I accepted the defense as necessary, essentially, and at no time did I push for affect or for fantasies relating to me. I understood that such insistence would be experienced as a gross violation of her boundaries and would lead to overwhelming anxiety. During her 136th session— now experiencing the solidity of a more cohesive and integrated self—she commented: "What I don't understand is that you haven't existed very long, and all I've read about transference." She became aware of my existence as a separate person for the first time. We were able to explore why she had needed to deny this up to that point. (See pp. 186–188.) With the structuralization that took place in this context, she was now able to let herself experience me as a person, and to deal with transference issues at this more evolved level.

Giovacchini (1972) reminds us that analysis of resistance is not the same as overcoming resistance (p. 291). The analysis of resistance must not become an exhortative struggle to make the patient give up something in the interest of analysis. This is especially so when the transference resistance lays bare the object relations pathology. Under these conditions our interventions should be aimed *first* at correcting these deficits of psychic organization. Our interpretation of resistance should enhance structuralization—should say to the patient in effect, "I fully understand and appreciate the necessity of making me not be—that right now your sense of survival as a self is what is most important." With this attitude on the part of the therapist, the basic trust that is built will eventually enable the frightened patient to move closer to relationship issues.

THE FALSE SELF AND RESISTANCE

Thus far I have described how problems of cohesion and of object relatedness are manifest in the transference resistance. The third desideratum of the self representation—reality-relatedness— becomes an issue when there is a false self identity and false self representation that is brought into the treatment relationship. Winnicott (1965), in his analysis of this kind of problem, became aware of a disturbance in identity that he referred to as the false self. With such patients, the working alliance may be with the false self and, as a result, the work of therapy is not experienced as real and cannot be integrated or sustained. The mobilization of the real self is crucial to the effectiveness of treatment.

Through her empathic responses to the child, the mother becomes a bridge to reality. She is the link between the child's inner world of experience and the outer world. When she fails in this capacity, and instead is experienced by the child as an impingement, the child's inner representational world, and thus his identity, becomes consolidated around *reactions to* the other. The real self remains cut off from external reality, and a split-off, emotionally isolated, sometimes autistic self may exist alongside the false self through which the individual relates to others. When the patient relates to the analyst through the false self, the transference resistance permeates all that goes on in the treatment situation.

Case Example

A therapist in training was working with a 30-year-old woman who seriously abused drugs, often endangering her life. There were frequent hospitalizations. It was clear that she related to the therapist as "good patient" and that this identity constituted a major transference resistance. For her own reasons, the therapist was not able to follow through on her supervisor's recommendation that the false self alliance should be a focus of work. Instead, she simply attempted to handle the resistance by reassuring the patient that she could say whatever was on her mind or in her feelings. This reassurance led the patient to feel that she was not being a good-enough patient. In one session she had reported that she was unable to go to her daughter's father for money anymore because he had developed a sexual problem, and she could not be of any use to him anymore. The therapist was advised to explore the implications for treatment. Did she miss appointments when she thought she had failed to meet the therapist's needs, whatever she imagined them to be?

One day the patient reported the following dream:

It was about my stepfather, mother, and sisters. I'm living with them. They want me to stay in. I went out against their wishes. My stepfather brought me home and beat me. My mother beat me. Everyone said how much she loved me and wanted to help me and I didn't respond. Then my mother said she would stop beating me and let me be, let me do what I wanted. But my stepfather said I can't because I blew his image of himself. I hurt his ego.

Then she commented that her stepfather never beat her. She was angry in the dream. She couldn't understand how they could say they loved her. Her sisters were angry at her for hurting her mother. She was angry at the mother for not meeting her needs and was punished because she did not meet her mother's needs.

In supervision there was a discussion of how the patient attempted to meet her therapist's narcissistic needs, how when she was a "bad patient" she blew the therapist's image of herself. At the same time, her own needs were suppressed, leading to frustration and anger. This activated the image of the bad self representation which was tied to the image of the bad object. She defended against the bad self image with projection, and then reported that she was afraid to go outside.

The following week the therapist was ill and canceled, and the patient called back saying she was suicidal and had gotten high on drugs. The therapist interpreted that she tried to cover up her negative feelings with pills or thoughts of suicide and that she needed to explore these feelings. The patient then said contritely, "I really try in therapy. I really do the best I can." She said she felt like a failure.

In treatment this patient played out the immature object relational situation. She desperately clung, like an insecure rapprochement child who is afraid that if she does not meet the needs of the important other she will be abandoned. The way to maintain the attachment with the good object is to meet the narcissistic needs of the object. But then there is an annihilation of the real self. Furthermore, the sacrifice does not pay off, and she is enraged. Then she feels that she is bad, and when this is projected she becomes fearful. There is a *wish* to have the total love and devotion of the important other. There is a *belief* that the way to get this is to meet the needs of the other. The *reality* is that no matter how hard she tries, the other is still separate and has a life apart from her. The *consequences* are that she is angry and bad and feels she has failed and that she is inadequate. The use of drugs is both a rebellion and, in a roundabout way, a self-affirming (albeit self-destructive) act. At the same time, the drugs wipe out the threatening rage. The problems that the therapist now has to manage in the treatment of the patient concern the aftermath of the failure of the fantasy, which she tries to play out in the treatment situation.

As long as the core transference and character resistance are not interpreted, everything the therapist says is taken in by the false good self, and is experienced as something else she has to try to do right if she is not to be abandoned.

THE NEED FOR PERFECTION

A positive transference is essential to the therapeutic alliance. However, this becomes a contaminated alliance when the positive transference is also a source of resistance. This will be the case when the fantasy of a special relationship with the therapist is maintained, often secretly. In the following clinical example, the transference resistance—the wish to be the "preferred child"—was latent through most of treatment, whereas the need to maintain the image of the perfect self was most conscious.

Case Example

The patient was a 30-year-old professional woman whose presenting problem related to marital dissatisfaction, and who was clearly developing acute anorexia nervosa at the time. She was troubled by a pervasive detachment and "deadness" that had also developed. She was concerned that all she really wanted to do was sit around and eat bonbons—what came to be understood as a metaphor for her passive dependent yearnings. She was the oldest of five children; her sister was born when she was 18 months old—the height of the rapprochement crisis. She recalled that as a small child she had experienced severe anxiety relating to fantasies of anything or any person—be it a green pea or one of her dolls—being lost and alone.

Her major character defense rested on her identification with her idealized intellectual father, with a corresponding devaluation of her "bumbling" mother. The father was not only the object of oedipal strivings, but, more important, was the recipient of the displaced feelings and wishes for the pre-oedipal idealized omnipotent early object. A moral perfectionism, Calvinistic and stoic, was the fabric of this identification, and its heir was an idealized perfect self. This was not the ego ideal of a mature superego, but an ego *identity*, the self representation of the prematurely individuated and intellectually precocious child as it came to be further elaborated in her identification with her father.

A major resistance throughout treatment was the protection of this image of the self inasmuch as any deviation from it threatened the sense of self. At the height of the anorexia, the number of the scale that indicated her weight also became a statement of her identity.

Therapy focused primarily on the identity issue, although oedipal and sibling rivalry dynamics were also dealt with. The transference resistance (the need to have me see her as she wanted to see herself) came more into focus and discussion in the termination phase of treatment. Just prior to my summer vacation, and after a termination date four months hence had been set, she brought in a long and complex dream. One aspect related to the sibling rivalry issues vis-à-vis the therapist and her other patients. Another related to abandonment rage. A dream about an invisible thing that ate people and made pasta from their blood was readily understood as related to cannibalistic castration fantasies with respect to her envied baby brother, oral sex, and her loathing of anything "icky." Other imagery related to the female genitalia and fantasies of castration. What is notable is how this difficult, repressed material could emerge and be reported at the same time as the transference resistance was being dissolved after long and diligent interpretation.

After she reported the dream and her associations to it, I wondered about her competitiveness with my other patients. She thought she was competing for who could be the most interesting—not pathetic or needing help, but "struggling nobly and not whiny." Here we see the rejection of the passive–dependent yearnings and the idealized self representation that was the product of the defensive, schizoid, grandiose self as elaborated by her identification with her father.

I inquired about the boarded-up school in her dream and its relation to my vacation. "This is like a school. You go to learn and to be judged on your performance. Then you graduate." She noted that in her dream, when she came back to the boarded-up school, she had to make it habitable. I commented on her fear that it wouldn't be the same, and she acknowledged that now I wouldn't be worried about her because she would be a "short-termer."

Therapist: Now you'll be displaced by the other patients—by all the brothers and sisters.
  Patient: By *Donna*! (The next younger sibling.)
Therapist: So now there's the danger of the horrible thing.

> **Patient:** Me in my coat (referring to the dream).
> **Therapist:** An *aspect* of you.
> **Patient:** The angry dangerous one that would hurt my sister.

At this point the cannibalistic associations and fantasies, going back to witches in fairy tales, emerged, as well as their relation to sexual and eating inhibitions.

In this session she commented that she was, in fact, the only one in the competitive race, and that what was important was that she persevered and finished. Then she noted, "I'm not detached today, and I can talk about this and not feel it's so farfetched. And I'm not bothered because I'm not so unusual and I'm not so terribly evil."

I noted that as she experienced therapy less as a competition for my love, she could bring out these things without fear that they might alienate me. She agreed that they could alienate but thought I was used to "stuff like this." Then she dealt further with the persisting wish to be at least near the top of the list when it came to my feelings for my patients. It was especially important now that I knew all these secret and real things about her.

So as the defenses of perfection yielded to the therapeutic efforts, the underlying transference resistance emerged into consciousness in the form of a wish. As it was interpreted and was in the process of being dissolved, repressed unconscious material related to the symptomatology was able to come into consciousness and be reported.

The specific object relational issue here was the defense against remembering and reexperiencing the rage and object loss that was evoked by the birth of the sister when the patient was 18 months old. The defensive character structure that came into play was that of the pathological grandiose self. The need for both physical and moral perfection were aspects of this defense. The perfect body that needed nothing from the outside—the wish and fantasy associated with the anorexia—was a further elaboration of this defense. The anorexia had abated by the time we moved into the termination phase of treatment. As we began to talk about ending, she reported buying two cookbooks. The compulsive purchase of cookbooks is part of the anorexia syndrome. The regressive and defensive nature of this behavior and its relevance to ending was interpreted, and she was able to accept the interpretation.

TIMING OF INTERPRETATION OF RESISTANCE

It is my feeling that when the patient is unable to experience the transference without losing the observing ego or without destroying the therapeutic alliance, the defenses manifest in the transference resistance should be left alone until later on when working around these specific defenses has achieved adequate structuralization.

In the face of object relational pathology, the management, handling, and interpretation of the transference resistance will be the key to treatment. Its timing, tone, and precision are exquisitely important. With a basic understanding of and concern for the structural issues, one can make these clinical decisions in a more appropriate and correct manner, and therefore with a higher level of expected outcome.

21

The Oedipus Complex

Short-term therapy does not permit the luxury of an exploratory, wait-and-see attitude. It demands a plan of action based on clear-cut formulations leading to specific goals. Psychoanalytic theory has been built on the data of observation and clinical experience. Short-term treatment reverses this process and entails a vigorous application of theory to the clinical situation. The selection of patients on the basis of the applicability of this theory is critical to the treatment process. The theory is the basis for our psychodynamic formulations, for the definition of our goals, and for our treatment strategies.

The approach to short-term treatment discussed here follows the work of Sifneos (1979), with its concentration on the Oedipus complex as it is manifest in the patient's developmental history, in her current life situation, and in the transference. The therapist's concentration and focus on oedipal issues rapidly heats up the treatment situation, generating anxiety and oedipal transference on the part of the patient and, at times, countertransference reactions and anxiety on the part of the therapist. The interventions that bring this about are derived from the therapist's understanding of the nature of the Oedipus complex and its resolution—or "dissolution," according to Freud (1924).

As in long-term therapy, we have with the short-term approach the four phases of (1) uncovering, (2) working through, (3) resolution, and (4) termination. The steps necessary for the resolution of the Oedipus complex have been "operationalized" for purposes of evaluating progress as well as to indicate what must yet be dealt with in treatment. A summary of these steps is provided in Table 21-1. The steps are based on existing theoretical formulations, as well as on clinical experience.

UNCOVERING

The work of the uncovering phase of treatment will bring into awareness the wishes and fantasies of the oedipal period—the wish to either have sexually the parent of the opposite sex or to be the preferred object by that parent. Although some patients may never acknowledge the sexual component of the wish, they can acknowledge the competitive wish to be special. They may also be aware of the specialness inherent in the sexual relationship and be angry that they were unable to compete because of the incest taboo. Along with the wish to be preferred by the parent of the opposite sex is the wish to defeat the rival, the parent of the same sex. In cases of extreme ambivalence, this competitive wish may have murderous overtones.

Associated fears that accompany the oedipal strivings need to be understood in terms of their role in the establishment of certain defenses against these strivings, whether they be neurotic and symptomatic or characterological. The fear may be of the loss of control of the intensely experienced impulses, a fear that will be exacerbated by uncertainty as to the reliability of the controls of the opposite-sex parent. Fear of punishment or retaliation by the same-sex parent depends on the quality of that relationship as well as on the fantasy fears of the child. Punishment by either parent may be withdrawal of love, or there may be castration anxiety as

Table 21-1
Steps Necessary to Resolving the Oedipus Complex

Steps	Opposite-Sex Parent	Same-Sex Parent
1. *Uncovering*		
Acknowledge wish, fantasy, or desire	To have sexually and/or to be the preferred object	To defeat in competition and to displace, to murder
Understand fear associated with the wish	Loss of control	Punishment (e.g., castration or withdrawal of love), guilt
Understand negative affect associated with frustration	Anger, feelings of betrayal, sense of failure or inadequacy, sadness, yearning	Humiliation, envy
2. *Working Through*		
Insight into how conflicts are played out (a) in present-day life (b) in the transference	Interference with heterosexual relationships	Interference with achievement of goals and ambitions
3. *Resolution*		
Renunciation of the wish	To have sexually and/or to be the preferred object	To defeat in competition and to displace
Acceptance of parents as real people	Without the need to idealize or disparage	Without the need to idealize or disparage
Acknowledgment of identifications	With opposite-sex parent without endangerment of gender identity and/or the ego ideal	With same-sex parent without endangerment of the ego ideal
Neutralization of drive	Desexualization of affection toward parent of opposite sex	Deaggressivization of strivings for success and achievement
Redirection of strivings	To new love object. Reunion of sex and affection without guilt or anxiety	Toward ambitions. Strivings for success and achievement without guilt or anxiety
4. *Termination*		
Therapist perceived in realistic terms as adult equal	Patient withdraws emotional investment in treatment and redirects it toward his real life	Patient actively takes over full responsibility for own life

well. Fear of punishment of the superego—that is, guilt—also motivates defenses against the oedipal strivings.

Along with impulse and fantasy, the oedipal child (and later
the oedipal patient) has to deal with feelings that are associated
with the inevitable frustration of infantile wishes. Feelings associated with the opposite-sex parent are anger, feelings of betrayal,
and a sense of failure or inadequacy, as well as sadness and yearning. Feelings evoked by the rival are those of envy or humiliation—
or both.

WORKING THROUGH

With the uncovering of the several facets of the conflict itself, the
patient develops insight into the manner in which these conflicts are played out both in everyday life and in the transference.
They can be seen to interfere with the establishment of satisfying
heterosexual relationships and with the achievement of goals and
ambitions, as competitiveness must be inhibited and defended
against.

With these insights there has to be a renunciation of the
infantile strivings along with an acceptance of the parents as real
people. This means letting go of the idealization and disparagement
of either or both parents that were part of the fantasies and the
defenses against them.

Recall Freud's (1923) observation that as the object cathexes
of parental objects are relinquished, they are replaced by identifications, both as part of the ego and as the nucleus of the superego.
The acknowledgment and acceptance of these identifications are
essential to the resolution of the Oedipus complex. Identification
with the opposite-sex parent will no longer jeopardize gender identity, and identification with either parent will be freed from con-
tamination by negative perception of the parent, rendering those
identifications no longer a danger to the ego ideal.

The concept of penis envy is anathema to feminists of all ages
and is ego-alien to women with a strong feminine identification
who are in conflict over identifying with the father and resist doing
so. Instead, they cling to the wish to have him as the libidinal

object. Yet moving past that point in analysis of the eroticization of father's power, to the recognition that the woman holds her husband responsible for providing her the power and prestige she previously felt vicariously through her attachment to her father, we must address the issue of the envy of that power and prestige and the competitive wish to have one's own. Clinically we may see that the competitive issues are evident between the girl and her father and between the woman and her husband and her boss. Clinging to the wish to be special by being nice and helpful, she passively and defensively continues to derive that power vicariously, envying it, enraged when it is not forthcoming, but still disclaiming the wish for her own. Returning to the issue within the family, where her father was both adored and seen as weak in the power balance with a domineering mother, one patient was able to see that she still idealized her father's maleness. The concept of maleness is less likely to be rejected as a source of envy than the concrete symbol of the penis.

> **Patient:** I want the status, but I don't want to work to earn it. But I don't want it given to me when I don't earn it.
>
> **Therapist:** The man just *is* powerful. You have to *do something* to be powerful. But then you would be more like a man.
>
> **Patient:** Right. Should we talk about my father?
>
> **Therapist:** Does something come to mind?
>
> **Patient:** I always get the same picture of that incident when I was on my knees at his feet reading and he uncrossed his legs and accidentally kicked me. He didn't know I was there. I made a big fuss and cried. He was surprised. I cried, but I think I enjoyed having that lump on my lip, like my medical emergency. That was really being special. There was pleasure in it. It was the most exciting thing that ever happened to me.
>
> **Therapist:** Like the lump on your lip. What did that mean interpersonally, with you and your father?
>
> **Patient:** I wanted to show he did something bad, maybe to

prove he was a bad person. Maybe to break away
from the feeling that he was wonderful.

Therapist: Why did you need to do that?

Patient: I didn't want to think it. It was babyish. Or I was
ashamed of how I felt about him. It was a weapon
he had. If I cared about his feeling for me, he
could control me. I looked for a reason not to
care.

Therapist: You envied what you admired and needed to bring
it down.

Patient: I could see it in relation to his being male, the
envy. I tried to show him as being less. That
makes a lot of sense that a little girl in *my* house
would want to be male. Though I'm glad to be a
woman. It's easier. The trying and exerting part of
being male is what I don't want. I don't want to be
a man, but wish to have that—the aggressiveness.
I think I'm developing it more. But the conflict is
deep and severe and mysterious.

Eventually, the woman must be able to own her identifications
with the admired father without feeling her gender identity compromised if she is to be able to give up the father equivalent as the
object of her infantile libidinal strivings. It is not the penis she
wants but the power and status attributed to her father's maleness,
which she must assimilate into her femaleness by identifying with it
in an ego-syntonic way.

RESOLUTION

Resolution of the Oedipus complex entails neutralization of drive,
the desexualization of affection toward the parent of the opposite
sex, and the deaggressivization of strivings for success and achievement. Concomitantly, there will be a redirection of those strivings
away from the early objects toward a new love object, with the
reunion of sex and affection without guilt or anxiety; as well as
toward the ambitions, also without guilt or anxiety.

TERMINATION

With termination and resolution of the transference, the therapist will be experienced in realistic terms, as an adult equal. There should be a concomitant withdrawal of the emotional investment in treatment, with a redirection of emotional energy toward real life. At the same time, the patient now actively takes full responsibility for her life. This step forward may generate its own guilt insofar as it constitutes what Loewald (1979) calls a kind of parricide, an overthrow of the authority of the parents.

Although these steps are presented in a specific order, in practice our patients do not always obey our formulations so closely. Nevertheless, if the overall schema is well understood by the therapist, he will be able to move freely with the patient with respect to which of the issues is in the forefront and still maintain the focus on the oedipal issues throughout treatment.

Presented in this chapter is an expanded theoretical formulation of the oedipal situation as it dovetails with the final stage of the separation–individuation process (Mahler et al. 1975). A clear understanding of the latter is essential if the therapist is not to be lured back into preoedipal issues, a strategic error of the first magnitude in oedipally focused, short-term treatment.

IDENTIFICATION AND STRUCTURALIZATION OF THE EGO AND SUPEREGO

Identification is the process common to the completion of the separation–individuation process and to the resolution of the Oedipus complex. Freud (1923) wrote that with the dissolution of the Oedipus complex there will be both a mother identification and a father identification. The identification with the father both replaces the object relation with him and preserves the object relation with the mother, whereas the identification with the mother replaces the object relation with her and preserves that with the father.

But Freud (1921) notes that there is an earlier identification with the parent of the same sex that sets the stage for the Oedipus complex. The little boy wants to be like his father, who he takes as his ideal. This is typical of little boys. The object cathexis of the early mother and this identification with the masculine father exist side by side for a time with no mutual influence or interference. The normal Oedipus complex, Freud notes, originates from their confluence. When the little boy becomes aware that his father stands between him and his mother, the identification takes on a hostile coloring and becomes identical with the wish to replace the father. Just as identification may be an expression of tenderness, so can it readily turn into a competitive wish for the removal of the other. That is, the identification may stand as a substitute for the actual love relationship, or it may make the relationship unnecessary, rendering the other a rival.

Freud (1923) anticipated modern object relational thinking when he wrote that the character of the ego is a precipitate of abandoned object cathexes and that it contains the history of those past choices. He noted, "It may be that this identification is the sole condition under which the id can give up its object" (p. 29).

Identification as a process leading to a change in the structure of the ego must be distinguished from the kind of gross identification that serves as an ego defense against object loss or other dangers to the ego. The internalizations that allow one to *give up* the object are not the same as the identifications that *defend against* the anxiety and depression of loss. An example of the latter would be the identification with a depressed or suffering mother. I have seen patients who reacted to the death of a mother during their late childhood or adolescent years by taking on, in toto, the personality of the mother as they viewed it. Defensive identification does not lead to a structural change in the self representation. Developmental identifications do.

In his discussion of the relationship between identification and individuation, Schecter (1968) defines the process of identification as "*the means by which part of the psychic structure of one person tends to become like that of another to whom he is emotionally related in a significant way*" (p. 50). He elaborates further, saying that identification can also be conceived as a "*relatively enduring modification of the self in the direction of similarity to the object as it is perceived and 'personified' by the ego.*"

Schecter (1968) also distinguishes the conscious wish to become like another person, as happens in the formation of one's ideals, from the actual tendency to become like another—that is, from the basic developmental processes leading to structural likeness. He also distinguishes both of these from "pseudoidentification," which involves an attempt to reconstruct an internalized object with which the self may then fuse. "The severely disturbed, often psychotic patient attempts to cling to the internal object, to fuse with it, to 'become' it, or to destroy it" (p. 74). In the evaluation of the patient in either long- or short-term treatment, we must be able to differentiate normal, developmental identification from defensive or "pseudoidentification."

He concludes (Schecter 1968) that identification grows out of primarily active and relatively conflict-free individuating processes and that it contributes to the ego structure or strength that is necessary for the gradual relinquishing of the more primitive object ties; that is, "Identification and the partial loosening of primitive object attachments may be simultaneous and part and parcel of the same individuation process" (p. 64).

Freud saw the identifications that mark the dissolution of the Oedipus complex as forming a precipitate in the ego that consists of the two identifications (with mother and father) as in some way united with each other. This modification of the ego, he says, then "confronts the other contents of the ego as an ego-ideal or superego."

IDENTIFICATION AND OBJECT CONSTANCY

The end of the separation–individuation process (Mahler et al. 1975) is marked by a fully established sense of a separate identity and object constancy. Object constancy is the outcome of a series of internalizations of parental, and particularly maternal, functions and modalities (Giovacchini 1979, Tolpin 1971). From an object relational viewpoint, failures of identification result in an ego insufficiency that constitutes the port of entry to preoedipal symptoms in a regressive fashion. This insufficiency—the incomplete securing of object constancy—is the basis for an ongoing dependency vis-à-vis the object, for the lack of full intrapsychic autonomy that generates fears of abandonment, separation anxiety, and depression (Horner 1979, 1984).

Burgner and Edgcumbe (1972) understand the concept of object constancy as "the individual's capacity to differentiate between objects and to maintain a relationship to one specific object regardless of whether needs are being satisfied or not" (p. 315). It is the "capacity to recognize and tolerate loving and hostile feelings toward the same object; the capacity to keep feelings centered on a specific object; and the capacity to value an object for attributes other than its functions of satisfying needs" (p. 328).

Eventually this must entail the ability to see parents as they really are without a dependent idealization or a defensive disparagement. This constitutes one of the steps in the resolution of the Oedipus complex.

Mahler describes object constancy in terms of the internal good object, the maternal image that is psychically available to the child just as the actual mother was previously available for sustenance, comfort, and love. Mahler and co-authors comment that object constancy seems to come about during the third year and that with this achievement the mother can be substituted for, in part, by the now-reliable internal image. The security that comes with this step toward intrapsychic autonomy makes it possible for the child to sustain the anxieties of the oedipal conflict and thus to maintain the forward thrust of development.

And so the end of the separation–individuation process is marked by the assimilation of maternal functions into the self even as the object is separated out as fully differentiated from the self. This involves not only the assimilation of nurturant and executive modalities, but also of maternal anxiety-reducing interactions that lead to the development of signal anxiety (Horner 1980). The assimilation of the imperatives that leads to the structuring of the superego (Schecter 1979) is an integral aspect of the resolution of the Oedipus complex.

The assimilation of the functions and qualities of the object into the self representation at this point of development—that is, the process of identification—is thus a sine qua non for the achievement of intrapsychic autonomy and for increasing autonomy vis-à-vis the object relationships of the oedipal period.

With the failure to make the identifications that mark the close of the separation–individuation process, we can anticipate that there will be prominent oedipal issues, since the same identificatory process is essential to its resolution, and since the lack of emotional autonomy will aggravate the anxieties associated with oedipal strivings. Anything that interferes with the identification process will prevent the ultimate resolution of both separation–individuation and the Oedipus complex.

As long as the significant attributes of the object belong to the object rather than to the self, the self will remain dependent on the external object for the provision of these attributes and what they contribute to the security and self-esteem of the individual. Clinically, these patients present with a picture of exaggerated dependency and depression in the context of a relatively well-differentiated and structured ego. These dependencies are often played out in current adult-life relationships, and there is often a clear oedipal cast to them as well. A defensive refusal to identify—as described on pp. 56–59—protects gender identity in males and the ego-ideal in females. These refusals to identify interfere with the establishment of object constancy. (See also pp. 62–65 for more on this subject.)

THE "COMPLETE" OEDIPUS COMPLEX

Freud (1923) distinguished what he calls the simple, positive Oedipus complex in a boy—an ambivalent attitude to the father and object relation of a solely affectionate kind to his mother—from the complete Oedipus complex in which there is also an ambivalent attitude to the mother and an affectionate object choice toward the father. The same dual strivings would be true of the little girl. Freud writes:

> In my opinion it is advisable in general . . . to assume the existence of the complete Oedipus complex. . . . At the dissolu-

tion of the Oedipus complex the four trends of which it consists will group themselves in such a way as to produce a father-
identification and a mother-identification. [p. 33]

There is implicit in the concept of the complete Oedipus
complex a bisexual potential in every child. The ultimate course of
development will depend not only on the balance of parental forces
during the oedipal period, but also on the vicissitudes of earlier
object relations development.

It has been my experience in the treatment of homosexual
women that there are two groups. One group, like the woman
described on pp. 62–64, are bisexual in behavior as well as in the
dream life, and it becomes clear that they have retreated from the
dangers of the oedipal situation. For these women the dangers were
those of maternal abandonment alongside an unavailable father.
Furthermore, potential maternal narcissistic rage led these daughters to a stance of placating the feared and needed female, behavior
evident in their adult homosexual relationships. They more fear
women than love them.

In the heterosexual development of the female child, the oedipal father, if emotionally available, may become a substitute for an
unavailable mother (or for the mother actively rejected by the little
girl), and there will be a fusion of dependency and oedipal strivings
vis-à-vis the male. Because of the disruption of the line of development through the primary attachment to the mother, the achievement of object constancy is aborted.

The second group of homosexual women whom I have treated
are those with a character disorder—either a narcissistic personality
or a borderline character. Oedipal strivings, if we can call them
that, have as their aim the undifferentiated mother. That is, sexual
strivings were assimilated into the incompletely differentiated self
and object constellation. The symbiotic-like quality of their adult
relationships is also marked in the transference. The need and
demand for merger, for total mirroring, and the rage when it was
not forthcoming are in strong contrast to the more highly differentiated stance in the transference of the first group. In their interpersonal relationships, triangular situations have the same competitive
cast as in the positive Oedipus complex situation, although perhaps

possessive is a better word than *competitive*. We need to distinguish what here is essentially a dyadic setup and not a triangular one, insofar as the third person has no significant relational meaning to the individual. The concept of an earlier negative Oedipus complex in the female as described by Freud is thus open to question in these instances. Can we apply a triadic concept to a dyadic situation?

All in all, since positive oedipal strivings pull the little girl away from the preoedipal mother, we can regard them as essentially progressive. On the other hand, the oedipal wishes of the little boy pull him back toward the preoedipal mother and stand in opposition to his drive toward individuation; that is, they tend to have a regressive impact. I would hypothesize that the little boy who turns to his father as oedipal object choice must do so, in some cases, to counter the threat to the loss of separateness vis-à-vis the primary attachment object, the mother. It is a flight from engulfment and annihilation of the separate self. At the same time, a secondary identification with the mother compensates for her loss. The inverted complex in the male child may also come about in the context of an emotionally unavailable mother vis-à-vis a more available father. Blos (1984) conceptualizes the negative complex in boys as dyadic—that is, the boy's preambivalent attachment to the father whose love enables him to escape the engulfment of the preoedipal mother.

In effect, then, the father as oedipal object choice assists individuation and/or substitutes for the inadequate mother for both boys and girls. The specific balance of maternal and paternal emotional availability as well as their support of individuation will be unique to each situation, and the outcome of any line of development can be understood in those terms if we look at the situation with minute care.

THE FATE OF THE OEDIPUS COMPLEX

Freud (1913, 1917a) noted that analysis of adult neurotics reveals the unresolved Oedipus complex, and he came to the conclusion that it was the nucleus of the neuroses.

With puberty, when the sexual demands are experienced in their full strength, the old familiar incestuous objects are once again cathected with libido. The adolescent is faced with the task of detaching himself from the parents, and Freud asserts that it is not until that task is achieved that the individual can cease to be a child and take his or her place in the social community. This task involves giving up the libidinal attachment to the parent of the opposite sex and reconciling with the parent of the same sex. He says of the neurotic solution:

> No solution at all is arrived at: the son remains all his life bowed beneath his father's authority and he is unable to transfer his libido to an outside sexual object. [p. 336]

Freud (1924, p. 177) notes that what he calls the "dissolution" of the Oedipus complex is more than a repression, and that if indeed the "ego has in fact not achieved more than a *repression* of the complex, the latter persists in an unconscious state in the id and will later manifest its pathogenic effect." These are the pathogenic effects, as they interfere with the capacity both to love and to sustain an intimate adult sexual relationship and with the capacity to achieve one's goals and ambitions (i.e., the conflictual nature of competition and success) that we observe in the patients who are identified as candidates for short-term, oedipally focused psychotherapy.

Freud notes that the absence of success of the oedipal strivings leads both the boy and the girl to turn away from the hopeless oedipal longing. He writes that the destruction of the Oedipus complex is primarily brought about by the threat of castration. For the boy there are two ways to satisfaction: the active way, in which he puts himself in his father's place and has intercourse with mother as father did, in which case father is a hindrance; and the passive way, in which he takes the place of mother and is loved by father, and mother is superfluous. According to Freud, both routes entail castration—the masculine one as punishment and the feminine one as a precondition.

He writes:

> If the satisfaction of love in the field of the Oedipus complex is to cost the child his penis, a conflict is bound to arise between

> his narcissistic interest in that part of his body and the libidinal
> cathexis of his parental objects. In this conflict the first of these
> forces normally triumphs: the child's ego turns away from the
> Oedipus complex. [p. 176]

As the object cathexes of parental objects are relinquished,
they are replaced by identifications. Their authority is taken into
the ego and forms the nucleus of the superego, perpetuating the
prohibition against incest. The libidinal trends are, in part, desexualized and transformed into impulses of affection toward the parents.

Loewald (1979) does not believe that there ever is a final
resolution of the Oedipus complex but comments that there is a
"waning" that can be expected both developmentally and as the
outcome of treatment. With respect to the outcome of analysis and
the establishment of a relationship of equality with one's parents,
he says, "It is not established once and for all, but requires continued internal activity; and it is not necessarily obvious at the
point of actual termination" (p. 764).

THE SUPEREGO AND THE EGO IDEAL

Freud's concept of the ego ideal changed over time. In his introductory lectures (1917b) he wrote that the ego ideal is created "for the
purpose of recovering thereby the self-satisfaction bound up with
the primary infantile narcissism, which since those days has suffered so many shocks and mortification." In object relational
terms, I view this kind of ego ideal as related to the grandiose self, a
defensive and compensatory structure that may be activated by
those very "shocks and mortification." A defensive and compensatory ego ideal must be distinguished from that of the mature
superego, which is the outcome of the transmuting internalizations
of parental imperatives (Schecter 1979b) at the end of the separation–individuation process and with the resolution of the Oedipus
complex, both of which continue on through adolescence.

Freud made that shift in 1933 in the "New Introductory
Lectures" when the superego was referred to as the "vehicle of the

ego ideal." He saw the ego ideal as derived from the child's perception of the admired parent, "an expression of the admiration which
the child felt for the perfection which it at that time ascribed to
them."

Sandler and colleagues (1963) related the ego ideal to the ideal
self, which they view, in object relational terms, as one of the
shapes that the self representation can assume. They trace the
development of a mature, reality-oriented ideal self as it takes place
in the healthy individual. They see the ideal self as far more fluid
and flexible than are the ideals that were held up to the child by his
introjects, even though the ideal self still contains a solid core of
identifications with the admired parents of his earliest years. They
note that in the healthy individual, the ideal self undergoes continuous modification according to the person's experiences of reality.
In states of regression, however, the ideal self becomes more like
certain aspects of the idealized pregenital objects. The authors add
that parental ideals are modified and displaced over time and
integrated with ideals taken over from other figures throughout
life. This will apply to what is taken in of the therapist in psychoanalysis. Bromberg (1983) notes that it is not the analyst's functions with which the patient identifies, but the analyst's superego,
as perceived by the patient.

The question must be raised about those instances in which
the parents were not admired. One woman found substitute models in the idealized television family of "Father Knows Best." There
may be a need to reject available identifications to maintain a more
primitive ideal with its core of narcissistic perfection. The short-
term approach would not be suitable for such a patient, and,
indeed, assessment of superego functions is an intrinsic aspect of
evaluation for short-term treatment, which requires a core of reliable, realistic self-esteem.

Loewald (1979) notes that the essence of the superego as an
internal agency involves owning up to one's needs and impulses as
one's own. This is a necessary step in the uncovering process of
therapy. It means "granting them actively that existence which they
have in any event with or without our permission" (p. 761). He
comments that this involves facing and bearing guilt for acts we
consider criminal, even if these acts exist only in fantasy. The

criminal acts he refers to are the incestuous fantasies of the Oedipus complex and what he views as a form of parricide—the murder of parental authority and the assumption of responsibility for one's own life that takes place with the severing of the emotional ties with parents. Incest is the "crime" associated with oedipal wishes, and parricide is the "crime" associated with the resolution of the Oedipus complex. "Not only parental authority is destroyed by wresting authority from the parents and taking it over, but the parents, if the process were thoroughly carried out, are being destroyed as libidinal objects as well" (p. 757). He does note that if things go well, what will be left is tenderness, mutual trust, and respect—the signs of equality. Freud, too, notes that the libidinal trends of the Oedipus complex are desexualized, aim-inhibited, and changed into impulses of affection.

Loewald (1979) sees the repression of the Oedipus complex as evading the emancipatory murder of the parents and as a way to preserve infantile, libidinal-dependent ties with them. He notes that when parricide is carried out, "aspects of oedipal relations are transformed into superego relations (internalization), and other aspects are, qua relations with external objects, restructured in such a way that the incestuous character of object relations gives way to novel forms of object choice" (p. 758). Even so, he tells us, these novel choices will still be under the influence of those internalizations.

Loewald concludes that oedipal issues are new versions of the basic union–individuation dilemma. "The superego, as the culmination of individual psychic structure formation, represents something ultimate in the basic separation–individuation process" (p. 755).

THE THERAPEUTIC FOCUS: OEDIPAL OR PREOEDIPAL?

Patients accepted for short-term therapy (see Chapter 22) should have a high level of development, with no significant character pathology. If we keep in mind that any new developmental phase or event takes place within the context of a preexisting character structure, we can expect that the form and expression of oedipal issues will vary from child to child and from patient to patient. At the emergence of oedipal strivings, one child may still be struggling with the task of differentiation from an engulfing mother. Will the little boy have to withdraw into schizoid detachment to protect his sense of self? Will the little girl so fear object loss that she brings her sexuality to the mother figure? Another child may be consumed with rage at an abandoning mother. Will the boy's frustrated oedipal yearnings fan the flame of his narcissistic rage? Will the little girl sense the anger with which she turns to father, later experiencing her interest in men as a bad and hostile wish? Will she flaunt her involvement with father as a way to torment the mother at whom she is so angry? A more evolved child may have negotiated the tasks of the separation–individuation process, attaining a modicum of object constancy, and as an adult patient, present with some of the more classical issues pertaining to the Oedipus complex.

The oedipal dynamic can be discerned in somewhat altered form in the patient from another culture. An Asian man, raised in a traditional Asian home but living in the United States, presented with the problem of being unable to advance in his managerial position. His unwillingness to challenge authority, his passive placating behavior, his wish to hide behind a more powerful other were all addressed in the transference and in the work situation. At the twelfth session he said he felt something was still missing. Up to that point he had claimed he did not remember his early years. Turning the focus backward in time, he was able to perceive the same dynamics in the family situation.

There was a large extended family living in one household, with the father's older brother the veritable ruler of the clan. The children of this man carried his status as well, and challenging them was as forbidden as challenging the uncle. The mother and father bowed to the uncle's authority, although the mother complained bitterly about him.

The patient denied affectional feelings for his mother at first, although later he could say that he wanted her love. He was able to experience hatred for the uncle and disappointment in the father, who would not stand up to his brother. The worst thing one could do to another was to make that person look bad. The patient recalled the time he did stand up to the uncle on his mother's behalf, wishing to protect her. He acknowledged that there probably was a wish to be special to her. But the mother was furious at him for making her look bad, furious that he, her son, should be so disrespectful to the uncle. The patient was able to say that he felt betrayed by his mother and angry at his father for not backing him up. As he talked about this, he experienced "fear" and then a sense of emptiness.

Although sexuality seemed far from the scene, the wish to be special to mother vis-à-vis a powerful male figure is clear. The failure of the father (by virtue of the cultural demand as well as his own character) to provide a model worthy of emulation led to a wish for the powerful protecting authority figure, as well as the acceptance of the passivity and the development of passive–aggressive strategies. The wish to be special to father was played out in rivalry with his younger brother and centered on money. The father–son dynamic was also being played out with his own son, with the patient angry that his son didn't do well in school, making him look bad. He was also aware that with the model he was providing, he was repeating the very dynamic he hated.

Assuming that oedipal and preoedipal factors affect one another in a reciprocal fashion and that character structure in terms of object relations development is a central issue, a developmental diagnosis is essential for the proper selection of patients for short-term treatment and for the decision not to treat when there is significant character pathology. Where borderline or narcissistic issues prevail, they are more than likely to dominate the transference. Just as immature or pathological character structure will interfere with the resolution of the Oedipus complex developmentally, so it will interfere in treatment focusing on oedipal issues. As stated earlier, the successful completion of the separation–individuation process dovetails with the resolution of the Oedipus complex, with both coming about as the result of identificatory processes.

Shapiro (1977) writes:

> The Oedipus complex is presented as a universal, developmentally determined mental organization that incorporates pregenital factors in a new hierarchic structure. [p. 559]

He says further:

> With maturation there is a discontinuous hierarchic organiza-
> tion such that structuralization at each stage reorganizes the
> mnemic traces of the prior stages. Thus, the oedipal constella-
> tion may supersede earlier experiences, rendering them less
> 'toxic' than their previous level might suggest. [p. 565]

He minimizes the impact of severe character pathology, saying that
its only effect is to make oedipal themes more intense, more rigid,
and more externally unstable.

Shapiro says, in effect, that the pregenital character is assimilated into and transformed by the Oedipus complex. In my experience with character disorders I have observed that quite the
reverse is often true—that oedipal issues are assimilated into and
transformed by preoedipal themes. In some instances the deficit of
structure aborts the development of the Oedipus complex. Competitive dynamics are assimilated into a dyadic structure rather than
into a truly triangular one in which both "others" are of equal
emotional significance. The oedipal situation is, by definition, triangular. It requires a mother who is sufficiently differentiated from
the self and a father who is sufficiently differentiated from the
mother. The following is from the session of a young woman who
presented with borderline lack of differentiation from the primary
object, alongside a schizoid self.

> Recently when I've called my parents, I didn't make any effort
> to chat any more. I'm taking the offensive of what my father
> does. He always says, "Talk to Mother." Now I just say, "Hi,
> where's Mommy?" I have a sense that my struggles are with my
> mother. I feel they exclude my father. In my mind I'm saying,
> "Wait your turn. I want to work all this out with Mother." In a
> way, thinking of them separately seems a big change. To sepa-
> rate them and think of them in relation to me is very different.
> In the past I've been conscious of my mother's relationship
> with me. My father was lumped onto the side. Now the picture
> I get is one of an equilateral triangle, but the focus is on my
> mother. I don't consider the other. [Horner 1984, p. 170]

Her father's historical failure was that of failing to be available in a way that would have supported and even enabled her separation from mother. Her failure to differentiate herself from her mother was paralleled by her failure to differentiate mother from father. "My father was lumped onto the side." The Oedipus complex requires that there be three separately perceived people and that the third element has some significant relational meaning for the individual. Sibling rivalry is triangular, but not oedipal. As a result of the young woman's analytic work, which focused on the issue of differentiation and boundary structuring, she approached the possibility of a true oedipal situation.

I have also worked with patients who presented with pseudo-triangular conflicts that appeared oedipal at first glance. However, they were situations in which object splitting was acted out with a separate good, idealized object, and a bad, persecutory object. The demand is often made of the "designated good object" (Horner 1979, 1984) to comfort when hurt by the bad one, and to "validate" the anger experienced toward the bad object so that the anger is good and righteous rather than the bad and dangerous rage of the infantile self. I refer to this as the "masochistic triangle" (p. 174). The idealized, omnipotent, good object representation is projected onto one parent, while the other parent is experienced as the all-bad, persecuting object. That is, oedipal strivings are assimilated into the split self and object representational situation, and narcissistic issues become intensely sexualized. Transferences with these patients are particularly intractable.

The answers to two important questions enable the clinician to make the diagnostic distinctions that are critical to determining a patient's ability to work in short-term therapy: Are the major issues oedipal or preoedipal? Will the character structure lend itself to this treatment approach?

The achievement of our goals—the resolution of the Oedipus complex and its attendant conflicts—in short-term treatment depends on an appropriate selection of patients, on a thorough understanding of the issues involved, and on an assiduous attention to the maintenance of focus lest we find ourselves drawn retrogressively into preoedipal issues.

22

Preoedipal Factors in Selection for Brief Psychotherapy

Critics of brief psychotherapy have characterized it as "wild analysis." Schafer (1985) reminds us that conceptions of what is wild, sound, or too tame are system-bound, that from the differing theoretical vantage points there are preferred lines of interpretation as well as differing technical opinions with respect to tact, timing and dosage. He reminds us that there are analysts of every persuasion who work abusively, at least at times, but that it cannot be useful to present one system as somehow morally superior to the others. Although Schafer focuses his remarks around the work of Kohut, Gill, and Melanie Klein, we would do well to adopt his wisdom in our consideration of brief therapy which is based on psychoanalytic concepts.

Greenson (1978) points out the difference between "unanalytic" procedures and "antianalytic" procedures. An antianalytic procedure is one that blocks or lessens the patient's capacity for insight and understanding. "Any measure which diminishes the ego's function or capacity for observing, thinking, remembering, and judging would fall into this category" (p. 366).

No matter what the modality of treatment, over and above its specific technical requirements should stand the dictum *do no harm*. In Greenson's terms, although there is room for "unanalytic" procedures, we must be on guard against those which are "antianalytic." Whether a given intervention proves to impair the ego's functioning or not will depend upon the nature of the organization of the ego and its strengths and resources as well as its deficits and vulnerabilities. It is our concern for these deficits and vulnerabilities that leads us to consider certain caveats in the application of brief psychotherapy techniques in the treatment of patients whose object relational worlds and interpersonal relationships continue to be dominated by preoedipal issues.

In the treatment of the patient with preoedipal structural deficits, the potential for diminishing the ego's functions or capacities is far greater than it is with the more evolved individual. By using the principles of brief treatment, can we help such a patient within the time limits imposed by external forces and still do no harm? Can we, within these limits, produce enduring structural change, the outcome that marks the distinction between brief psychotherapy and crisis intervention?

De Simone Gaburri (1985) writes with respect to termination that a moment comes in every analysis when the idea of temporality arises for the first time. She notes that we must deal with incompleteness and what it means to us if we are to be able to terminate at all. Winnicott (1962) makes the point that one of the aims of psychoanalytic treatment lies in its termination.

Temporality, incompleteness, and termination are intrinsic to brief psychotherapy, and the method does not allow for their denial. The patient must be able to deal with these realities without being unduly traumatized by them or rigidly defended against awareness of them.

In both long-term and brief psychotherapy, there is always the possibility of built-in, undetected resistances related to the very choice of treatment modality. A preference for brief treatment may contain defenses against the regressive dangers associated with long-term psychotherapy. On the other hand, a choice of an ongoing and open-ended approach may just as possibly carry built-in, undetected resistances related to higher-level conflicts. These possibilities do not disqualify either method. Rather, they call for the therapist's attention to them if they exist, and for their analysis in an appropriate manner.

TRANSFERENCE RESISTANCE

Transference resistance may be defined as a characteristic manner of relating to the therapist that has as its aim the realization of a wished-for interaction or the avoidance of a feared one. As an overall manner of relating, it is often so subtly woven into the process that we may not give it the attention it merits, particularly with the patient who uses passivity and helplessness in the service of defense. How many people are in an unterminable treatment because the very act of being in therapy is itself the acting out of a stance of needing help, as a characterological defensive posture in the world? I worked confrontively within the brief treatment model with such a man. He had come to me seeking long-term treatment, having had at least twenty years of treatment with well-known therapists who had assigned him a variety of diagnoses. The "sick" posture proved to be a compromise formation that defended against the dangers of aggression toward his ambivalently regarded father and the dangers of sexual potency vis-à-vis his mother. At the same time, it offered a safe and reliable vehicle for establishing a special and gratifying bond with his mother and later, transferentially, with his therapists.

In contrast, a woman who seemed to meet all the criteria for brief therapy came to me specifically requesting it. It became evident at the start of treatment that she wanted to avoid the dangers of dependency and subsequent loss imposed by commitment to a long-term therapeutic relationship. Her father, with whom she had had a favored relationship in the family, had died unexpectedly when she was 12 years old.

From my point of view as their therapist, engaging with either of these patients in what, at face value, seemed a clear choice of treatment approach, carried with it the danger of collusion with the resistance.

IMPLICATIONS FOR THE FUTURE

The discipline imposed by the demands of brief psychotherapy, and the sharpening of skills with respect to detecting and analyzing transference resistances, seems to accelerate, and thus shorten, long-term analytic therapy; recognition of this has led many to propose that we push even more vigorously at the frontier of our profession and extend the techniques of brief psychotherapy to our work with patients who do not fit the criteria so rigorously imposed by the pioneers in the field.

Is there now a danger of the inevitable pendulum shift after a decade of Kohut's influence and the demands and self-discipline imposed by our deeper understanding of the structural vulnerabilities of the borderline patient? Do we seek to justify confrontation so as not to have to endure the existential annihilation we experience as our patient's "selfobject"? In our ongoing dedication to self-awareness and self-understanding, we must be alert to ways in which countertransference plays a role in our clinging to or turning away from any given treatment philosophy. The ultimate questions with respect to choice of treatment must always be, With which patient, and when, and why?

Unfortunately, it may not be an issue of treatment of choice so much as an issue of treatment of necessity. Limitations imposed by third-party reimbursement and by clinic and training structures demand a more creative approach to helping, and it may well be that a marriage of brief therapy principles with our knowledge about character disorders will allow for the most fruitful use of available human and financial resources. The wisdoms of psychoanalytic theory and clinical practice have much to offer toward these creative solutions.

CHARACTERISTICS OF BRIEF PSYCHOTHERAPY

First, let us consider the major features that characterize brief psychotherapy based upon analytic principles. These are (1) the establishment and maintenance of an agreed-upon treatment focus, (2) the early and consistent interpretation of transference as a resistance and/or as it relates to the agreed-upon focus, and (3) the activity of the therapist.

In considering the use of brief psychotherapy with the oedipal patient, we should look during the evaluation interview for the following necessary ego capacities: (1) the ability to form meaningful give-and-take relationships; (2) the ability to tolerate strong affects associated with anger, guilt, depression, and anxiety; (3) characterological flexibility; and (4) positive response to interpretation. Patients with simple, focused complaints related to oedipal material can be interviewed with little attention paid to characterological issues. On the other hand, patients with many characterological problems, such as obsessional defenses, passivity, and dependency, require immediate attention to characterological resistance in order to assess potential for affective responsiveness. These interviews use the techniques developed by Davanloo (1978) and have a flavor that is less cognitive and more confrontational.

Three triads of interpretation (Horner 1985) are consistently formulated:

1. Exploration within the determined focus of the triad of conflict, anxiety, and defense.
2. Analysis within the oedipal focus of the triangular interpersonal situation with mother, father, and the patient, where both legs of the triangle are explored and then interrelated with respect to parents as well as within the context of derivative triangles.
3. Exploration of the focus within the triad of past relationships, present-day relationships, and the transference.

The presence of the core conflict, anxiety, and defense in each of these situations is laid out.

THE PATIENT WITH PREOEDIPAL ISSUES

In working with the patient with significant preoedipal issues, the focus may be defined in terms of the specific structural and interpersonal issues that generate the presenting problem, as well as the nature of its attendant anxieties and the defenses used against these anxieties. Although Davanloo relies upon the patient's ability to respond to interpretation in a trial therapy of a few sessions, rather than relying on diagnosis as a major selection criterion, it seems to me the two go hand in hand. Certainly the patient's response to trial therapy will provide data upon which a structural diagnosis can be postulated. This information will enable an appropriate definition of focus, which may not always be oedipal.

I use the term *structure* to refer to the nature of the inner representational world, its reality-relatedness, and the quality of its cohesion and object-relatedness (Horner 1979, 1984). This kind of structural formulation allows us to predict with some degree of reliability what strengths we can count on in our therapeutic work and what dangers are to be avoided. It also defines treatment goals, such as the facilitation of cohesion, differentiation, integration of split-off aspects of the self, or consolidation of identifications, or the resolution of oedipal conflict in a well-evolved individual.

Our interventions will depend upon the level of psychic organization in structural terms. Do we have to function as an auxiliary ego, to provide an integrating matrix in the face of the fragmenting self of the patient? Do we listen to and respond to the alienated, empty, schizoid, and buried true self despite the patient's pleas to collude with his defenses? Do we interpret passivity as a defense against a feared retaliation for self-assertion in a competitive context, or do we view the passivity as a defense against dissolution panic associated with the loss of the object, who is still experienced as part of a fragile self? If we overestimate the patient's structural integrity, we may traumatize him, leading to an intensification of defenses, a paranoid reaction, or a flight from treatment. On the other hand, if we underestimate the patient's strength, we may reinforce regression as a defense against the anxieties of oedipal conflict.

In long-term treatment of the patient with preoedipal pathology, the formulation of the structural diagnosis in terms of the core developmental issues enables us to make interventions that directly address these issues. The information we use to make the structural diagnosis comes from the data of the individual's interpersonal relationships within the family, within the world of peers and friendships, in adult work and love relationships, and—most important—in the specifics and subtleties of the therapeutic interaction. Once we understand the core developmental issue with respect to the self and its feelings of cohesion as opposed to fragmentation, and its reality-relatedness as opposed to false self organization, and the quality of its relatedness with its objects in terms of differentiation and integration as opposed to boundary blurring and splitting, we must articulate this core issue to the patient in a manner that—when accurate, of course—makes the patient feel profoundly understood and hopeful that something can be done to help him.

There is no reason that this should not also be true within a time-limited framework wherein this core issue becomes the agreed-upon focus. The core issue then becomes the organizing principle for our work together, for understanding the experiences and material reported by the patient, as well as for understanding the process that goes on between patient and therapist. Thus, what is structural is brought into the here and now of the interpersonal situation, where new experience and the application of adult understanding of primitive experience allows for the amelioration of distorted development. Just as the self structure first evolves within an interpersonal matrix, so the self of the patient can be more fully experienced and more maturely structured within the interpersonal matrix of the therapeutic relationship. In a time-limited treatment we will rely less upon the transforming effects of the relationship matrix, although it will still be a factor, and more upon appropriate and nontraumatizing interventions, anticipating that cognitive change will effect some degree of corresponding structural change.

Kavanagh (1985) reports studies that suggest that "a good therapeutic relationship in both supportive and expressive therapy enables structural change to occur in a patient's internalized object relations." He points out that "through a process of learning, a person becomes able to represent objects internally in a more mature manner," adding that through psychotherapeutic treatment the individual "is enabled to unlock the cognitive and perceptual potentials that physiological maturation has already provided" (p. 588).

Viewing the self and object representations as cognitive schemas in the Piagetian sense, Kavanagh's findings suggest that inasmuch as changes in the representational world are largely a cognitive achievement, a predominantly cognitive approach to brief psychotherapy of the patient with a structural deficit, with the core developmental issue as the agreed-upon focus, might in fact lead to some degree of enduring structural change.

Kavanagh reports Appelbaum's (1977) findings that "some more disturbed patients receiving supporting psychotherapy unexpectedly showed structural change too, becoming better organized with respect to basic ego functions" (p. 560). In his research, Kavanagh found that regardless of the kind of treatment or initial level of ego strength, in both psychoanalysis and psychoanalytic psychotherapy, patients showed "both an increase in the maturity of perceived interactions and freer access to structurally lower levels of object representations" (p. 561).

These findings encourage us with respect to applying the principles of brief psychotherapy to the treatment of some patients with significant preoedipal features in their character structure. The choosing of a focus and the cognitive elucidation of the core issues as they arise alongside an appropriate approach to transference interpretation would be determined by qualities specific to the patient. In his discussion of the treatment of borderline patients, Horwitz (1985) notes that "interpretations that convey dynamic and genetic content within the context of communicating empathy differ in important ways from the more classical drive-defense interpretation, which inevitably strains the patient's self-esteem" (p. 539). The latter style is characteristic of brief psychotherapy with the oedipal patient as it has been developed by Sifneos (1979), Davanloo, and others.

The continuous dissolution of transference by interpretation within the focus is central to success in brief therapy. The ability to tolerate transference interpretations within the structural–developmental focus will also be critical in the application of principles of brief treatment to the patient with significant preoedipal pathology.

Horwitz (1985) notes that, with the borderline patient, there has to be some capacity to tolerate a degree of both closeness and separateness in order to do transference work, lest interpretations be experienced as traumatic abandonments or intolerable intrusions. He suggests that "patients who rigidly adhere to either a symbiotically close or aloofly distant relationship are not amenable to transference work, while patients who alternate between these extremes show signs of readiness for both the intimacy and separateness involved in transference exploration and interpretation" (p. 534).

Horwitz does caution that we have to make a distinction between pathological and healthy alternation. In the former we see the involuntary, automatic, poorly controlled alternation of ego states that reflect a split in self and object representations. "On the other hand," Horwitz notes (1985), "oscillations that have the earmarks of greater integration between good and bad internal representations are a positive sign" (p. 543).

Case Example

I worked with a young woman with whom the brief format was imposed by a training situation. She had tended to form idealizing relationships with women. The mother failed to support her strivings toward either individuation or mastery. She had an intense and special relationship with her father. Although he supported her intellectual development and achievement, he did not support her defining herself as separate from the mother's selfobject demands. Her intellectual development outside the arena of compromised functioning is a major resource in therapy. The focus agreed upon was her need to control in all relationships, an aspect of her character that was both necessary and, at the same time, dystonic and hated.

The need to control proved to be highly over-determined. We had barely begun our work when I had to cancel because of illness. She did not bring this up at the start of the next session, but I did, realizing that the issue of control within the transference would surely have been activated by this event. She acknowledged that she had felt rejected and that she had been in a needy mood, which embarrassed her. She was concerned about living up to the expectations that would exist at her next placement. I brought the issue back to how my canceling made it clear that she was not in control. She said, "I saw you as someone with power, and people with power reject me." She spoke of trying to be the perfect patient so that she would not be rejected. She also spoke of a pressure to perform for me, to be interesting in the way she had been with her father in order to maintain her place of specialness with him. In this example, the careful and prompt attention to transference and its relationship to the agreed-upon focus is demonstrated.

The patient had earlier expressed concern that the therapy would be cold and intellectual; however, in the sixth session she expressed surprise that—as she started to think about how she has to be in control, how she devalues others and never lets herself lean on anyone else—she could feel herself changing in this respect, particularly with her boyfriend. Understanding that what she had called depression was the consequence of the emotional isolation she imposed on herself as a result of her self-protective posture, she came to redefine the depression as loneliness.

THE OEDIPAL PATIENT WITH PREOEDIPAL ISSUES

Is brief psychotherapy an appropriate form of treatment for that most difficult of all patient groups? I am referring here to a particular segment of the patient population whose members are diagnosed as everything from high-level borderline to neurotic. These are individuals who, developmentally, have one foot in the rapprochement phase of the separation–individuation process, and the other clearly in the realm of the Oedipus complex. Therapists generally tend to view these patients as borderline, and oedipal dynamics in and out of the transference are ignored, leading to long-standing stalemates in treatment. One is reminded of Zetzel's (1971) distinction between borderline states and borderline personalities. Many of these patients might respond well to treatment oriented in the brief model, in which regression under stress might well be interpretable within the focus.

Pine (1979) writes cogently on the distinction between pathology of the relation to the *undifferentiated* other and pathology of the relation to the *differentiated* other. He also describes a third group, the one to which I refer here, drawing a further distinction within the concept of pathology of the relation to the *differentiated* other, and showing that some of this pathology is in fact tied to the *differentiation process itself*. He reminds us that the power of the *cognitive* differentiation of self and other—"though contradicted by preverbal memory and by wish, yet anchored in perception of the real world—is indeed great and ordinarily provides a context in which likeness is safely distinguished from undifferentiated merging" (p. 231). He does note that there may be pathological exceptions to this.

Elsewhere (1979, 1984) I described this same group of patients as "preneurotic," in consideration of what happens to the Oedipus complex when issues of individuation remain unresolved. I described these individuals as having a well-defined and ambivalently experienced separate self, but also as having failed to assimilate significant maternal functions and attributes into the self in the service of either the ego ideal or gender identity, resulting in a state of continued dependency on the object. The final step toward an autonomous self and toward object constancy and consolidation of identity has often not been accomplished because of a resistance to identification with the ambivalently regarded object.

Mann's (1973) twelve-session time-limited psychotherapy has as its focus preoedipal separation–individuation issues. He first invites a regressive merger with an empathic stance, and then shifts to a confrontation of overcompliance and dependence. In my view this would evoke a catastrophic reaction when structural deficit and compromised ego functioning are part of the picture. On the other hand, patients with a well-differentiated and integrated self who nonetheless continue to struggle with issues related to the separation–individuation process itself—that is, Pine's third group, whom I have referred to as preneurotic—may well be able to tolerate this approach. The diagnostic distinction would be critical.

In my view, it would be an error to diagnose this group of patients as borderline, inasmuch as there is a cohesive, differentiated, and relatively well integrated self representation. If these patients are included in brief psychotherapy-outcome research under the label of "borderline," conclusions that are drawn from that research with respect to treatability of the borderline by dynamic brief psychotherapy will also be in error.

Loewald (1985) describes the oedipal phase as "a crucial stage of transition . . . from lack of, or rudimentary, subject–object differention . . . to the level of sexual–aggressive object relations" (p. 437). He adds: "The more mature sectors of the personality are unattainable without the narcissistic patient's having reached this stage, however shakily, although in the overall mental life of the patient it has failed to gain sufficient dominance."

The trial therapy suggested by Davanloo will test whether or not the oedipal phase has indeed gained sufficient dominance to tolerate the confrontive element of brief psychotherapy. If this is not the case, the unmodified application of brief techniques as developed for the treatment of the oedipal patient may very well do harm. In recognition of the difficulty of assigning an accurate diagnosis to the patients just described, trial therapy should be considerd as one way to determine whether or not the individual is indeed a suitable candidate for brief treatment. If the patient fails the crucial test, it would be incumbent upon the clinician to deal promptly with any negative consequences. If, on the other hand, brief treatment is the modality of necessity, then modifications in terms of focus and working with the transference that take into account the preoedipal pathology may still be an option.

INTERPRETING UPWARD

In elucidating principles for the brief treatment of the oedipal patient, I have described the process of "interpreting upward" (Horner 1985):

> Inasmuch as there are bound to be perseverating preoedipal issues with every oedipal patient—unresolved orality in psychosexual terms, rapprochement issues in object relations terms, or narcissistic vulnerability in self psychology terms—

one has to make a clinical decision when these issues emerge. They can be interpreted with the earlier metapsychology as an organizing principle, but if we do this we encourage or facilitate a more regressive stance vis-à-vis the treatment process and transferentially. Since regression is to be avoided in brief therapy, we interpret this same material within the context of the oedipal triangle and its conflicts. The fear of maternal punishment by the withholding of maternal support and love is interpreted as a consequence of the competitive strivings vis-à-vis the father. The narcissistic wound of the oedipal defeat is interpreted within the framework of the competitive evaluation of the self vis-à-vis the rival. If the patient is unable to work with this kind of material within the oedipal framework, but seems traumatized by such interpretations, we have to assume that he is not a candidate for this approach. [p. 80]

If we modify the technique, however, and formulate a focus that elucidates the core developmental issue, will we be able to contribute to the development of a more mature structure as described by Kavanagh?

A point of discomfort for many therapists and analysts who have always worked within the long-term model is the incompleteness of this approach. Is a "complete analysis" necessary to the achievement of the patient's goals, or, once the core conflict is well along toward resolution, does further change continue without therapeutic intervention? Is there an unraveling of interrelated conflicts and defenses once the central knot is untied? Malan (1963) wonders whether the therapist's own need for perfection may not be more the issue here. Alexander (1964) noted that the aim of psychotherapy is to bring the patient to the point where his or her natural growth can be resumed. In brief psychotherapy it is assumed that the working-through process will continue through and beyond termination.

The principles of brief therapy are often useful for bringing to a close long-term therapies that have become bogged down because of a failure to address a major transference resistance related to the necessary "overthrow" of the therapist, an intrinsic aspect of the ultimate dissolution of the Oedipus complex (Loewald 1979). Setting a termination date and applying the principle of brief therapy can enable the therapist to bring the treatment to a constructive close.

We must endeavor to view the changing world of psychotherapy as a challenge to our creativity rather than as a death knell to psychoanalytic treatment. However, despite a changing world and changing social and economic demands on both patient and therapist, certain basic principles should endure. Whatever our therapeutic goal, we should continue to begin with as thorough an understanding of the person as is possible—how he or she is put together psychologically, how this particular mind was organized from the beginning of life onward, and how this organization is now manifest in the individual's way of being in the world. With such understanding, our therapeutic endeavors will be appropriate to this person and to his or her character structure.

Bibliography
of Author's Writings

PUBLICATIONS

1965 An investigation of the relationship of value orientation to the adaptive-defensive system of the personality. Doctoral dissertation. Ann Arbor: University Microfilms.

1968 The role of education in the goal-setting process (with C. Buhler). In The Course of Human Life, ed. C. Buhler and F. Massarik, pp. 231–245. New York: Springer.

Genetic aspects of creativity, ibid., pp. 123–139.

The evolution of goals in the life of Clarence Darrow, ibid., pp. 64–75.

1969 Protesting students. American Psychologist 24:876.

To touch or not to touch. Voices 4:26–28.

Existential and humanistic psychology (with C. Buhler). In *The Future of Psychotherapy*, ed. C. Frederick, pp. 55–73. Boston: Little, Brown.

1970 Self-deception and the search for intimacy. *Voices* 6:34–36.

1971 Letting go. *Voices* 7:38.

A topography of early marriage: critique. *Family Process* 10:249.

1973 Ego boundaries: the last line of resistance in psychotherapy. *Psychotherapy: Theory, Research, and Practice* 10:83–86.

1974 Early object relations and the concept of depression. *International Review of Psycho-Analysis* 1:337–340.

1975 A characterological contraindication for group psychotherapy. *Journal of the American Academy of Psychoanalysis* 3:301–305.

Stages and processes in the development of early object relations and their associated pathologies. *International Review of Psycho-Analysis* 2:95–105.

1976 Oscillatory patterns of object relations and the borderline patient. *International Review of Psycho-Analysis* 3:479–482.

1977 *Psychology for Living*, 4th ed. (with G. Forehand). New York: McGraw-Hill.

1978 *Being and Loving*, 1st ed. New York: Schocken Books.

Character Detachment and Self-Esteem (tape). New York: Jason Aronson.

1979 *Object Relations and the Developing Ego in Therapy*. New York: Jason Aronson.

1980 Object relations and the primacy of structure. *Issues in Psychology* 3:27–35.

The roots of anxiety, character structure, and psychoanalytic treatment. *Journal of the American Academy of Psychoanalysis* 8:565–573.

Object relations, the self, and the therapeutic matrix. *Contemporary Psychoanalysis* 16:186–203.

1981 Discussion, "The rhetoric of intimacy" by Edgar Levenson. *Group* 5:12–15.

1982 Discussion, "The compulsive personality disorder" by Douglas Ingram, M.D. *The American Journal of Psychoanalysis* 42:199–205.

Psychoanalysis: a discussion of contemporary issues (with M. Brenner, H. Halpern, and R. Stolorow). *Voices* 18:30–39.

Little Big Girl. New York: Human Sciences Press.

1983 The soul of a profession. *Journal of Smith College School for Social Work* 10:11–14.

Refusal to identify: developmental impasse. *Dynamic Psychotherapy* 1:111–121.

Will, transcendence and change. *Contemporary Psychoanalysis* 19:471–482.

1984 The creative alliance. *Lydia Rapoport Lectures Monograph* no. 10. Northampton, MA: Smith College School for Social Work.

Object Relations and the Developing Ego in Therapy, 2nd ed. New York: Jason Aronson.

1985 *Treating the Oedipal Patient in Brief Psychotherapy* (editor and co-author). Northvale, NJ: Jason Aronson.

1986 Foreword. In *The Psychology of Today's Woman*, ed. T. Bernay and D. Cantor, pp. xv–xvii. Hillsdale, NJ: Analytic Press.

Object relations and transference resistance. In *Techniques of Working with Resistance*, ed. D. Milman and G. Goldman, pp. 227–248. Northvale, NJ: Jason Aronson.

Comments on "Self-direction and schizophrenia." *Journal of Humanistic Psychology* 26:80–82.

Comments on "Reconstructing radical therapy." *Journal of Humanistic Psychology* 26:83–85.

Being and Loving, 2nd ed. New York: Jason Aronson.

1987 Book review, *Assessing Object Relations Phenomena*, ed. M. Kissen. *FORUM of the American Academy of Psychoanalysis.*

The "real relationship" and analytic neutrality. *Journal of the American Academy of Psychoanalysis* 15:491–502.

The unconscious and the archaeology of human relationships. In *Theories of the Unconscious and Theories of the Self*, ed. R. Stern, pp. 27–39. Hillsdale, NJ: Analytic Press.

1988 Book review, *The Twenty-Minute Hour. Journal of the American Academy of Psychoanalysis* 16:558–561.

Book review, *Gender Identity: A Developmental Model*, by Irene Fast. *FORUM of the American Academy of Psychoanalysis* 32:18–19.

The constructed self and developmental discontinuity. *Journal of the American Academy of Psychoanalysis* 16:235–238.

Comments on "The life of dialogue." *Journal of Humanistic Psychology* 28:134–135.

Developmental aspects of psychodynamic supervision: parallel process of separation and individuation. *The Clinical Supervisor* 6:3–12.

1989 *The Wish for Power and the Fear of Having It*. Northvale, NJ: Jason Aronson.

Pseudo-schizoid development: the little boy's dilemma. *Journal of the American Academy of Psychoanalysis* 17:501–503.

1990 *Being and Loving*, 3rd ed. Northvale, NJ: Jason Aronson.

Creativity and pathological solutions: variations on a not-me theme. Presented to the American Academy of Psychoanalysis, New York, May. Submitted for publication.

The double approach–avoidance conflict and obsessive disorders. Unpublished paper.

Money issues and analytic neutrality. In *Money and Mind*, ed. S. Klebanow and E. Lowenkopf (in press, Plenum).

From idealization to ideal—from attachment to identification: the female analyst and the female patient. *Journal of the American Academy of Psychoanalysis* 18:223–232.

UNPUBLISHED PRESENTATIONS

1981 *Object relations and the resolution of the Oedipus complex.* Paper presented at the meeting of the American Psychological Association, August.

1982 *Burnout: a countertransference phenomenon.* Paper presented at the meeting of the American Academy of Psychotherapists, New York, February.

Innovation by prescription. Paper presented at the meeting of the Institute for Psychoanalytic Training and Research, New York, January.

1985 *Bulimia: a complex compromise formation.* Paper presented at the Center for the Study of Anorexia and Bulimia, New York, November 17.

Falling in love and the idealization and sexualization of the power attributed to the male figure. Paper presented at the meeting of the American Psychological Association, Los Angeles, August 25.

The structuralization of the self in the context of therapy. The Self in Context, UCLA Continuing Education Program, Los Angeles, April 27.

1986 *Preoedipal factors in selection for brief psychotherapy.* Paper presented at the meeting of the American Academy of Psychoanalysis, Washington, DC, May 9.

1990 *Before we start: perceptions of the treatment.* Paper presented at a conference entitled *Psychoanalytic Beginnings: The Opening Phase*, Santa Monica, March 11.

References

Alexander, F. (1964). Psychoanalysis and the human condition. In *Psychoanalysis and the Human Situation*, eds. J. Marmorston and S. Stainsbrook. New York: Vantage Press.

Alexander, F., and French, T. (1946). *Psychoanalytic Psychotherapy*. New York: The Ronald Press.

Appelbaum, S. A. (1977). *The anatomy of change: A Menninger Foundation report on testing the effects of psychotherapy*. New York: Plenum.

Arlow, J. (1980). Object concept and object choice. *Psychoanalytic Quarterly* 49:109–133.

Atkin, A. (1974). A borderline case: ego synthesis and cognition. *International Journal of Psycho-Analysis* 55:13–19.

Bak, R. C. (1973). Being in love and object loss. *International Journal of Psycho-Analysis* 54:1–8.

Balint, M. (1968). *The Basic Fault*. London: Tavistock.

Basch, M. (1976). The concept of affect: a re-examination. *Journal of the American Psychoanalytic Association* 24:759–778.

Beres, D. (1956). Ego deviation and the concept of schizophrenia. *Psychoanalytic Study of the Child* 11:164–235. New York: International Universities Press.

Bergmann, M. (1980). On the intrapsychic function of falling in love. *Psychoanalytic Quarterly* 49:56–77.

Beukenkamp, C. (1968). Comment. *Voices* 4:28–29.

Bion, W. R. (1959). *Experience in Groups and Other Papers*. New York: Basic Books.

Blanck, G., and Blanck, R. (1974). *Ego Psychology: Theory and Practice*. New York: Columbia University Press.

Blos, P. (1984). Son and father. *Journal of the American Psychoanalytic Association* 32:301–324.

Bowlby, J. (1969). *Attachment and Loss: Attachment*. Vol. 1. New York: Basic Books.

Brenner, C. (1979). The components of psychic conflict and its consequences in mental life. *Psychoanalytic Quarterly* 48:547–567.

Bromberg, P. (1983). The mirror and the mask: on narcissism and psychoanalytic growth. *Contemporary Psychoanalysis* 19:359–387.

Buhler, K. (1927). *Die Krise der Psychologie*. Jena: Fischer.

Burgner, M., and Edgcumbe, R. (1972). Some problems in the conceptualization of early object relationships, Part II: The concept of object constancy. *Psychoanalytic Study of the Child* 27:315–333. New Haven, CT: Yale University Press.

Button, A. D. (1969). *The Authentic Child*. New York: Random House.

Coates, S. (1989). Conflict in gender identity of boys. Paper presented at the American Academy of Psychoanalysis, New York City, January.

Chrzanowski, G. (1978). From ego psychology of the self. In *Interpersonal Psychoanalysis: New Directions*, ed. E. Witenberg, pp. 33–46. New York: Gardner Press.

Davanloo, H. (1978). *Basic Principles and Techniques in Short-Term Dynamic Psychotherapy*. New York: Spectrum Publications.

——— (1980). *Short-Term Dynamic Psychotherapy*. New York: Jason Aronson.

De Simone Gaburri, G. (1985). On termination of the analysis. *The International Review of Psycho-Analysis* 12:461–468.

Deutsch, H. (1942). Some forms of emotional disturbance and their relationships to schizophrenia. *Psychoanalytic Quarterly* 11:301–321.

Diagnostic and Statistical Manual of Mental Disorders (1987). 3rd ed., revised. Washington, DC: American Psychiatric Association.

Eissler, K. R. (1953). The effect of the structure of the ego on psychoanalytic technique. *Journal of the American Psychoanalytic Association* 1:104–148.

Erikson, E. (1950). *Childhood and Society*. New York: Norton.

——— (1968). *Identity: Youth and Crisis*. New York: Norton.

Escalona, Sibylle K. (1963). Patterns of infantile experience and the developmental process. *Psychoanalytic Study of the Child* 18:197–244.

Fairbairn, W. R. D. (1952). *Psychoanalytic Studies of the Personality*. London: Tavistock.

—— (1954). *An Object Relations Theory of the Personality*. New York: Basic Books.

Fantz, R. L. (1966). Pattern discrimination and selective attention as determinants of perceptual development from birth. In *Perceptual Development in Children*, ed. A. J. Kidd and J. L. Rivoire, pp. 143–173. New York: International Universities Press.

Federn, P. (1952). *Ego Psychology and the Psychoses*. New York: Basic Books.

Framo, James L. (1965). Rationale and techniques of intensive family therapy. In *Intensive Family Therapy*, ed. Ivan Boszormonyi-Nagy and James L. Framo, pp. 143–212. New York: Harper & Row.

Freud, A. (1965). *Normality and Pathology in Childhood: Assessments of Development*. New York: International Universities Press.

—— (1968). Remarks in panel discussion. *International Journal of Psycho-Analysis* 49:506–507.

—— (1969). Discussion of John Bowlby's work. In *The Writings of Anna Freud*, vol. 5. New York: International Universities Press.

Freud, A., with Sandler, J. (1981). Discussions in the Hampstead Index, "The ego and the mechanisms of defense." *Bulletin of the Hampstead Clinic* 4:5–30.

Freud, S. (1908). Creative writers and day-dreaming. *Standard Edition* 9:141–153.

—— (1910a). Five lectures on psycho-analysis. *Standard Edition* 11:9–55.

—— (1910b). Observations of "wild" psycho-analysis. *Collected Papers*, vol. 2, pp. 297–304. New York: Basic Books.

—— (1912). The dynamics of transference. *Standard Edition* 12:99–108.

—— (1913). Totem and taboo: the horror of incest. *Standard Edition* 13:1–17.

—— (1914a). On narcissism: an introduction. *Standard Edition* 14:73–102.

—— (1914b). Remembering, repeating and working-through (further recommendations on the technique of psychoanalysis). *Standard Edition* 12:145–156.

—— (1915). Instincts and their vicissitudes. *Standard Edition* 14:117–140.

—— (1916). The premises and technique of interpretation. *Standard Edition* 15:100–112.

—— (1917a). The development of the libido and the sexual organizations. *Standard Edition* 16:320–338.

—— (1917b). Introductory lectures on psycho-analysis: the libido theory and narcissism. *Standard Edition* 16:412–430.

—— (1917c). Mourning and melancholia. *Standard Edition* 14:243–258.

—— (1921). Group psychology and the analysis of the ego: identification. *Standard Edition* 18:105–110.

—— (1923). The ego and the id. *Standard Edition* 19:3–66.

—— (1924). The dissolution of the Oedipus complex. *Standard Edition* 19:72–79.

—— (1926). Inhibitions, symptoms, and anxiety. *Standard Edition* 20:87–172.

—— (1931). Female sexuality. *Standard Edition* 21:225–243.

—— (1933). New introductory lectures on psycho-analysis: the dissection of the psychical personality. *Standard Edition* 22:57–80.

Friedman, L. (1984). Picture of treatment by Gill and Schafer. *Psychoanalytic Quarterly* 53:167–207.

Giovacchini, P. (1972). *Tactics and Techniques in Psychoanalytic Therapy.* New York: Jason Aronson.

—— (1975). *Psychoanalysis of Character Disorders.* New York: Jason Aronson.

—— (1979). *Treatment of Primitive Mental States.* New York: Jason Aronson.

Goldberg, A. (1981). One theory or more. *Contemporary Psychoanalysis* 17:626–638.

Gorkin, M. (1985). Varieties of sexualized countertransference. *The Psychoanalytic Review* 72:421–441.

Great Books of the Western World (1952). Vol. 3: The Great Ideas: A Syntopicon, pp. 1071–1101. Published by The Encyclopaedia Brittanica.

Greenberg, J. (1986). Theoretical models and the analyst's neutrality. *Contemporary Psychoanalysis* 22:87–106.

Greenson, R. (1954). The struggle against identification. In *Explorations in Psychoanalysis*, pp. 75–92. New York: International Universities Press, 1978.

—— (1962). On enthusiasm. In *Explorations in Psychoanalysis*, pp. 171–190. New York: International Universities Press, 1978.

—— (1965). The working alliance and the transference neurosis. In

Explorations in Psychoanalysis, pp. 199–224. New York: International Universities Press, 1978.

———— (1967). *The Technique and Practice of Psycho-Analysis*. New York: International Universities Press.

———— (1968). Disidentifying from mother: its special importance for the boy. In *Explorations in Psychoanalysis*, pp. 305–312. New York: International Universities Press.

———— (1969a). The origin and fate of new ideas. In *Explorations in Psychoanalysis*, pp. 333–358. New York: International Universities Press, 1978.

———— (1969b). The nontransference relationship in the psychoanalytic situation. *International Journal of Psycho-Analysis* 50:27–39.

———— (1971). The "real" relationship between the patient and the psychoanalyst. In *Explorations in Psychoanalysis*, pp. 425–440. New York: International Universities Press.

———— (1978). *Explorations in Psychoanalysis*. New York: International Universities Press.

Group for the Advancement of Psychiatry (1966). *Psychopathological Disorders in Childhood: Theoretical Considerations and a Proposed Classification*: 62. New York: GAP.

Grunes, M. (1984). The therapeutic object relationship. *The Psychoanalytic Review* 71:123–143.

Guntrip, H. (1969). *Schizoid Phenomena, Object Relations, and the Self*. New York: International Universities Press.

———— (1971). *Psychoanalytic Theory, Therapy, and the Self*. New York: Basic Books.

Hartmann, H. (1964). *Essays on Ego Psychology*. New York: International Universities Press.

Held-Weiss, R. (1986). A note on spontaneity in the analyst. *Contemporary Psychoanalysis* 22:2–3.

Horner, A. (1968). To touch or not to touch. *Voices* 4:26–28.

———— (1973). Ego boundaries: the last line of resistance in psychotherapy. *Psychotherapy* 10:83–86.

———— (1974). Early object relations and the concept of depression. *International Review of Psycho-Analysis* 1:337–340.

———— (1975). Stages and processes in the development of early object relations and their associated pathologies. *International Review of Psycho-Analysis* 2:95–105.

———— (1979, 1984). *Object Relations and the Developing Ego in Therapy*. New York: Jason Aronson.

———— (1980). The roots of anxiety, character structure, and psychoanalysis. *Journal of American Academy of Psychoanalysis* 8:565–574.

—— (1985a). The Oedipus complex. In *Treating the Oedipal Patient in Brief Psychotherapy*, ed. A. Horner, pp. 25–54. New York: Jason Aronson.

——, ed. (1985b). *Treating the Oedipal Patient in Brief Psychotherapy*. New York: Jason Aronson.

—— (1988). The constructed self and developmental discontinuity. *Journal of the American Academy of Psychoanalysis* 16:235–238.

—— (1989). *The Wish for Power and the Fear of Having It*. Northvale, NJ: Jason Aronson.

Horowitz, M. H. (1987). Some notes on insight and its failure. *Psychoanalytic Quarterly* 56:177–196.

Horwitz, L. (1985). Divergent views on the treatment of borderline patients. *Bulletin of the Menninger Clinic* 49:525–545.

Hurwitz, L., with Sutherland, J. D. (1983). The self and object relations. *Bulletin of the Menninger Clinic* 47:541–544.

Ingram, D., ed. (1987). *Final Lectures of Karen Horney*. New York: Norton.

Ingram, D. (1989). Personal communication to the author.

Jacobson, E. (1964). *The Self and the Object World*. New York: International Universities Press.

—— (1971). *Depression*. New York: International Universities Press.

Kavanagh, G. (1985). Changes in the patient's object representations during psychoanalysis and psychoanalytic psychotherapy. *Bulletin of the Menninger Clinic* 49:546–564.

Kernberg, O. (1974). Contrasting viewpoints regarding the nature and psychoanalytic treatment of narcissistic personalities: a preliminary communication. *Journal of the American Psychoanalytic Association* 22:255–267.

Khan, M. M. R. (1963). The concept of cumulative trauma. *Psychoanalytic Study of the Child* 18:286–306. New York: International Universities Press.

—— (1974). *The Privacy of the Self*. New York: International Universities Press.

Klein, M., Heimann, P., Isaacs, S., and Riviere, J. (1952). *Development in Psychoanalysis*. London: Hogarth.

Kohut, H. (1971). *The Analysis of the Self*. New York: International Universities Press.

—— (1977). *The Restoration of the Self*. New York: International Universities Press.

—— (1982). Introspection, empathy, and the semi-circle of mental health. *International Journal of Psycho-Analysis* 63:395–407.

Kris, E. (1983). The analyst's conceptual freedom in the method of free association. *International Journal of Psycho-Analysis* 64:407–412.

Krystal, H. (1978). Trauma and affect. *Psychoanalytic Study of the Child* 33:81–116. New Haven: Yale University Press.

Laing, R. D. (1962). Ontological insecurity. In *Psychoanalysis and Existential Philosophy*, ed. H. Ruitenbeek. New York: Dutton.

––––– (1967). *The Politics of Experience*. New York: Ballantine.

Langs, R. (1975). Therapeutic misalliances. *International Journal of Psychoanalytic Psychotherapy* 4:77–105.

––––– (1976). *The Bipersonal Field*. New York: Jason Aronson.

Lawrence, D. H. (1919). *Women in Love*. Toronto: Random House, 1950.

Lewin, B. (1951). *The Psychoanalysis of Elation*. London: Hogarth.

Lichtenberg, J. (1981). Implications for psychoanalytic theory of research on the neonate. *International Review of Psycho-Analysis* 8:35–52.

Loewald, H. W. (1979). The waning of the Oedipus complex. *Journal of the American Psychoanalytic Association* 27:751–775.

––––– (1985). Oedipus complex and development of self. *Psychoanalytic Quarterly* 54:435–443.

Luborsky, L., Crits-Christoph, P., Mintz, J., and Auerbach, A. (1988). *Who Will Benefit from Psychotherapy? Predicting Therapeutic Outcomes*. New York: Basic Books.

MacKinnon, D. W. (1961). The personality correlates of creativity: a study of American architects. *Proceedings of the 14th International Congress of Applied Psychology*. Copenhagen: Munksgaard.

Mahler, M. S. (1968). *On Human Symbiosis and the Vicissitudes of Individuation*. New York: International Universities Press.

––––– (1971). A study of the separation–individuation process, and its possible application to borderline phenomena in the psychoanalytic situation. *Psychoanalytic Study of the Child* 26:403–424. New Haven: Yale University Press.

Mahler, M. S., Pine, F., and Bergman, A. (1975). *The Psychological Birth of the Human Infant*. New York: Basic Books.

Malan, D. (1963). *A Study of Brief Psychotherapy*. New York: Plenum.

Mann, J. (1973). *Time-limited Psychotherapy*. Cambridge, MA: Harvard University Press.

Masterson, J. (1972). *Treatment of the Borderline Adolescent*. New York: Wiley.

May, R. (1969). *Love and Will*. New York: Norton.

Meissner, W. W. (1988). *Treatment of Patients in the Borderline Spectrum*. Northvale, NJ: Jason Aronson.

Mitchell, S. (1986). The wings of Icarus: illusions and the problem of narcissism. *Contemporary Psychoanalysis* 22:107–132.

Mullahy, P. (1949). *A Study of Interpersonal Relations.* New York: Hermitage.

Munn, N. L., Fernald, L. D., and Fernald, P. S. (1972). *Introduction to Psychology.* 3rd ed. Boston: Houghton Mifflin.

Murdoch, I. (1957). *The Sandcastle.* New York: Viking.

Myerson, P. (1981). When does need become desire and desire need? *Contemporary Psychoanalysis* 17:607–625.

Perls, F., Hefferline, R., and Goodman, P. (1951). *Gestalt Therapy.* New York: Dell.

Phillips, J. L. (1969). *The Origins of Intellect: Piaget's Theory.* San Francisco: Freeman.

Phillipson, H. (1955). *The Object Relations Technique.* London: Tavistock.

Piaget, J. (1936). *The Origins of Intelligence in Children.* New York: International Universities Press, 1952.

Pine, F. (1979). On the pathology of the separation–individuation process as manifested in later clinical work: an attempt at delineation. *International Journal of Psycho-Analysis* 60:225–242.

Poland, W. (1984). On the analyst's neutrality. *Journal of the American Psychoanalytic Association* 32:284–299.

Rank, O. (1945). *Will Therapy, Truth and Reality.* New York: Knopf.

Rees, K. (1987). "I want to be Daddy": meanings of masculine identification in girls. *Psychoanalytic Quarterly* 56:497–521.

Reik, W. (1949). *Listening with the Third Ear.* New York: Farrar, Straus.

Richardson, W. (1987). *Language and Psychoanalysis.* Paper presented at The American Academy of Psychoanalysis, Chicago, May.

Rimland, B. (1964). *Infantile Autism.* New York: Appleton-Century-Crofts.

Robbins, M. (1989). Primitive personality organization as an interpersonally adaptive modification of cognition and affect. *International Journal of Psycho-Analysis* 70:443–460.

Sandler, A. M. (1977). Beyond eight-month anxiety. *International Journal of Psycho-Analysis* 58:195–208.

Sandler, J. (1981). Unconscious wishes and human relationships. *Contemporary Psychoanalysis* 17:180–196.

Sandler, J., Holder, A., and Meers, D. (1963). The ego ideal and the ideal self. *Psychoanalytic Study of the Child* 18:139–158. New York: International Universities Press.

Schafer, R. (1960). The loving and beloved superego in Freud's theory. *Psychoanalytic Study of the Child* 15:163–188. New York: International Universities Press.

——— (1983). *The Analytic Attitude*. New York: Basic Books.

——— (1985). Wild analysis. *Journal of the American Psychoanalytic Association* 33:275-300.

Schecter, D. (1968). Identification and individuation. *Journal of the American Psychoanalytic Association* 16:48-80.

——— (1979a). *Developmental Roots of Anxiety*. Paper presented at the American Academy of Psychoanalysis, November.

——— (1979b). The loving and persecuting superego. *Contemporary Psychoanalysis* 15:361-379.

——— (1980). Early developmental roots of anxiety. *Journal of American Academy of Psychoanalysis* 8:539-554.

Searles, H. (1965). *Collected Papers on Schizophrenia and Related Subjects*. New York: International Universities Press.

Segal, H. (1964). *Introduction to the Work of Melanie Klein*. New York: Basic Books.

Shapiro, T. (1977). Oedipal distortions in severe character pathologies: developmental and theoretical considerations. *Psychoanalytic Quarterly* 46:555-579.

——— (1984). On neutrality. *Journal of the American Psychoanalytic Association* 32:269-282.

Sifneos, P. (1979). *Short-Term Dynamic Psychotherapy: Evaluation and Technique*. New York: Plenum.

Stolorow, R., and Lachmann, F. (1980). *Psychoanalysis of Developmental Arrests*. New York: International Universities Press.

Stolorow, R., Brandchaft, B., and Atwood, G. (1987). *Psychoanalytic Treatment, an Intersubjective Approach*. Hillsdale, NJ: The Analytic Press.

Sullivan, C. T. (1963). *Freud and Fairbairn: Two Theories of Ego-Psychology*. Doylestown, PA: The Doylestown Foundation.

Sullivan, H. S. (1953). *The Interpersonal Theory of Psychiatry*. New York: Norton.

——— (1954). *The Psychiatric Interview*. New York: Norton.

——— (1956). *Clinical Studies in Psychiatry*. New York: Norton.

Sutherland, J. (1983). The self and object relations. *Bulletin of the Menninger Clinic* 47:525-541.

Szurek, S. A. (1973). Attachment and psychotic detachment. In *Clinical Studies in Childhood Psychoses*, ed. S. A. Szurek and I. N. Berlin, pp. 191-277. New York: Brunner/Mazel.

Tolpin, M. (1971). On the beginnings of the cohesive self. *Psychoanalytic Study of the Child* 26:316-352. New Haven: Yale Universities Press.

Wachtel, P. (1986). On the limits of therapeutic neutrality. *Contemporary Psychoanalysis* 22:60-70.

Waelder, R. (1930). The principle of multiple function: observations on over-determination. *Psychoanalytic Quarterly* 5:45–62.

Watzlawick, P., Beavin, J. H., and Jackson, D. D. (1967). *Pragmatics of Human Communication*. New York: Norton.

Winnicott, D. W. (1951). Transitional objects and transitional phenomena. In *Through Paediatrics to Psycho-Analysis*, pp. 229–242. New York: Basic Books, 1975.

—— (1962). The aims of psycho-analytic treatment. In *The Maturational Processes and the Facilitating Environment*, pp. 166–170. London: Hogarth, 1965.

—— (1965). *The Maturational Processes and the Facilitating Environment*. New York: International Universities Press.

—— (1971). *Playing and Reality*. London: Tavistock.

—— (1974). Fear of breakdown. *International Review of Psycho-Analysis* 1:103–108.

Wyatt, G. L. (1969). *Language Learning and Communication Disorders*. New York: Free Press.

Zetzel, E. (1971). A developmental approach to the borderline patient. *American Journal of Psychiatry* 127:867–871.

Index

Production Editor: *Adelle Krauser*
Editorial Director: *Muriel Jorgensen*

This book was set in 11 point Goudy Oldstyle by Alpha Graphics of Pittsfield, New Hampshire.

It was printed and bound by Haddon Craftsmen of Scranton, Pennsylvania.